PENGUI
WHAT TOOK

Kitty Sewell was born in Sweden and later spent twenty years living in Spain and Canada before settling in South Wales with her family. With a background in business and law, then art, she trained in Britain to become a psychotherapist and counsellor working both within the NHS and in private practice. She now combines her practice with being a freelance journalist and writer. She contributes regularly to various publications and writes a popular agony column.

Raymond Thompson is an artist and lives in South Wales with his partner Lorretta.

RAYMOND THOMPSON WITH KITTY SEWELL

What Took You So Long?

A Girl's Journey to Manhood

PENGUIN BOOKS

PENGUIN BOOKS

Published by the Penguin Group
Penguin Books Ltd, 27 Wrights Lane, London W8 5TZ, England
Penguin Books USA Inc., 375 Hudson Street, New York, New York 10014, USA
Penguin Books Australia Ltd, Ringwood, Victoria, Australia
Penguin Books Canada Ltd, 10 Alcorn Avenue, Toronto, Ontario, Canada M4V 3B2
Penguin Books (NZ) Ltd, 182–190 Wairau Road, Auckland 10, New Zealand

Penguin Books Ltd, Registered Offices: Harmondsworth, Middlesex, England

Published in Penguin Books 1995
1 3 5 7 9 10 8 6 4 2

Copyright © Raymond Thompson and Kitty Sewell, 1995
All rights reserved

The moral right of the authors has been asserted

Filmset in 10.5/12 pt monophoto Bembo
Printed in England by Clays Ltd, St Ives plc

Except in the United States of America, this book is sold subject
to the condition that it shall not, by way of trade or otherwise, be lent,
re-sold, hired out, or otherwise circulated without the publisher's
prior consent in any form of binding or cover other than that in
which it is published and without a similar condition including this
condition being imposed on the subsequent purchaser

Contents

	Introduction	vii
1	When I Grow up to be a Man	1
2	I'm Getting out of Here	27
3	Locked up	60
4	I Abandon All Former Names	86
5	All My Hopes and All My Dreams	107
6	A Sober and Industrious Life	138
7	Removing Everything That Didn't Belong	161
8	A Man with a Mission	186
9	Tolerating Ignorance	216
10	Tolerating Pain	247
11	What Took You So Long?	274
	Epilogue	312
	Afterword by Dr D.H. Montgomery	314

Introduction

Transsexualism has become a household word in the last two or three decades. A lot has been written about the condition and the public continues to be intrigued by transsexualism and 'gender reassignment surgery'.

It is estimated that there are approximately 50,000 transsexuals in Britain, and of those only a proportion seek help. Out of those who have consulted a 'Gender Clinic', only about 10 per cent go on to be considered for reassignment surgery. A very small percentage of these are female-to-male transsexuals.

Raymond Thompson was one of them.

He is a primary transsexual, an unusual status even among transsexuals. From the very first moments of conscious thought, Raymond knew that the body he was born in, the body of a girl, could and should not be his. By the age of five he knew beyond any doubt that he was male, and every moment thereafter was a struggle to hold on to this identity.

As a teenager, when he became aware of the fact that his condition was recognized by science and had a name, and that there could one day be a 'cure' for his body, he set out on a journey to achieve this end. Only then would he rest.

Through the trauma of his childhood, through years of turning to drugs and alcohol, petty crime and pimping, periods of imprisonment, through college, and then the struggle to lead a sober and industrious life, he continued his quest for a solution to his condition. This was at last achieved at the age of thirty-two, when he had the last of several operations that finally made him into a whole man.

Raymond was referred to me as a client for counselling in a General Medical Practice in his hometown, where I worked as a counsellor/psychotherapist. This was just after his operations had been concluded, and he was struggling to put together the pieces of his fragmented life. Raymond had a persistent suspicion and dislike of any kind of therapy, having had several rather negative experiences of enforced 'treatment' in his youth. Instead, after our initial session, we decided that we would look at his life and experiences together, and I would write them down in the form of a biography. Raymond had often in the past thought of 'setting the record straight' to defend and explain his condition. With my background in journalism, he placed his trust and confidence in me to do this for him. I was fascinated by his extraordinary story and determined to meet the challenge. We both found this to be a purposeful way of us working together. Indeed, the remembering and the telling of his life's events proved as cathartic as any therapy.

It was the first time he had looked at his life willingly and tried to make some sense of it. At first his story came pouring out in a jumbled and fragmented fashion, but as we journeyed through his life the memory of events, feelings and conversations sharpened. It took the best part of two and a half years to piece together the facts. My job was to tell Raymond's story with dignity and sensitivity, and this is what I have attempted to do at all times, without ever departing from the truth as he remembers it.

Raymond is an attractive man with jet black curly hair and piercing blue eyes, 5 foot 7 inches tall with a strong build. In spite of his moustache and beard he looks younger than his age, but a slightly haunted countenance and the scars on his hands off-set this. He has a deep, penetrating voice and an assertive and forthright manner. He is a man of passionate emotions, caring and sensitive to all nuances of life, particularly sensitive to those creatures, human or otherwise, who have suffered handicaps, discrimination and personal struggles. On the other hand, he carries his share of rage and outrage. I felt his anger was based on the constant pressure that society puts on someone like him, his perpetual need to justify who he is and also the fact of having to internalize his frustrations and the torments he suffered. Whenever the lid is lifted on these powerful and sometimes destructive forces, it has always had a detrimental effect on his life, as his story will tell. But Raymond's sensitivity and intuitiveness reveal a softer quality. He would deny having experienced life from any feminine perspective, although I cannot help thinking that the sum total of his experiences must have given him some insight into, and from, both sides of the gender divide. Surely we all possess our share of both masculine and feminine elements? Jung believed that an inner feminine figure, the anima, played a distinctive, and archetypal, role in the unconscious of man, just as animus played the corresponding masculine role in woman. This may help us towards an understanding of the spiritual aspects of Ray's condition, although speculation about the origin of primary transsexualism, whether it be genetic, mental, emotional or spiritual, could be discussed endlessly and is beyond the scope of this book.

Ray's best quality must be a very dry and wicked sense of humour, and so despite the agony and the arguments we invariably had, the writing of this book has provided me with large doses of hilarity and laughter. From quite a complex and trying start, we grew to be friends and partners and working together was always a lively and demanding experience.

My own difficulty with the completion of our work together is that Raymond never wavered in his resolution to shun the gender he was born into. He was resolutely sure that he had never been other than who he is, and had made a silent pact with himself not to acknowledge the child in whose body he was born. The only part of his child-self that has a voice is a very angry, very bitter little boy. As much as I respected and honoured this stance, as a therapist I felt the urge on his behalf for a merciful embrace and acceptance of his total past self. As a human being I felt painfully for that long-forgotten, scorned and beaten part of his child-self that had to be sacrificed. At the same time I understood that in order to keep his balance and sanity he needed to preserve and express his true nature. And I realized that we born into our rightful bodies can never truly imagine what it is to be trapped in a body we cannot call our own.

Kitty Sewell
February 1995

I
When I Grow up to be a Man

My name is Raymond.

Once upon a time, a very long time ago I had another name. I don't care to think of that name, perhaps I don't even really remember it. The life that I led, when this other name was assigned to me, is a life that is no longer part of me. In a sense I am reborn.

The first time I was born, it was in a body which was other than male. By some cosmic mistake, as a budding human being I had somehow chosen the wrong body, or the wrong body had chosen me.

I am a transsexual person, a man really. It took me more than thirty years to reach a stage when my body started to fit my identity as a man, but now there is no doubt about it. Here I am, well and truly the male that I have always known myself to be.

It's a long story. It starts now and goes backwards, because it is not until now that I am whole. It is not until now, safe and sound in my male body – well, just about – that I feel I have the strength and the courage to look back to see what it was all about.

It began at the time I was starting to be conscious of myself. Maybe when I was three or four years of age. I felt that something was wrong with me, that I was not like other children. When you are little you don't have the ability to figure it out, but the sense of 'wrongness' was there.

At about the age of five I started to understand what the wrongness was all about. There was something contradictory about the way I felt to the way my body was. I must have become aware of the differences between girls and boys because gradually it came to me: 'I am not what everyone thinks I am, I am a boy.' Once this realization had dawned I began to feel an aversion to parts of my body and I taught myself to ignore those parts that didn't belong to boys.

In my own way, I kept trying to make things come true for myself. I was always trying to stand in front of the toilet rather than sit to pee. I would stand there and hold what I thought should be there, my penis. It wasn't only the thought, but the act and the posture that made me feel right. It was a very private gesture, not something I would have shown anyone even at that young age.

I also managed to persuade my parents that I should have my hair cut. Ever since I was a very young child, people had been complimenting my mother on my thick, black, curly hair, saying how beautiful it was. I saw this word as implying girlishness and was bothered by it. I didn't want to be beautiful, I wanted to be handsome. My mother was so proud of my hair and she wasn't keen on letting me have it cut, but finally she relented. I had it cut very short and felt a great sense of relief.

My parents obviously didn't know anything about the feelings I had. I was the child my mother had given birth to and she treated me accordingly. If anybody in the family, or friends, made any comment about the boyish way I presented myself, she would reply that I was just a tomboy and I would grow out of it.

To me, these conversations between adults were embarrassing. They would talk as if they 'knew' all about me, and what I was feeling had nothing to do with it. I cringed hearing these things said about me, hearing that soon I was supposed to grow out of who I was.

As I became more aware of myself it became harder for me to relate to my body and it affected, in turn, the way I related to the world around me and to people, including my parents. I was puzzled and disturbed by their expectations of me since they didn't fit with my own experience of myself. These expectations of how I should be and how I should look and behave became unacceptable to me. I simply wasn't the person that they imagined me to be. Why was I the only one who could see that obvious fact? One of my strongest memories of early childhood is a feeling of embarrassment, an all-encompassing embarrassment, about the way I looked and the way I felt. I was a confused, lonely, angry and very restricted little boy. My anger at the unfairness of it, and my frustration with my own inability to put right this wrongness in me, made me volatile and moody.

I must have really believed in God because I was sure that in him lay the answer to my predicament. It must have been his mistake and he must have the power to set it right. Safely tucked up in bed at night, I didn't pray for God's help but I would ask him what I should do. My desperate need for help would get my imagination going so that I could hear God's voice saying, 'I'll try to help you, but you must lie flat on your back and keep perfectly still, and while you sleep I will try to put things right.'

Full of hope, I immobilized myself by twisting my arms and legs around in awkward positions in order to stay flat on my back. This would help me keep absolutely still because if I tried to move in my sleep the discomfort would wake me. If only I didn't budge an inch through the night, never moved or turned over, God would be able to put things right, he would make me the boy I should be. By staying motionless I thought that I was helping him to do the job properly, allowing him to 'see' what needed to be done.

Each morning when I woke up I would lift up the blankets to have a look, only to find that I must have turned over in my sleep, since the transformation had not taken place. Each time I managed to convince myself that I had moved during the night and made it impossible for God to get on with the job, and this made me resolve to try again and again, night after night.

For a long time this ritual provided me with the hope which kept me from the very pits of despair.

I wasn't an only child. I had a little sister, Anna, who at this time was about three years old. I was quite pleased to have her around and felt very protective towards her. She was late speaking so I spoke for her. She would signal to me or point at things when she wanted something, and I would tell my mother what she wanted. Often I knew instinctively. My mother would ask me, 'What's the matter with her, what does she want?'

'She wants her shoes,' I would say. My mother would go to get her shoes.

'No, she doesn't want her blue ones, she wants her red ones.' Anna hadn't opened her mouth. My mother would always laugh and give me a puzzled look: 'How do you know?' I liked being able to help Anna in this way, but there did come a time when I longed to hear her speak and I would ask my mother when she was going to start speaking. 'When she is good and ready,' my mother would tell me. One day I went along with my mother to the chemist to get a prescription for Anna. When I saw the bottle of medicine for my sister I felt relieved. 'Will she be able to talk now?' I asked my mother. My mother and the pharmacist both had a laugh and said, 'No, love, it's for her cold.' Anyway, she started speaking not long after.

I did have a few friends, mostly cousins and extended family and I used to enjoy spending time with them. I liked to visit my Aunt Kathleen's house which was just down the road, especially when there was some kind of celebration, like bonfire night. We would build a bonfire on the green just outside the house. I loved the smell of hot dogs and baked potatoes, there always seemed to be more than you could eat, and we had great fun playing ducking apples and setting up different kinds of fireworks. It was exciting to watch them explode and burst into so many colours in the darkness.

Even though I did enjoy playing with the other children I became a loner. The easiest way to deal with people's expectations of me was to avoid spending time with them. I had an urge to cry a lot, and for that I needed privacy too. There was always a vague sense of time running out. Sometimes when I was performing my nightly ritual calling on God's help, I would beg him, 'Please, *please*, God, let it be tomorrow.' I longed for an end to my frustration and my tears.

I can't remember how long I carried on with this particular strategy involving God's goodwill, but it persisted in different forms for years and years. The sense of urgency and time running out increased as the years went by, yet still I didn't lose hope.

But there were other ways for my mind to escape – I developed an imaginary world of my own. When I was alone I would conjure up a world where I could release the boy that lived inside me. I used to lose myself in my thoughts: being the boy I knew myself to be. At first my world didn't differ from the real world except in the way that I myself was different, not sad, not odd, but full of joy, feeling carefree and whole. It felt so good and so right to be there.

Gradually as I came to know my environment better, my imaginary world developed and reflected how I was when I was outside in the countryside playing, running, climbing trees, looking under leaves and stones to see what I could find, listening to birds and the wind rustling through the trees. The smells and the noises of the outdoors would be clear and sharp even in my thoughts. Soon I was able to stay with these daydreams when around other people. My vivid pictures also brought me relief and protected my sense of self from reality.

Anyway, it was only a matter of time before God would put things right. I really believed there was a simple solution. It would happen just like that, overnight, and no one would know that I had been 'wrong'. But everyone kept treating me as if I were a girl. I was a boy. Why did I have to feel this humiliated? Why couldn't everything be easy, like it seemed for everybody else? Why did I spend so much time crying, or being angry? Little comments made by my family or other adults sometimes pierced my protective shell. I didn't want to hear what they had to say about me, because they always got it wrong.

If I could have spoken about myself, what would I have said? My condition was more obscure and mysterious to me than it would have been to anyone else. All I knew was that people's expectations of me were getting further removed from how I felt. No one could possibly have understood even if I had tried to explain it. But I didn't have the words to express my feelings or explain my predicament and there was such shame and mortification in the way I felt about myself that I knew instinctively it was not something to speak of. Anyway, it was in my actions and in the way I attempted to look that I was expressing who I really was.

One of my older cousins, Patrick, had a cap which was part of his school uniform. I took a real liking to this cap and was allowed to keep it. Just the act of putting this cap on my head gave me a good feeling; I felt more like my real self. I would take this cap off last thing at night and hang it on one of the bedposts, and the first thing I did when I woke up in the morning was to put the cap back on. I would have done anything to wear the same school uniform as Patrick.

The beginning of my school years brought more pressures to bear on me. I had difficulties in conforming and being told what to do, and I felt imprisoned, being required to stay in school for the whole day. My behaviour was scrutinized and the restrictions were piled on: 'You are late', 'Don't play over there', 'Get off the grass', 'Walk tidy', 'Don't fidget', 'Be quiet', and so on. At least at home when I was under pressure, I could walk out.

I started to 'mitch' the odd day. I would get to school and then hide in some bushes in the park across from the schoolyard. I would look over and think how good it felt to be sitting over here, and how lousy the other kids must have felt over there, all queuing in rows waiting to walk in to school. These queues bothered me.

'Now, we want the boys over here, and the girls over this side,' the teacher would shout while briskly sorting and pushing us into the right queues. 'Come on now, make it quick, hurry up.'

'Why do I have to be over this side? Why am I here anyway?' I would think, not just about being in the wrong queue but the whole idea about being told what to do. 'I won't be standing by here tomorrow, I'm not going to be coming in,' would be going through my mind. I was defiant but I was just a kid, and I didn't want to be stuck in school. I felt much happier being able to run off up into the hills where no one would see me, and where I could be in my own little world. On my way to school I would slip away up a mountain path and spend the day up there and then come wandering home at the right time.

I always liked to do my own thing, which sometimes got me into mischief, like smoking. I had my first cigarette when I was about six. A friend's mother had left a pack on the mantelpiece and I nicked one and smoked it. I liked the feeling of smoking. I started to nick my father's fag-ends from the ashtray. He smoked thick roll-ups, and always stubbed them out leaving a substantial end. I would take a couple and shove them in my pocket. Later, when I was up on the mountain, I would practise my smoking, coughing my guts up.

One day I told my friend Paul to sneak in and nick some cigarettes from his mother, but when he came back he had a fiver with him. He'd found it in his father's pocket. We went straight to the shop and bought pop, chocolates, cigarettes and matches. I had never been on a bus on my own, so we got on the bus and went back and forth from one end of town to the other. We were sitting at the top of the bus in the front seat, as if we were driving it, eating our chocolates, drinking our pop and smoking our fags.

Having met no opposition, we became more daring and decided to take another bus, which went to the beach. The bus-stop was just around the corner from where I lived. Walking past the house, my little sister Anna saw us and asked, 'Where are you going?'

'We're taking the bus to the beach,' we told her.

'I'm telling Mum,' she said. I tried to persuade her not to, but then I remembered I had a bag full of chocolate éclairs.

'If I give you these, will you keep your mouth shut?'

'Yeah!' She grabbed the bag. But she didn't keep her mouth shut, which surprised me at the time, and when we got back all hell broke loose. Also, in the meantime Paul's father had discovered that the fiver was missing, so 'there were murders'. I told Paul, 'You tell your father that I had anything to do with this and you are in for it.' He knew not to implicate me in any trouble, even if it had been my idea. We had had a few fights before, and I'd always come out on top. Once we had quite a scuffle. I had given him some of my tadpoles to look after. When I went to his house the next day I found him in the garden trying to pull the little legs off the tadpoles. I couldn't believe what I was seeing, he was shocked to see me too, and in a fury I dived on him. I really laid into him and we were wrestling on the ground and he started to cry. His mother heard the commotion and poked her head out the window. 'For Christ's sake, pack it in,' she shouted and put an end to it.

We got grounded for a few days on account of the fiver.

Paul's father was furious and I heard that he had marched Paul to the police station in order to teach him a lesson.

I was happy when I had to take a couple of weeks off school due to an accident. I had put a swing in a massive oak tree up on a wooded hillside but it hadn't been used since the previous winter and the rope had rotted – it was just a long rope with a stick on the end. My cousin Sheila gave me a push, and the next thing I knew I was in the bottom of a pit which was full of rocks. One of my legs was bent underneath me, bruised and twisted, but in the end the only thing broken was a little bone in my ankle.

However, there were a lot of fun times too, and life often seemed a big adventure, particularly when I was on my own. I spent ages rummaging through the woods, exploring, trying to find caves and secret places. Drawing was something I was very keen on and had some talent for. I used to draw anything I could find in the countryside. I have always felt passionately about nature and animals. Some of my earliest memories are of my fascination with everything in the outdoors. I loved the high hills around the town. Up behind our house was a virtual wilderness, where there was a pond. It was quite narrow, but very deep and had green slimy edges that went down sharply. Once my cousin Patrick accidentally slipped down the edge into the pond and if a friend hadn't come to his aid he would have drowned. The pond is no longer there, it was filled in. As a child I spent a lot of time up there, particularly around a smaller offshoot of the pond which was shallower and excellent for collecting newts and frogs and frog-spawn, which I kept safely in tanks. I was forever running off with my steel bucket, coming back covered from head to foot in mud.

One day I came running down the path to the house shouting to my mother that I had rescued thirty-six newts. It was late in the autumn and the pond was freezing over and I thought the newts would freeze to death. I had dug down into the mud with the whole length of my arms and I could see their little tails wiggling in the clumps of mud that I brought up. Well, of course that is what they do, dig down into the mud to keep warm, but to me they were in grave danger. I did look after them well though, keeping them with plenty of mud and green slime to make them feel at home. I loved watching frog-spawn grow into frogs. I kept them to look at and to sketch, until they had legs and then I would let them go back into the pond.

Once I found a huge toad which had no front feet. Its front legs were just stumps. I ruminated quite a bit on how he got that way. Had his feet been trapped somewhere and pulled off? But then again maybe they never grew in the first place. Maybe these things happen, maybe things don't always grow where they should. I felt strongly about this toad and his predicament. I kept him with me for a while and took him places where I thought he couldn't get on his own. I carried him about in my bucket.

One day I met my father on his way to the newsagent's. He said, 'Come on, I'll take you down to the shop and buy you some sweets.' I had my bucket with me.

'What have you got there?' my father asked, looking into the bucket. 'Cor, look at the size of 'im. That's the biggest toad I've ever seen,' he exclaimed. Once we were in the shop my father nudged me and whispered, 'Go on, take it out and put it on the counter,' which I happily complied with. The women in the shop became hysterical and were screaming for me to remove it. I must have been pleased with the effect because later I did the same thing at my cousin's wedding. I wanted a pint of bitter just like my father, but of course I couldn't have one. So I went over to the pond in the garden and got a frog, not a toad – toads are dry – but a really slimy frog, and put it on the bar. It did cause quite a stir. The barman told me in no uncertain terms to remove it. My father smiled at me and said, 'I'll give you a beer if you take the frog back to the pond.' So, I got the beer.

That autumn I turned seven. I desperately wanted a bicycle and had been asking my parents for one, but my father told me I'd have to ask Father Christmas. I had already tried various ways of making my own transport. First, I made a forerunner of the skateboard, literally with a board screwed on to a skate. Next, Paul and I made a 'gambo'. It was a four-foot-long cart with a wooden box on the back. You sat in this box on a plank with your feet on a crossbar. It had a rope for steering and a piece of wood that pushed down into the wheel for braking. Of course, it was only good for going downhill. What I really needed was a bike.

My father could play some wicked tricks on us sometimes, it was his kind of humour. That Christmas he was winding us up by saying that since there were no kids living either side of our house, Father Christmas would not realize we were there and he would probably miss us altogether. Anna and I got very anxious about this, and we set about drawing signs on large bits of paper saying, Father Christmas, This Way, which we sellotaped in the windows with arrows pointing to our door. I can imagine my father having a good laugh about this as he helped us put these signs up. He told us that Father Christmas liked a drop of brandy to warm him up and a mince pie, so we left these on the side of the fire grate along with a list of presents we wanted.

Anna and I both woke up at the crack of dawn on Christmas morning and ran down to the living-room while outside it was still pitch dark. The brandy and the mince pie were gone but there were only an apple and an orange in each of our stockings, and a couple of books; I had *Beano* and *Dandy*. That was it. We sat on the sofa together feeling really disappointed and I tried to console Anna saying, 'At least he didn't miss us out completely, at least we got something.' But then it occurred to me to investigate the other rooms. When I opened the kitchen door I discovered that the kitchen was absolutely packed with toys. The whole kitchen smelled of new things and when I switched the light on I immediately spotted the bike I had asked Father Christmas for, a red bike with a white seat and big, chunky, white tyres. I shouted for Anna and she came running. Her whole face lit up when she saw it all; there was the doll in a high chair that she wanted so much. I was over the moon with all my presents, the Lego that I had asked for, walking robots and a Dalek from the *Dr Who* series.

On Boxing Day I took my new bike over to show it to my grandparents. My cousin Sheila, who was thirteen at the time, was walking with me.

'Nice bike,' she said.

'I got it from Father Christmas,' I told her.

'There is no such thing as Father Christmas,' she said.

'There is,' I said sharply. 'He brought me the bike.'

'Your mother and father got you the bike. There is no such thing as Father Christmas,' she insisted.

My stomach started churning as her words sank in. In a rage I picked up the bike and threw it away from me with all my strength. All kinds of thoughts and feelings welled up inside me. If Father Christmas did not exist, what about God? Was it all just pretend? Were there no mystical, magical unseen powers? The implications of it all were profoundly distressing for me. Sheila could see that I was hurt and troubled so she tried to retract what she had said, but the damage was done.

When we arrived at my grandparents' house my spirits lifted a bit. They were admiring my bike and telling me how lucky I was to have it, but I still felt uneasy. Had Sheila just been pulling my leg? Were my mixed-up feelings justified? I had always trusted Sheila and we got on well, so I decided to question it further with her.

'When I grow up to be a man, I'm going to have a motorbike,' I said to her casually.

'But you won't,' she said, puzzled, 'you won't grow up to be a man.'

'I will,' I argued.

'No, you won't, mun!' she exclaimed, exasperated. 'You won't.'

I couldn't believe her, but this conversation substantiated my conviction that this subject was best kept to myself. I didn't quite understand why, but I realized I wouldn't be able to argue the point with anyone. Everyone would think I was lying, I simply didn't have the proof to show that I was right. That night I asked God more vehemently than ever, 'Please let it be tonight ... please, *please* God.' The confusion and the doubts generated by what Sheila had told me made my stomach churn with anxiety. What I felt was true, wasn't it? It had to be true. How could it not be true? How could I possibly be so wrong about myself when I knew with absolute certainty that I would grow up to be a man?

My new bike brought me a lot more freedom and I could get

about the town and explore much further afield. Those days were different, it was quite safe for a kid of seven to get about on his own, or so it seemed. I went everywhere on my bike. I loved going to the graveyard and finding slow-worms and grass snakes under the stone slabs. It was the ideal habitat, with the stones and grass and trees around them. One day I was coming home from the graveyard on my bike, and my mother was on her way out to work, it was early in the morning.

'What have you got around your wrists?' she said.

'Two snakes,' I answered.

'Get off it, they're not real are they?' she asked anxiously. I rode in a straight line towards her.

'Jesus Christ!' she screamed. 'Throw them away, throw them away, get away from me, put them back wherever you found them!' These were slow-worms, which are snakes that look slimy but, in fact, are not. They're lovely and silky to the touch and very colourful with nice markings on them. I just liked to hold them, and keep them with me for a while, and at the end of the day I would let them go. I would always put them back where I had found them, in case they had a family.

My Aunt Colleen, my father's sister, always said that I would become either a vet or an artist – she was right on one count. I don't think I would have had the stomach to be a vet, I would have got too attached. I felt close to animals, protective, and I used to get very emotional about them, particularly about the idea of them being so vulnerable.

Of course, it happened that I sometimes killed them accidentally myself. That spring we were going on holiday to Butlin's. My parents were running about getting ready and packed to leave; I was sniffing around in the grass when I spotted a lizard under a stone. Well, I didn't have a lizard, did I? So I was chasing it all over the garden while my parents were urging me to get ready to go. Eventually I caught it and put it in a container, but in the rush I forgot to give it grass and leaves to keep it happy. When we got back from holiday I went straight out the back to take a look at the lizard, but it was dead and dried up. I was extremely upset about the death, particularly because I had been responsible for it.

Another incident affected me deeply. I was out for a walk on the sand dunes with my father and grandfather when I found a curlew's nest which had three eggs in it. I had not seen a nest made in the sand before and I was intrigued. Collecting eggs was something that I had never done but I wanted to take one of these, perhaps as a memento of the occasion. My father and my grandfather tried to warn me against it, saying it was the wrong time, but I was determined to have one and wouldn't let up until I could. So they let me take one, perhaps in order to teach me a lesson. When we got home, I asked my father to blow the egg for me, but when he tried the shell cracked and there was an almost fully formed little chick inside and there was lots of blood. I went berserk and and started punching my father in the head as if it were all his fault. He tried to calm me down, saying, 'We tried to warn you but you wouldn't listen.' I never took another egg. The memory and the image of that incident stayed with me for a long time.

My father also got the brunt of my anger when once he opened a window, which accidentally pushed a container of tadpoles off the outside window-sill and it crashed on the ground. I was outside sorting out my frog tanks, lost in my own thoughts, when the crash brought me abruptly back to earth. I completely lost my temper and shouted at my father, 'Look what you have done! If anything happens to any of my tadpoles, you're in for it!' Both of us scrambled around on the ground trying to pick them all up. They were wriggling, slimy and slippery, which made it difficult. I wouldn't calm down: 'If any of them die, you're in for it.'

'For Christ's sake, you don't think I did it on purpose, do you?' my father exclaimed. I could get quite nasty. I was fiercely protective towards my animals; they had to be safe while they were with me.

I was almost too sensitive about animals and wildlife in general. Nature felt so real to me, and it was the one thing that I felt I was really part of. I knew that I was a living, breathing being surrounded by life. So much goes on in nature all the time, you can spend hours feeling, hearing, seeing and touching things, just watching nature. It always gave me tremendous inner joy watching birds swooping down among the trees and squirrels jumping from branch to branch. I would get totally absorbed and it set me free from my own confusion about the world and myself. When I was on my own, surrounded by wilderness, I could enjoy being the boy I was, within my own world, whereas when I was with people I had to behave in a certain way and do certain things considered appropriate for a girl.

One day when I was cleaning out my trays where I kept my frog-spawn, a friend came to visit at my house. An urge came over me to have some kind of intimate contact with this little girl, and I pushed her over and lay on top of her. She didn't understand what I was doing, nor did I really, but she asked me to get off and leave her alone. I let her up and she looked a bit startled and said, 'You frightened me then.' I felt confused by what I had done because it felt natural to me, but at the same time I knew instinctively that others would see it as wrong.

Suddenly I put my hands around her neck, wanting somehow to blot her out. More than that, I think I wanted to blot out the fact of her being witness to how I was. I felt bitter and humiliated by my behaviour. It seemed that it was a disgraceful thing for me to want to do to a girl, but at the same time it didn't seem unnatural for a little boy to want to do it. I felt very bad about wanting to strangle her, and embarrassed, so I just pretended that the whole thing hadn't happened and got on with cleaning the trays. She didn't hang around, and thankfully never referred to the incident again.

These confrontations between what I was and what I was supposed to be, began to turn my frustration into anger and aggression. It had no other outlet. My aggression could be quite unpredictable. When I was speaking to or playing with someone I could lose my temper in a flash, having no control over it myself.

As an adult man, twenty years later when I got to know my parents all over again, I talked quite a bit to my father about the past: he agreed that something had not been right about the way I was as a small child. He told me that he had always known I was different but he didn't understand it, at least not correctly. I was not like my sister, either in personality or in behaviour. I had a thick patch of dark hair on my lower back and my father remembers wondering if it was due to a hormone imbalance. My entire posture and the way I presented myself were masculine. On one occasion he remembered us going to the beach with another family on the street who had a son the same age as me. He had a set of snorkelling gear, and I decided that I wanted this set.

'It was the way you held your body, and put your fists up,' said my father. 'It was your whole stance. It made me look at you again.

'And you were like a match. You didn't take kindly to being told what to do, or being questioned in any way. I couldn't say anything to you at all, you would just flare up.'

I asked my father if he remembered the time we were watching a film on television about a little boy who befriended a giant turtle. In the film the turtle takes the boy swimming all around the coral reefs and in deep caves. I was so taken with this film that I desperately wanted a giant turtle. A turtle of my own could take me to hidden places where nobody could find me. He would protect me and I would protect him. I was determined to have one.

'It's not possible for you to have one,' my father said time and time again. 'They don't live in this country, the climate isn't right for them.' I just wouldn't let up, I didn't want to know about the explanations. If only I could have a turtle I could take it down to the beach and we could go swimming off together. My father tried various explanations as to why I couldn't have a giant turtle, but I got more and more angry and frustrated, and in the end I stormed off.

We also talked about my obsession with Red Indians.

'You always had to know *why*,' my father recalled. 'You used to get so angry and exasperated about why the Indians were never allowed to win. Every time they were beaten by the white man, you would fly into a rage. I tried to tell you it was only a film, that things didn't always happen that way, but you wouldn't have it.' I felt strongly about the fact that the Indians were always killed, it seemed so unfair. I think I also hated the way that they had their freedom taken away from them. I thought they too should be able to live any way they wanted.

My father asked me if I remembered the many holidays we had been on when I was young. I tried to explain to him that although I remembered quite a lot, I could only relate to the memories as I am now, as a male, because inside it's the way I'd always been.

These conversations between my father and myself were light-hearted at first and we tended to play it safe, especially if my mother was around. Talking about my childhood was difficult enough; what happened as I grew older was a subject still too sensitive and painful for us to broach.

Taking us on holiday was my parents' way of showing that they cared, apart from the fact that they both worked very hard and needed breaks themselves. They always made sure that they could take us kids away somewhere every year. Sometimes it would be in a caravan by the seaside, or to Blackpool or Butlin's. My maternal grandparents often came with us, or joined us half way through the holiday. My father and grandfather got on very well together and were good friends. I would go off with the two of them during the holidays; it felt right to be with them. It was their company I sought out, not my mother's, grandmother's or sister's. Once at Butlin's they entered me into a drawing competition. I drew a Disney cartoon character and around it I drew a strip of black and white film that depicted several other cartoon characters. I won first prize for it. My grandfather in particular was impressed by this and started to encourage me with my drawing.

I was still very much a loner and I would take off on my own if possible. My mother says she never saw me on holidays. I didn't mind joining in with all of them for meals and activities, but the sense of belonging was always missing. I wasn't ever really a part of things, I would just be there lost in my own thoughts.

My parents often had a hard time agreeing about things. At around this time, it was about where they were living. For my mother it was very important to live near her own mother, as was traditional at that time and place, mothers and daughters tending to stick close to one another. My grandparents lived in another small town a couple of miles away. These arguments between my parents eventually led to a split, and my mother, myself and my sister went to live with my grandparents.

My parents were only human and they had their problems to sort out. Although they did have problems with me, I never felt or was made to feel responsible for their difficulties. The time they spent apart did bring about constructive changes in my parents' relationship, so the separation was very beneficial.

They had married when they were in their early twenties. They were both quite quick-tempered and hotheaded. My father was a very hard-working man, he never took a day off except for holidays. He worked shifts so we didn't see very much of him. His job was arduous, working on the blast furnaces in the steel works. He always had to wear thick protective shirts and trousers and heavy-duty boots. Over the years he had different jobs within the steel works, progressing up to operating the cutting machine that eventually took his fingers. He always provided well for the family, and so did my mother. She always worked in some capacity, either in cleaning jobs, factory or office work. Later she trained to be a data processor and earned almost as much as my father.

As a result of living with my grandparents, I saw a lot more of my grandfather and became much closer to him. I thought very highly of my grandfather and for a few years I was very attached to him. He took a keen interest in me and in my drawing in particular when I was very young, but our really good times together began when I was around eight and we went to live with him.

I think he was the most important male role model in my life. He always had time for me, and we shared an interest in and a passion for nature. He was passionate about football and he was a very good player. He amused himself for hours in the backyard, kicking the ball and catching it on his knee or on the back of his head and rolling it down one arm or the other. He was full of tricks. I loved kicking a football around probably because I saw my grandfather getting so much pleasure from it, but mostly I enjoyed diving through the air for it. I was happy to play this game by myself, kicking the ball against a wall, and then diving for it.

He was very good at drawing too, even though he had lost the use of his right arm in an accident at the docks where he was working when he was a young man. He had a thick fleshy scar which ran from his wrist up into his armpit. He had fallen in a skip of slag and ripped the main artery in his wrist. If it wasn't for the fact that he was a good runner and very fit, it might have been the end of him. His friend ripped a piece off his shirt and made a tourniquet at the top of his arm, and my grandfather ran a very long way to the hospital to get the injury stitched up. He still had the use of his thumb, but the rest of the fingers curled over and stayed closed. When I was little I used to try to prise them open, but it wasn't until he died that his fingers uncurled and opened.

He received substantial compensation for this injury and could have stopped working at this point, but he continued working at the docks after the accident. He went in the very early hours of the morning to light the coal fires that drove the giant cranes, and he was back home again before breakfast, so he always had the days free. He was a great expert at lighting fires. Even at home he did a thorough and meticulous job of it.

I never thought of him as old. He was not tall, but gave that impression because of his straight posture. His hair was black, greying a bit, and his eyes were blue; he had exactly the same colouring as me.

From the age of five or six onwards he used to take me out into the hills or to the beach for long walks, he just loved walking, and we would collect wild flowers, shells, dried-up shellfish and other natural objects. When we weren't outside, he would make me sit and draw from pictures and postcards and the stuff we collected on our walks. Once we found a perfectly preserved wing of a seagull which we took home to draw. From him I learned a lot about seeing things and conveying them on to paper. He taught me about perspective and how to bring light into a drawing by the use of shading. He gave me a lot of encouragement and I remember this time with him as being very special.

He liked making decorative bottles with sea shells we collected on the beach; it was his hobby. On a fine day he used to make them outside in the backyard. He was quite particular about the way they were done and didn't want any assistance. I was allowed to mix up the glue for him and I enjoyed watching him work. He would put his bad hand on the top of the bottle and tilt it and put the shells on with his good hand. He did a fine job of it, and the really exceptional or unusual ones were always seized by members of the family.

Many, many years later when I was back in my home town, I dropped in to see my grandmother and we talked about him over a few tots of whisky. She missed him a lot and really wanted to talk about him. I told her about our long walks and all the different colours, sizes and shapes of shells we found.

'If he'd left me as many pennies as he left me shells, I'd be a millionaire,' she laughed.

My grandfather must have been fit even in his old age because it wasn't until I was an adult and rediscovered my old surroundings that I realized the huge distances we had walked together. He knew the area like the back of his hand and all the good places for picking blackberries, dewberries and mushrooms and the best beaches for collecting shells. In the spring, when the wild flowers came out, he would pick a bunch of the very first ones to give to my grandmother.

He was the one who taught me about money and even got me to save some. We had a secret hiding-place for my stash in the back of his old grandmother clock. My grandfather was also quite domestic and enjoyed helping my grandmother around the house. He would often look after us kids, and sometimes several cousins, while my grandmother was off to bingo for the evening. If there ever were any arguments or disruptions in our household or those of my aunts, us kids would be bundled off to my grandfather's house. Those were fun times, there would be loads of us, we all knew each other well and I felt quite secure.

My grandmother seemed to be always making Welsh cakes and the smell of them would fill the house. We would dive on them as soon as they came off the grill. My grandfather liked to have a go at turning them, but he wasn't very good at it and he broke quite a few because of his bad arm. He had to turn them with his left hand. When we all gathered in their house to watch a movie on television, my grandmother would get frying chips in industrial quantities. She'd open the hatch from the kitchen and shout to us, 'Right, how much do you want? Do you want three penneth worth or six penneth?' We'd all scramble to the kitchen hatch shouting 'Six penneth!' and she would wrap them in brown paper for us, just like at the chippie. Then we would all sit around the television eating our chips. My grandmother was a bingo fanatic, and she would have us all playing bingo in the house. There would be a hell of a din with us all shouting, including my grandfather. We played cards and all kinds of games and my grandparents would sing to us. They both loved singing. When we were sleeping over at their house my grandfather would put bricks in the fireplace, then wrap them up and put them in our beds to warm them up. When we were settled in for the night we would shout to my grandparents in the next room to sing to us. As soon as they finished one song we would ask for another, and so it went on until we were asleep.

My grandfather enjoyed looking after us on his own too, and he would happily see his wife off to bingo and get stuck into cooking for us and then he would tidy up and make sure everything was in order before she returned home. He always wanted to give her a thorough and graphic description of everything he had given us to eat, which used to make me feel full all over again.

He was a really nice guy but, like all of us, needed time to himself. He was quite a betting enthusiast, and on weekends he was not so keen to have us around. Nothing could interfere with the times of the races. He used to do stints as a bookie's runner – this was years earlier. When the horses were running, no one was to say a word, except to shout along with him for his horse to win.

One Christmas when my parents fell out with each other, and my Aunt Kathleen fell out with her husband, all of us piled into my grandparents' house. There were three Christmas trees, one in each room; we had all brought our own. My grandparents were very tolerant, since they enjoyed having us around.

The feelings of being unacceptable and different didn't come into it with my grandfather, with him I was always comfortable. He never challenged me about my boyish interests and behaviour, in fact, he seemed to take me exactly the way I was, even encouraging me to be myself. My grandmother thought I was very much like my grandfather and used to describe me as a sensitive child, which would make my mother smirk somewhat. My mother saw me as detached and headstrong, anything but sensitive.

My grandmother and grandfather each came from a family of eleven children, although two of my grandmother's brothers died young of tuberculosis. My grandfather's father married two sisters. By the first he had five children but sadly she died in childbirth. Her sister came to live with him to help out with the new baby. They eventually married and had six children of their own.

My grandmother often told us stories about her own life. Her mother died when she was only twelve, and being the second oldest she had to work very hard helping to bring up the little ones. My great-grandfather and his brother had come over from Ireland in their youth. My great-grandfather stayed in Wales but his brother went on to America. My grandmother showed us a photo of her father and said that he was a very quiet man. I thought he was stern looking with a great long handlebar moustache. He worked in the docks and liked a drop of whisky in the evenings. After his wife died he spent more time in the pub, but he held his whisky very well and could always walk a straight line.

'God bless him,' my grandmother would say, 'he missed my mother something terrible.' They could have been better off, but most families in the area were very poor, particularly at that time. One night my great-grandfather came home from work and asked my grandmother what she had made for tea. There was literally nothing to eat that day, and she had put a block of wood in the oven to warm up.

'Well,' said my grandmother as she opened the oven, 'if you can get your knife and fork into that, you're welcome to it.' Like all members of my family, she had a great sense of humour, and we would have a lot of laughs at her stories. One Christmas my grandmother's little sister wanted a doll, but there was no money to buy one. Finally my grandmother found an old shoe and painted a face on it in order for her sister to have her doll. My grandmother told us that she loved the doll and would wrap it in an old cloth and nurse it. We would all be in stitches when my grandmother explained how they had to wash their hair when she was young. There was just one source of water in the house and it was a tap on the outside wall, only twelve inches off the ground. They all had to lay themselves out flat on the ground and stick their heads under this tap and rinse their hair in the cold water.

She told us how she had met Bap – that is what we called my grandfather – at a dance when they were very young. They lived in different villages and Bap would walk quite a distance along the canal to meet my gran at an old bridge. He would call to her across the canal and she would cross the bridge to meet him. She told us that my grandfather was good-looking and all the girls were after him, but he only had eyes for her. They married when they were sixteen and eighteen years old in spite of a lot of opposition because of their age. Bap's brother Peter was very sceptical and said he gave the marriage no more than six months. On their fiftieth wedding anniversary I remember my grandmother saying, 'I wish Peter was alive to see us now.'

'Once we were married,' my grandmother said, 'I never looked back.' They moved in with my grandfather's aunt and uncle and her life improved immensely. She was taught all kinds of things, including baking. And that was it, she loved baking and baked forevermore.

My other grandfather died before I was born and my paternal grandmother did not figure as much in my life. What I remember most about her was that she gave me some very appropriate Christmas presents, robots. I loved my robots. She made homemade beer, ginger beer, ale and cherry brandy to drink herself and to give away to other people, especially around Christmas time. She was an unofficial midwife and well known for her skills in delivering babies. Lots of women in the area would come to my grandmother for help.

During the time that we were living with my grandparents, which lasted a few months, my parents patched up their differences, and my father bought a house down the road, just as my mother had wanted. The transition was easy for me because, since we were now neighbours, I continued my close association with my grandfather.

Once we had moved into our new home I made some friends in the neighbourhood, three boys and a girl. I felt comfortable with these friends and they treated me the way I wanted to be treated, like a boy. I kept asking them to call me different names. One day it would be Mike, another day Dave, Luke, Jud and so on. I also got to know two brothers whose father bought and sold horses. One of the brothers was nicknamed Clinker; I was quite friendly with him for a time and enjoyed helping him out with the horses, feeding them and brushing them. There was also lots of interesting land to explore in this new community. I was always sniffing about, looking in derelict buildings and along the railway line, finding bits and bobs. I would be running and ducking and diving, hiding or rolling down slopes to avoid being seen, living in my fantasy land where I was escaping or being a fugitive or exploring new territory.

In my travels I found a beautiful horse carriage. I was wandering down the railway line, past the signalbox used for the shunting trains coming from the foundry, and saw some old buildings. Inside one of them, there it was, yellow, red and blue. I decided to come back for it and a couple of days later I enlisted Clinker to help me. We pulled it all the way to the waste ground where Clinker's horse was kept, and strapped it up to him. We had a wonderful couple of hours riding around in it until a big smart silver car appeared. Someone had seen us and alerted the owner. He got out of the car. 'You get that carriage back to where you found it immediately, or I'm phoning the police!' he shouted at us.

Clinker's father got a horse once that was very fiery, all black. This horse could be quite excitable. One day we had to take this horse and another one to a field up the hillside where they could graze. We got on their bare backs, with me on the black one. As soon as we got to the bottom of the mountain my horse bolted off in a wild gallop. I can remember the sensation vividly. I wasn't scared, it was such an overwhelming feeling of exhilaration. As we got higher up the mountain the paths were narrow, often with sheer drops to one side, but he continued at a full gallop with such ease, as if I wasn't even on his back. I was hanging on to his mane, totally at his mercy, but he knew exactly where he was going. It was my first experience of a gallop and it felt great.

Although I was familiar with the area, having come there to visit my grandparents since early childhood, the move also proved to be the start of new difficulties for me. I had to adjust to a new school and was becoming aware of my limitations. Many aspects of my life seemed to become more oppressive and complex as I grew older.

For the first few months in the new house Anna and I shared a double bed. By this time our differences had really begun to show and we drifted apart. She was uncomfortable with my presence in the bed and would only agree to sleep there if my mother put a big fat bolster between us. As I remember, we were both pissed off at having to share a bed. My mother soon realized that we needed to be in separate bedrooms, and I was moved into the boxroom. They borrowed a very comfortable sofa bed from my grandparents for me to sleep on.

I did have one space at the new house which I liked and felt happy in, where I spent a lot of time. It was a tumbledown old shed at the end of the garden, damp as hell. This shed became mine. It had electricity in it, and I had a record player to play my music on: 'A Horse With No Name' was a favourite. I had all sorts of things in there, a knife and a dartboard and my fags. I smoked myself simple down there. Sometimes I spent all day in the shed throwing my knife. If I had a friend over, we played the game – I think it is called jackknife – where you take turns throwing the knife into the floor and the other person has to stretch for it, without moving one foot from its spot on the floor. I liked my knife. I also had an old gun that I had found, a German army hand-gun. I didn't have it for long. One bonfire night, when I was fooling around with it, my father took it off me. He had to chase me all over for it, I wasn't going to let it go easily. I was already like a match all over the place, and he probably thought, 'My God, give the child a gun as well...'

I remember painting over all the windows of my shed with white paint. Maybe it was to keep people from looking in, but I remember it as being more than that. I painted everything white. I had painted my Noddy, my brass horses and most of my toys white. I felt things needed filling in or blotting out. Reality for me didn't have the same weight and solidity as it seemed to have for others. I also had some doubts about whether things really were the same as the way they were presented, and often wondered if things were blank until somebody decided what they were going to be. Is what you see really what it is, truly? Noddy had his little blue jacket and his red shorts and his hat with the gold bell, but then again so did I, and the clothes I was supposed to wear said nothing about who I was and what I was; on the contrary, they lied.

With time I started to withdraw from my family, including my grandfather. I think that subconsciously I must have chosen to fail my eleven-plus. I must have been aware that if I passed I would end up in the grammar school which segregated boys and girls, and I knew which side I would have been forced into. I didn't want to be in any school at all, but at least I went to a mixed comprehensive school.

With the beginning of comprehensive school came the degradation of having to wear a girl's school uniform. I don't even like to talk about what that felt like, it can't really be described. At least when I was little I could wear what I wanted, and I was always in trousers. And, of course, in school, as you get a bit older, you are open to more ridicule in other ways too. It must have been obvious to most kids in school that I was extremely uncomfortable in myself, the way I acted, the activities I chose, my hostility and rebelliousness, and the way I looked. There were a tremendous number of new pressures, and I didn't want to be there at all. I started to mitch more often.

My parents didn't understand any of this. How could they? I don't think they'd ever heard or read about a condition such as mine. All they knew was that what they had on their hands was one very difficult child.

'You act as if you came into this world alone,' my mother used to say. 'You act as if you don't have any parents.'

And that is how it was for me: it felt as if I came into this world with no physical form to protect me. I was not a solid, tangible human being, like everyone else seemed to be. I felt vulnerable and alone.

2

I'm Getting out of Here

Most of my family had lived in this small Welsh town for generations and knew everybody. You were observed in everything you said and did. Any way of being that differed from the norm was either not known or not understood and certainly not accepted. Prejudice was rife, and life was about conforming and behaving like everyone else and striving for the same things as everyone else. For that reason it was particularly difficult for my mother to cope with the fact that she had given birth to a child that was becoming increasingly complex and unruly. This was coupled with the fact that she couldn't understand or make sense of me at all.

At some point, my father tells me, he tried to talk to my mother about my strange behaviour but no, no, no, she wouldn't have any of it, it was not to be discussed. She couldn't cope with any speculation about what could be wrong with me. She clung on to the idea that I was 'normal' and she kept hoping that I would grow out of it, whatever it was. I do understand now how she must have feared for me, even though she didn't understand at all what strange affliction I suffered. She, if anyone, knew that in a small community you are constantly being scrutinized, particularly as our family was well known to everybody. She was worried about what impression people would begin to have of me and unconsciously she must have been frightened for me, knowing the kind of prejudice I might encounter if I continued to be so out of tune with normality.

School was getting more difficult to endure. I was preoccupied with the way I felt, and my need to get away; there was nothing about school that interested me at all. I suppose I didn't even believe I could have done well. It wasn't that I didn't want to learn, but school was not the place for me to learn. There, the expectations of me were to act and behave according to the gender they believed me to be, and this was impossible for me. I had to push back all the harder to assert my sense of self. It made me resent authority and I became more and more anti everything.

As often as I dared I would take off after the register had been called. I would just fail to show up at my first lesson. Sometimes I didn't bother to show up at all. When my mother had my first school report she nearly had a heart attack. She couldn't believe that I had been off from school for that amount of time. Of course the school didn't let me get away with it: they tried various ways of keeping me in school, such as having my parents escort me there in the mornings, which I didn't take kindly to. I would sometimes run down to my grandparents' house and beg them not to let my parents force me to go to school. My grandmother would say to my parents, 'Don't make him go to school if he doesn't want to go, love 'im!' and she'd say to me, 'Go on, you run out and play, my handsome boy.' My grandmother often mixed up her grandchildren when she was talking to them. Most of the time, to her, I was her 'handsome boy' (at the time I didn't think anything of it, but later I wondered if she could have known that I was really a boy, on a subconscious level). My mother would practically go mental: 'What do you mean, don't make her go to school? They'll have me in court if she doesn't go to school. She has got to go.'

'All right, all right, I'll go, but please let me go by myself. At least let me get on the bus by myself,' I pleaded.

'You devious thing, you are nothing but a little thug, you'll be there waving from the bus and then you'll get off at the next stop,' my mother would say. And that is exactly what I did, maybe not at the next stop, but two or three down the road.

I became very secretive, and fierce about my privacy. My mother used to say, 'You act as if you have just two minutes to live, you don't want to be around, you don't want to stay in the house. You eat your food standing up and then you're off.' I had nowhere to go really but I just wanted to get out, to get away. I didn't want to take part in any family activity or meals. I don't ever remember being hungry anyway; food didn't interest me. I was happy walking along canal banks or disused railway lines, where I didn't have to feel the constraints that I felt around people.

At the age of eleven or twelve I had begun to realize that I had to be a lot more cautious about keeping bits of myself well hidden from others. Like my attraction to, what was for me, the opposite sex. It was also a time when I realized that my mother was not someone I would ever be able to confide in, where my feelings were concerned. This realization first came to me via a stainless steel lighter that I coveted. It was my father's, he had got it while he was in the army. He was forever dropping it down between the cushions of the couch, and this is how I got my hands on it. I just liked having it in my pocket, and I used it to light my cigarettes in bed. I hid it in a slit that I had cut in my mattress, but Anna got wise to it and told my mother where it was.

With the lighter was a letter. It was a letter that I had written to a girl I liked. When my mother found the lighter she also found the letter and read it. It must have been a love letter, because she went berserk over it and made me feel that I had done something absolutely wrong. She threatened to tell my father and grandfather about it and made it sound as if they would disown me if they found out. 'If they find out, there'll be murders.'

This incident really knocked me back. My mother's disgusted reaction drove it home to me how strongly people and society disapprove of anyone who is different, and how unacceptable it was for me to have these feelings. I suppose my mother's fear was that I was becoming a lesbian. Little did she know what was really ailing me. I was a boy.

Whatever she thought or believed, she was unable to handle the situation in a sensitive way, and both of us were very disturbed by this episode, each in our own way. Even now, just thinking about that incident, I can feel the humiliation of it all. It confirmed my feelings of inadequacy, my sense of not belonging anywhere or with anyone. And yet, in spite of all that, something about the way I was seemed perfectly natural to me. What was unnatural was relating to others in the way that they expected me to. The girl in question knew I liked her, we had even kissed a few times. Because it seemed OK with her, it seemed even more normal to me.

My Aunt Kathleen, Sheila's mother, let me be myself most of the time. She was not unlike my mother, full of fun but much taller, but because she wasn't my mother I didn't feel under the same pressure with her. She could be very stern when she had had a gutful of us all running about. We knew when it was about to happen because one of her eyelids would start to close, and it was time to run. Once, after a safe interval we rang on the doorbell and when she opened the door we all stood there with one eye closed. When she saw this she laughed like hell. She seemed to have some sympathy and understanding of the fact that I was different and struggling. When this incident with the letter happened, it was arranged that I should go and stay with her for a week. Whether it was a break for me to be there or not, leaving home after the incident increased the feeling of humiliation and made it seem magnified and drawn out. I was worried about seeing my mother again and wondered how she was going to feel about me and react to me.

My aunt was very relaxed about things. She was able to control me quite easily because I respected her. She let me smoke in front of her from that visit on, something my parents never let me do until I was thirteen, when there was a final showdown about it. My mother had for ever been going through my pockets and confiscating my cigarettes.

'It's fucking irritating the way you keep taking my cigarettes off me. If you don't let me smoke in front of you I'm going to do it behind your back anyway,' I said to her, 'so stop taking my smokes away from me.' From then on my parents, who at the time were both smokers, let me smoke in the house. Even so I didn't feel comfortable smoking in front of them, but on the odd occasion I did.

I was getting myself into trouble, and starting to go off the rails. I had my first real brush with the law when I was twelve and I nicked a motorbike with a couple of friends. We crashed it into the back of a car; someone saw this and reported us and that was how we were caught. We ended up in court and my parents had to pay a fine of £76. The judge had requested a report about me from my school. In this report, the deputy headmistress described me as truculent, among other things. My science teacher reported that my aggression and rebelliousness were unreasonable, that I was a disruptive influence on the rest of the class, I couldn't concentrate, I wouldn't communicate or be involved in anything, I wouldn't listen to anybody or cooperate, I was extremely aggressive and explosive and I made it quite obvious that I didn't want to be in school.

My parents were shocked at this damning report, and I suppose it described my behaviour, but also how inadequately my teachers interpreted my conduct. No one had an inkling where all this stemmed from. Once this report had been issued, the stigma of being a troublemaker stuck to me. I became a scapegoat for most of the trouble that went on in school. My mother would get letters blaming me for almost every misdemeanour going.

This started my parents worrying about what effect my behaviour would have on Anna, particularly as she would soon be starting in the same comprehensive school. Whereas I was aggressive, masculine and loud, she was quiet, feminine and reserved. My mother was very protective about both of us. She didn't like having teachers talk about me, putting all those labels on me, but even more she worried that they would think Anna was cut out of the same cloth. Anna herself was worried.

My behaviour generally was causing a lot of upheavals in the home. My mother felt that my father, being the man in the house, should take charge of the situation.

'You've got to control her, say something to her, for God's sake,' she would shout at him. He would be shouting at me because she expected it of him, but he was the more open-minded and easy-going of the two. I can't say that he was very lenient, but he did often try to smooth things over to keep the peace. Nevertheless I caused my parents a lot of grief and in their frustration and helplessness they blamed each other. My mother particularly blamed my father. He is a gentle guy, but he is big and very loud. If he raised his voice or shouted it was awesome and always sounded much worse and more aggressive than was intended. My mother felt I could be following him.

Soon I was also up for drinking under age and for disorderly conduct. I was very young when I started drinking. I used to, somehow or other, get hold of flagons of cider, and more often than not I was drunk. Later, when I was examined by a psychiatrist, she said it was quite possible that I would become a child alcoholic with the amount I was drinking.

Perhaps even more destructive was the lighter fuel and the Lady Esquire that we used to sniff. Lady Esquire was a solvent which was intended to strip the colour off leather shoes. It was taken off the market because of kids like me buying it in order to get high. When I got used to sniffing it and it no longer had the desired effect, I would soak a rag in the stuff, put it in my mouth, bite hard and inhale through it. Once I really went over the top after doing this. It stands out in my mind because it was the last time. Paula, a cousin of a friend of mine a few years older than me, found me in a hell of a mess walking down the middle of the road, totally out of my mind, high as a kite. There were buses and cars all over the place and I was just strolling among them, when she ran out into the road and pushed me out of the way. She took me home to her place and gave me a mixture of beans and ice-cream to make me sick.

After a while I left Paula's place not feeling too great; I walked down the lanes with the bottle of Lady Esquire still in my pocket. Good as the stuff was for a cheap high, it also caused severe stomach cramps, which doubled me up in pain. I read somewhere that it also strips the marrow out of your bones. So a combination of factors made me resolve to never use it again. I took the bottle out of my pocket and threw it against a brick wall where it smashed into a thousand pieces.

Most of my friends did the same thing, but their reasons for getting high were mostly pleasure and fun, although I am sure some of them had problems of their own. All I could think of was getting high and rebelling whenever I wasn't allowed to do my own thing; there was nothing else in my head. There was a recklessness about the way I lived, as if I didn't care at all what happened to me at the end of the day. I wanted to live, not die, but whether or not I got into trouble or got locked up or harmed myself in any way seemed totally unimportant. I already knew that getting locked up was a possibility. I had been warned by teachers and other adults that this was how I could end up. In fact, I didn't even care if I was put away or locked up. It seemed a way out of my life as it was and I'd be in another environment where perhaps I was not the only one who was different, or at least my difference would be better tolerated or ignored altogether, or so I thought. As a result I took all kinds of crazy risks.

One evening when I was out in the street causing a ruckus with my friends, I climbed up on the police cars right outside the police station, trying to kick off the flashing lights from the roofs. Amazingly I wasn't caught. I did learn from some of the situations I got myself into and I really made an effort to avoid confrontations where my aggression would get out of hand, mainly by keeping myself to myself.

Even so, word gets around, and there were a couple of occasions when someone came from one of the other villages to challenge me to a fight. Because of the way people perceived me, there were times when a confrontation became unavoidable and if I was pushed enough my aggression would take over, and I wouldn't care if the other person was male or female. Later on in my life, I became more respectful of the difference between men and women and would treat confrontations with women more rationally and calmly, but on reflection my experience has been that, although women are not as aggressive, they can be just as violent as men.

When I was around twelve or thirteen, on a hot summer's day a friend came up to me in town and said, 'Someone is looking for you.'

'Who?' I asked.

'It's some girl from out of town who has heard about you. She is supposed to be really hard.'

A while later this girl came on to me in the street and challenged me to fight her. I didn't really want to, but she kept provoking me and getting more confident as I refused to be drawn into it. I could see that I wasn't going to be able to avoid the confrontation. She was quite a big person, a couple of years older than me, and obviously thought herself invincible. She was taunting me into it and in the end I got pissed off. I punched her, and she went flying up against a car, fell over the wing and landed on the road. She got up and started to run and I went after her. Further down the street she ducked into someone's house and that seemed to be the end of it.

I went for a walk down the canal bank and then roamed around for a while, had a fag or two, and then I decided to go home. My father was sunbathing on the front steps. He was always a real sun worshipper, and when the sun went from the front he would move to the back of the house and stay there until the sun went down. I went up the stairs and stepped over him quietly, not to disturb him. I got two steps past him, and I could feel a hand closing around my ankle, pulling me back down the stairs.

'You bastard, what have you been up to? We've just had the police here looking for you.'

I was astonished, because I couldn't understand what it was all about. 'I haven't done anything.'

'You've beaten up some girl, and she is not only physically hurt, but she is in an extreme state of distress. You've been at it again, causing trouble for yourself and for us.'

The point is that I didn't really want to fight for the sake of having a fight. It was never my intention to give the impression that I was out to challenge everyone, but it was sometimes impossible to contain the envy and bitterness I felt at having to take a back seat in my own life. The anger would ignite in the pit of my stomach and then rise like a burning fuse and explode in my head. More often than not it was myself I hurt rather than other people. I could bash my head against a wall or punch myself in the face, or throw myself down banks, get soaking wet and covered with mud. It was as if I needed to feel pain externally in order to get away from the raging inside my head. It always happened involuntarily, in a flash, and it left me feeling empty and despondent at not being able to contain my frustration.

I had quite a few scraps with boys. But my aggression was also a tool for keeping people at bay; they knew not to mess with me. It automatically put a distance between me and others which I needed in order to maintain my equilibrium. My friends must have been quite confused about me anyway. They had a nickname for me: Crunch. It referred to a time when I punched a girl in the nose. Ironically, I had hit the girl in defence of a friend, whom she'd been bullying for some time. One day I saw this happening and said, 'Come on, fight me instead and leave her alone. She is smaller than you.' When I punched her, her nose broke with a crunching sound and thereafter everyone called me Crunch.

I did enjoy the rough and tumble of playful fighting. Once I took a swing at a mate and he literally flew backwards into a children's paddling pool (which thankfully was full of water) and got up with a bloody nose and a stunned expression on his face.

'Sorry mate, I really didn't mean to hit you so hard.' I was somewhat stunned myself. I had missed out on the normal games and contact sports that boys engage in, which might have helped create more of an awareness of my physical strengths and weaknesses.

Because I felt so restricted by my body, any external restrictions compounded my frustration and discomfort in myself. I think it was for that reason I seemed to do everything at odd hours; my whole life was upside down. I came home whenever I wanted to, and ate when I was hungry, and got drunk when I felt like it, be it morning, noon or night. Any form of authority over me also added unbearably to these feelings of constraint. It was like being suffocated. Any suggestions from my mother about clothes to wear were met with anger and refusal. If she asked me where I was going, it was: 'I don't know, do I, for Christ's sake? What's it got to do with you anyway?' I would never say where I was going, partly because most of the time I didn't have a clue myself. Once she asked me if I would be home for tea. To get her off my back, I said, 'Yeah, yeah, I'll be home for tea.' I was out all night and came home the following afternoon.

'I meant tea yesterday, not tea today,' she scowled at me.

Often my parents had heard from others about some of my antics, sometimes the police had been to see them about me, and

I could never be sure how the ground lay when I came home. Approaching the house I would sometimes catch them screaming about me, 'Where is the little bastard? . . . She is out of control . . . We can't do anything with her . . . Just look at the time,' and so on. I would think, 'Shit, I'm not going in there,' so I would turn around and run off and spend the night somewhere else. Sometimes Anna would come running to warn me that the police had been to the house so that I could make myself scarce.

I found it so difficult to be around most people, and around my family, that I continually ran away and took to the hills. The urge to escape would be overwhelming sometimes. I yearned to be able just to be myself, and that seemed possible only with no one else around. Sometimes, if I was drunk, I would stay at a friend's house, or sneak into somebody's garage, a vacant house, or sleep rough somewhere. My mother and father had the police out after me time and time again. They would give it a day, and a night maybe, and then they would have the family, my uncles and cousins out looking for me. If they didn't find me, they reported my absence to the police.

When I was thirteen I ran away and ended up in the city, about fifteen miles from home. Anna had run up to me in the playground to warn me that the police were looking for me. I can't remember what I had been up to, but I decided to take off there and then, rather than go home and face the music. On my way down the street I met a girl from school.

'Where are you off to?' she asked.

'I'm on the run. I'm taking off,' I said.

'I wouldn't mind running away myself,' she said. 'Things are not that great at home.'

'Right, well I am going. If you want to come it's up to you.'

We had enough money between us to take the bus into the city, and from there we hitched a lift along the bay to a nice part of town that had a marina and lots of boats. That night we tried to sleep in a rowing boat, which had another one turned upside down over it, like two halves of a walnut. It was extremely uncomfortable and awkward. We got out after a couple of hours and saw that the tide was right out. Resting on the sand a few hundred yards out was a nice comfortable-looking speed boat with a canvas top. We decided to walk out and spend the rest of the night on it. We were up to our knees in mud by the time we reached it and climbed in. We were soaking wet and freezing, all I had on was a thin blue cord jacket, but we had a packet of Woodbines and some matches, so we tried to warm up by smoking fag after fag.

We eventually got some sleep, but by the time we woke up and were about to hop out of the boat in the morning, the tide had come in and the shore seemed miles away.

'Jesus, did we walk all that way?' I couldn't believe how far out we were. We had no choice but to jump in the water, fully dressed. My friend could hardly swim, so she was hanging on to me. It's a miracle we didn't drown. After swimming for what seemed like an eternity, we found ground under our feet. But, of course, the seabed is not level so once in a while my friend would disappear under and I would have to grab hold of her and pull her along.

When we finally reached shore all she wanted to do was to get home. I didn't want to go home but I agreed to take her and make sure she got there all right, and then be on my way again. We walked around a while to try and dry off, and then we went to the bus-stop. There was a hut where a bus driver was drinking tea and eating sandwiches. We told him we had run away and were starving. He was a decent sort of person, because he gave us some sandwiches and then drove us back into the city and also gave us the bus fare to go home.

When we eventually got back, we could see in the distance that there were police cars outside my friend's house. Opposite her house was a graveyard, and that is where I took refuge to avoid being seen. As luck would have it, down the road strides my mother and spots me. There was nowhere to run. She grabbed me and marched me down the centre of the street all the way home. On the way we passed my grandparents' house. My grandmother was in the doorway, and when she saw me she shouted 'You little bastard!' That shocked me because she had always been on my side, telling my mother to leave me alone.

One place that provided me with refuge several times was a wartime air-raid shelter on a piece of wasteland outside of town.

It was hidden by trees and bushes and, conveniently, had a stream running past it. It was my secret sanctuary until it was discovered when I ran away and stayed there for about four days. It consisted of just a deep hole in the ground with a small room to one side. It was difficult to get in and out of, the walls were so high, somewhere between six and eight feet. The place was full of rubble which I had cleaned up and piled in a corner.

There was often no reason for me to run away except my need to be alone. This particular time when I stayed four days in the shelter I had taken nothing with me but I had a very thick warm coat which kept the cold out. A couple of friends knew where I was and they nicked tins of spaghetti and beans and brought them to me. In the day I would walk all over the mountain and along railway lines, keeping away from the roads, since the police would be on the lookout for me.

When eventually they found me, I was having a cosy time in my little pad. My football socks, which I had washed in the stream, were hanging on a line to dry. I was in the process of cooking some spaghetti hoops in a saucepan that a friend had brought me. I had a nice fire going with an upturned wire breadbasket acting as a cooker, with the pan on top. A friend was paying me a social visit and he cleared off in the nick of time. He was about to leave anyway and when he got up on to the ground he shouted down to me, 'The law, the law is coming!'

'Quick, run, don't let them see you!' I shouted back, so he scurried off.

And there was my mother and the cops looking down the hole. My mother was just so shocked and disgusted with my hide-out she said, 'What do you have, rats for cushions?' That's my mother's sense of humour, but make no mistake, she was not pleased. I was marched back into town and taken straight to see the 'boardman'. He is the man who takes charge of kids caught mitching from school. Truanting was also called being 'on the mung'. We used to call this bloke the 'Dickabordie', and he would catch up with you if you stayed away from school. It was even more embarrassing for my mother because the Dickabordie was a distant relative.

At the end of the interview he said that this was my final warning, whatever that meant. I didn't take a blind bit of notice anyway. I didn't even understand the purpose of me being there, except to frighten me, and frightened I was not. All the while my mother kept reminding me, 'Your father is going to kill you when we get home.' He did go for me, in fact, but as I recall I went for him as well. He seldom hit me, but this time he slapped me hard on the head. There is nothing more aggravating than being slapped on the head.

As usual, after this kind of performance, I would go up to my room and 'freak out'. The doors on my wardrobe had been ripped off long ago, and most things had been smashed up. I kept the wardrobe intact though, because I used it to barricade myself in by putting it up against the door. I had snapped all the coat-hangers in half. I would scream at everyone to get out and leave me alone, and I would butt my head hard against the walls. My parents must have really wondered what kind of creature they had brought into the world.

Later the police came to the house carrying my football socks and my Crombie coat, which had been left in the air-raid shelter in the commotion.

'Are these yours?'

'Yeah, thanks,' I said.

That same night, I climbed out of the window and was gone again.

Because I didn't get along with my parents at all they mistakenly believed I was running away simply to escape from them. They thought I really hated them, and I don't think I did very much to convince them that it wasn't so. Sometimes I thought I hated them but at the same time I knew deep down that they were not to blame. I didn't really want to cause them so much distress but I didn't know how to behave any differently. They couldn't have understood my craving to escape, and I couldn't have explained it even if I'd wanted to. Communication had broken down between us completely. It was impossible to talk on a rational level any more. By now we only seemed to interact through arguments, shouting and screaming at one another. It was difficult for me to feel any warmth towards them; it seemed they were never on my side. Other people happily brought my behaviour and my actions to my parents' attention, so they were constantly upset and angry with me.

I often barricaded myself in my bedroom and wouldn't come out, so my mother would leave me my food outside the door. In the night when the house was quiet I would put on my clothes and climb down the drainpipe and take off. I was like a fugitive, always trying to run away from something, but I was always much more at peace with myself if only I could be on my own, particularly in the wild. It used to give me quite a high: my train of thought about myself and who I was could take off and be free. I was able to stay in my reverie and forget the reality of my parents, school, the town, my friends. I was living on the wild side and pretended to be on the run permanently. At night I would make a fire to warm myself and wash in the streams in the morning. There were times when, sitting alone in the dark in front of a fire, I felt a little lonely and forlorn. But mostly I was elated when I was lost in my own little world.

When I was eventually found by either my parents or the police and I was dragged right back into the harsh reality of my parents' world, the world that was my enemy, it wasn't without a fight. Being yanked out of my dream world, which for me was my reality, was always a severe shock to my system. It was profoundly disorientating: a bit like when you are engrossed in a book, really living the story and someone comes out of nowhere and starts ranting at you about something. You don't want to tear yourself away from the story and you don't want to hear what is being said. I couldn't bear being brought back to reality and I'd go wild. I would scream and shout at my parents: 'I can't wait to get away from you! As soon as I'm sixteen I'm out of here!' In a frenzy I would try and upset them as much as I could. 'I hate you. I can't wait for you to die and I'm going to dance all over your fucking graves when you do,' I would shout. 'You are no parents of mine, and when I go you'll never ever see me again because I'm never coming back.' I would get so worked up that in my rage I didn't care how much I hurt their feelings.

My parents would be equally angry and shout back: 'You have to stay here and you have to go to school.' And they would try to have me believe: 'We'll have to go to prison or we'll get a big fine if you don't go to school. Look what you are putting us through – and your sister. You must really enjoy doing this to us. We're having all the neighbours talking about us and peering through the windows.'

'Well, soon I'll be gone and I won't have to fucking live around here no more, with all these bastard people. I can't wait to get out of here.'

I didn't understand that none of this was my parents' fault. Because, as my parents, they were mainly responsible for the restrictions in my life, they got the brunt of my anger. I didn't give a thought to the fact that my behaviour was affecting their marriage, that they worried constantly about my whereabouts, and that my anger and apparent hate for them were very hurtful. All I could see was that they had no understanding of the fact that I just wanted to be left alone. I felt desperately that I needed to make my own way in life, away from my short-lived past, so that I could live in my own reality. Naturally it was totally impractical and unrealistic.

Once, in a moment of insight into what my behaviour was doing to my parents, I wrote my mother a letter. I told her I was sorry for upsetting everybody, that I didn't mean to hurt her and that I didn't really hate them. I left the letter in a place where she would find it, but I felt quite nervous about how she would react to it. She went berserk.

'Don't you write me any more bloody letters!' she shouted at me. 'I want no more letters of apology from you.'

Her reaction made me feel totally humiliated and I regretted ever attempting to make amends with her. The incident made the divide between us even deeper. I saw that Anna was able to communicate quite well with my mother, but I no longer could nor wanted to.

My relationship with school was becoming a disaster. I was impossible to control when I was there. I wasn't afraid of anyone; my anger and frustration conquered all that. I felt so strongly about my predicament and about the school uniform I had to wear that anything else seemed trivial in comparison. I seldom attended any lessons, and when I did I always caused a disturbance of some sort. If it wasn't with a sling, it was with a peashooter. Letters were coming thick and fast to my parents, saying that I was disruptive, and that I was affecting the whole class, making it difficult to control, and that they couldn't get me to do any work.

'You are nothing but a little thug,' my mother would say.

It was absolutely true that I was misbehaving. I was smoking all over the place, impertinent to teachers, hostile and angry. I refused to conform and I couldn't stand anyone telling me what to do. It was as if even having someone encourage me, or tell me that I was good at something, would have been a defeat, a weakness on my part. I was told that I was artistic, but I didn't want to hear it from them. Apart from that, I don't recall any teacher ever trying to help me or understand me, not that I would have noticed it anyway – I neither wanted help nor allowed anyone to get close enough to offer any.

I remember only once taking a small stand in relation to learning. I insisted that I should be allowed to join the boys in a woodwork class, rather than the cookery class where I was supposed to be. I hated cookery class, and I don't suppose I was very popular with the teacher. To the school's credit I was moved to the woodwork class, but I didn't stay even there for long.

I could no longer make myself scarce or blend in; my behaviour was now being constantly scrutinized. I couldn't make a move without being noticed, both by teachers and by my peers.

My biggest torture at school was still how I had to be dressed. I couldn't stand it. I hated wearing a skirt so much. My legs were quite hairy and masculine anyway, but that wouldn't have mattered if I could have worn shorts. My difficulties were not with my legs as such, but with what was around them. I'm sure people thought I looked as stupid in my school uniform as I felt. It is hard for me even to think about how shameful and oppressive that was, so I won't say anything more about it. In any event, all I ever carried in my school bag was a pair of jeans that I would put on as soon as I was out of the school gates or when I was 'absent' from school.

After a time I decided that if I had to attend school, I was going to wear what I wanted. I changed into my jeans in the lane before going into school every morning. I was warned by teachers several times so instead I tried wearing a pair of black trousers. That didn't work either and I was finally taken to the headmaster and threatened with suspension if I refused to wear the proper school uniform. I left his office feeling very angry and went to find my friend, Jill, who was in the year ahead of me. I found her in the common room used by the fourth and fifth years and told her what had happened. She got quite worked up about it herself. After school we went back to her flat where she lived with her mother and continued talking about it. She looked at me quietly for a while. She knew I wasn't going to stop wearing trousers and she said, 'I'll come out in protest with you. You're already classed as a troublemaker, they're not going to take you seriously on your own. Cool down a bit and meanwhile I'll try and find others who will be prepared to wear trousers in order to help. They can't suspend us all, can they?' We laughed about this prospect and I felt a lot better.

I was able to have a pair of shoes that fitted with my image of myself: brogues with leather soles, horseshoe studs on the heel and metal tips on the toe. They were excellent for sliding along the pavement and were very tough.

My dinner money was spent daily at the corner store on five cigarettes, and if I got hungry I nicked my dinner from the bakery. It was easily done – the place was always packed with people at midday – I just had to stick my hand over a low glass partition and off I went. It was always the same, a hot loaf of bread and a pie. I used to break the loaf in half and stick the pie in between. A pie-butty – it was delicious.

If I was desperate for food in school I occasionally approached Anna: 'Hey, lend me a dinner ticket.' She would just keep on walking. I couldn't get her to stop and speak to me most of the time. She had started to walk around as if she didn't know me. I am sure it was her way of coping; it couldn't have been easy being my sister. Anna always behaved herself and never caused my parents any grief. She never smoked or drank and she kept herself well away from me. She must have been mortified about being related to me. I didn't mind because I knew what it was like to feel vulnerable and I felt protective towards her.

Loaves of bread were not the only booty. I remember coming home from school once and my mother had all these objects lined up on the floor, ridiculous objects, such as tin-openers, a thing to make round potatoes, a handful of crosses and St Christopher medals, braces (for my Stay-press trousers), records, and other bits and bobs.

'What shop did this come from?' she screamed at me, pointing at each thing in turn. I was wearing a maroon checked shirt, a Ben Sherman, the sort that skinheads used to wear. My mother knew that it wasn't mine and that I must have thieved it from somewhere.

'My God, not even what you're wearing is yours.' She went for me and ripped the shirt off me, and all the buttons went flying. She said that she was taking it all back to the shops, but I'm sure she didn't, it would have been too embarrassing. But I don't think for one minute that she kept them either; they probably all ended up in the bin. She could not have coped with the idea of handling stolen goods and actually using the potato scoop.

I often took a 'shopping trip' into town with my big parka coat on, one with many deep pockets. A very conspicuous garment, looking back on it. It was not uncommon for me to come bolting out of a shop with someone chasing after me. I would just keep running and not look back. I really don't know what the hell I needed some of those things for, but I remember it made me feel independent. If I wanted or needed something I would never have to ask anyone for it; it was as if I was really on my own, getting by.

I thought of myself as living on the edge, so I believed that none of the rules that applied to other people applied to me. I was pushing the limits all the time, seeing how much I could get away with. Being in control of any situation was a powerful feeling for me. Along with this was a complete lack of concern about what the consequences of my actions would be. If I was apprehended and in deep trouble, well so be it, that was the road that I was supposed to go down. Nothing could match the grief that I was constantly living with, so nothing made any real impact on me in that way.

One evening I was in our front room with one of my friends, Katrina, listening to music. I didn't often sit in there but when I did I would say to my mother, 'Don't come in and start asking me questions and talking to me. If I am going to be in here I want to be here alone.' I never wanted to be bothered or hassled by adults and I didn't want to talk. So, there we were left to our own devices. I said to my friend, 'Do you want to try and nick a car?' We sneaked out of the house – she was more or less tagging along – and across the railway line we found a car that was easy to get into. I had never driven a car and I didn't know the first thing about them. After tinkering around I got in, but I had no idea of what to do next and in any event that is when the police car came along. Someone must have alerted the police when they saw me break into the car. I got out and ran full pelt across the lines, down the hill and back into the house and just sat in the front room. I don't remember where Katrina disappeared to.

A little while later there was a knock on the front door. My mother opened it. I could hear her talking to the cops, she was adamant: 'Listen, she has been sitting in the front room all afternoon and evening. I know she can be trouble but this time you are wrong. Whoever it was you saw, it wasn't her; she hasn't left the house.' But my father thought differently. He came in and stood looking at me while my mother was talking to the coppers.

'Mind if you have been out, there is going to be murders.' He looked closer at me. 'You have been out, haven't you? I know you have.' He lowered his voice and hissed, 'For Christ's sake, don't let your mother find out that she has been out there telling lies to the police.' He left it at that. We both knew it was better if she didn't find out, so I got away with it.

Even though I belonged with no one I still had a few mates, a mixture of boys and girls, and I hung around with them quite a lot. We had some exciting times causing a riot and being up to no good. We used to hang out in one particular pub. I was only thirteen when I started drinking there. Quite a few of us there were under age. On occasion the landlord would shout, 'Police!' and most people would evaporate through the back window. God knows what the police thought when they came in there, the tables full of pints and nobody around.

One place where we used to hang out was at the flat of a girl from school. Her mother, Ginny, had been related to my family by marriage but she was divorced and was living in the flat alone with her daughter. She didn't have a lot of control, none in fact, and it was the daughter who called the shots. We were always at the flat playing records, smoking, and having a good time. If I was too drunk to go home I would often go to their flat instead and the mother would think nothing of having me in for the night and giving me some grub.

I was there one night, and my mother had the police looking for me. They came to Ginny's flat and we quickly turned off all the lights, pretending not to be there. The cops were trying to see in by shining flashlights through the letterbox and through the little window at the top of the door.

Ginny was whispering, 'I've got to open the door, you little bastards, let me open the door.'

Her daughter said to her, 'You open that fucking door, I'll fucking knock you out.'

She was scared of her daughter so she didn't open the door. In any event, Ginny was going through a rough time because of her divorce, and was 'not all there' at times. She could often be heard shouting out of the window in the middle of the night. Mostly she was ranting abuse at her ex-husband, screaming, 'You bald-headed bastard – stop shagging behind the Co-op!' so that it echoed around the blocks of flats.

She would wake us up in the night, saying that her dead mother was present. She had this notion, among others, that it was a bad omen if a red rose fell off a table or cabinet. Katrina and I played a cruel joke on her once. There was a plastic rose in a vase sitting on top of her television set. When she was out of the room we tied a thread around the stem of the rose and trailed it out through the door. Later, when she was sitting there in front of the television I was tugging at the thread, making the rose move. I finally gave it a yank, and the rose flew off the television. The poor woman was running around screaming, saying her mother was in the room, trying to warn her of something.

The flat was full of mice – they came from the empty flat underneath. When we turned the light out at night, they would come scurrying around on the floor. Nobody would ever volunteer to go and turn the light back on or fetch cigarettes or anything because of the fear of stepping on one or having them run across your feet. It was quite a household, and we had some good times there.

There was an alcoholic woman who lived in a flat opposite Ginny's. Sometimes, if we were drunk or were desperate for a place to crash, she would let us stay there. We would knock on the window and she would open it and in we'd climb. One night I was sleeping there with Katrina when we both woke up, startled to find her standing over us. 'Do you want a drop of cider?' she croaked.

'No, we don't want a drop of cider. What the hell time is it?' She didn't take kindly to my reaction, and started to rant and rave, so I said to Katrina, 'Let's leave discreetly, the same way we came in.' We opened up the window and climbed out.

A few other people of my parents' generation did appear to have a bit of understanding and tolerance of me, but not many. The mother of my friend Jill said to me once, 'I know what you are, and I don't mind as long as you don't touch my daughter.' I just looked at her. What could I say? She thought she knew what I was, like many other people thought they did as I grew older. I didn't mind so much that they thought I was gay, although they were wrong. Boys saw me as a mate, and this is what I wanted, it was safe. Even though these sorts of misinterpretations weren't causing me particular grief at the time, I had an inkling that to be myself was going to get increasingly complicated.

I didn't seem to care much about anything else, but I went through a lot of anguish leading up to my grandfather's death when I was thirteen. He had been diagnosed with cancer of the stomach two years earlier and had been given six months to live, but lived another two years. He couldn't keep anything down except liquid food, and later he wasn't able to keep anything down at all. I found it extremely distressing to see him deteriorate, since I had always known him as a very fit and strong man. Towards the end he was very ill. We were all there, the whole family, the day he left his house to go into hospital. He turned to my grandmother by the front door, and grabbing her arm, he winked, 'Don't worry Ma, I'll make our fiftieth anniversary.' And he did. As close as I was to him, I was the only one of all the grandchildren who never went to visit him in the hospital. Even though I wanted to, I couldn't bring myself to go. I was off the rails with drinking and in a lot of trouble, and perhaps also I didn't want him to know me in this state. I don't honestly remember.

One day I was walking through town when I suddenly had a strong urge to go to my grandparents' house. My grandfather was home from the hospital by then, and when I saw my whole family gathered there I started running up the stairs. Everybody gathered there tried to stop me. I ran up anyway, into his room. He knew I was there but he didn't even turn around to look at me. He was dead, of course, but my mind wouldn't register it. I ran downstairs where everyone was crying and asked what was happening, what was wrong.

Later they told me that he had shouted out my name before he died. I can't get over that. Was it because he had not seen me to say goodbye, or perhaps he knew something about the life I was going to have to face?

It was around this time, aged thirteen, that I finally smashed up my school and was expelled. One lunch-time I started to throw stones at the windows. I smashed as many windows as I could, and before anyone had time to stop me I ran down into the toilets, which were in the yard, and kicked all the lids off the toilet pans and hurled them all through an opening in the roof on to the road outside the school. Then I started to pull the doors off the toilet cubicles. A man who was driving past the school saw all the toilet lids spread all over the road and came in to report it to the headmaster. The schoolyard was full of kids and after I had finished my rampage I hid behind a large group of them. The headmaster marched through the yard, shouting, 'I *will* find out who is responsible for this, make no mistake about it.' I ran until I was out of sight of the school and didn't return home that night – I stayed with a barmaid who worked in a pub where I used to drink.

The next morning I went back to school, why, I cannot for the life of me remember. Perhaps just to see how the ground lay. Through the glass doors leading to the headmaster's office I spotted my parents. My mother turned her head and saw me. I ran for my life and she came bolting after me. I hopped over the fence and as I turned around I saw my mother trying unsuccessfully to climb over the fence herself. In that instant I did feel profoundly sorry for her; I saw clearly, for once, how incredibly distressing all this must have been for my parents.

I can't remember what had caused me to be so angry that I felt I had to destroy the school, I just know how I hated being there. And with this last rampage I had it coming to me. I was out, banned.

My parents were not about to keep me home all day, or rather let me roam the streets, as I was doing anyway when I was on the mung. They knew that they had no control over me any more and that I needed to be somewhere where I could be helped or at least controlled. I was placed in a small unit run by some child psychologists for kids with behavioural problems. My mother brought me there the first morning. Our first experience of the school was seeing one kid hitting another one over the head with a milk bottle. My mother looked at me sideways and I could only guess what she was thinking.

She tried to explain to the head of the unit that my behaviour was due to grief about my grandfather's death. This is how my parents tried to justify my conduct, to themselves and others. First attributing it to my grandfather's illness, then to his death. It is true that it had all affected me deeply, but my mother was trying to grasp at anything that would account for my erratic behaviour. It was simply too hard for her to accept that the problem ran much deeper than that, and that there was never going to be a 'cure' for what was fundamentally wrong with me.

There were only six to eight of us in this school, and all I can remember is that it was profoundly boring. We weren't taught a lot; mainly they retained us there to keep us out of trouble. Someone was determined to teach us about logarithms, which I don't remember ever having any use for. I didn't, in fact, mitch from there very often because there were no pressures put on me in this school. Perhaps my conscience was niggling me a bit as well. I knew that my parents were going to be in more trouble if I didn't toe the line, and there was not the same urgent need to get away as there had been in the comprehensive.

What I did like about this place was that you could wear whatever you wanted. This was so important to me; one huge source of humiliation was removed. I could be me, and nobody questioned it too closely. Until around this time, I had worn my hair fairly long, as was the fashion, but now I became a skinhead. My hair was close-cropped, and the standard uniform was Stay-press trousers with braces and a shirt.

My friend Jill had continued with the protest we started about the uniforms in the comprehensive school. By this time it had gone on for about six months, but she won the conflict with the help of a few friends and managed to get the school regulations changed. Jeans were not allowed, but from now on anyone could wear trousers so long as they were navy blue. It was a real achievement on her part – not just on my behalf – and it meant that in the future everyone would have a choice. This was one of the things I liked about Jill, she had the courage of her convictions and we have remained friends.

You could do what you wanted in the school I now attended, whatever amused you. There were things you could do, such as drawing, painting and crafts, but I was still in my rebellious mode and not really interested in anything. Just on principle I used to threaten to leave all the time, and one teacher used to say, 'Go on then, leave.' He gave as good as he got and would tell me to fuck off, which took me aback somewhat, especially when I thought I was telling him where to get off. I did respect him a little bit. I would walk out on him, but he would usually come after me and try and reason with me.

One thing that I couldn't figure out was how he knew so

much about me. He would come up to me and say, 'Look into my eyes. I bet I can tell you where you were last night.'

'Oh yeah, where?'

'In (such-and-such a place), drinking flagons.'

To this day I don't know how he knew these things; perhaps he was eavesdropping on me and my friends talking about what we were up to the night before. Sometimes I was convinced that they had a microphone in the classroom, to check up on what the kids were doing, or even that he had me followed. But he was OK, he wasn't a bad guy.

Because the school was at the other end of the town I had to walk through town on my way home, but I usually ended up going into pubs instead. By this time I didn't see much of my old friends; most of the people I associated with were older than me, worked and had their own money. Paula – the girl who had fed me beans and ice-cream – had a car that she had inherited, and I didn't even have to walk to the pub, she would pick me up from school. Cider was dirt cheap in those days and I was often getting drunk with these people after school, as well as getting drunk by myself.

One day when I was drinking in a pub, the cops just walked in and saw me sitting there with a friend. They arrested us for drinking under age; I was thirteen. Again my mother had to bring me to court.

One day at the school I got tired of having to go out on to the field to have a smoke behind a tree, so I decided that I should be able to smoke a fag in the classroom. I was in there with a girl, who wanted a cigarette as well, and I barricaded us in by putting a woodwork bench and other furniture up against the door and I closed all the blinds so that nobody could see in. Then I smashed open the metal cabinet where all the paints were kept, got out the squeezy bottles of paint and squirted them all over the floor and the ceiling. I felt all right after that and sat down and smoked my cigarette while outside the door people were shouting at me to open up and let them in. At some point I must have opened the door, but I don't recollect what happened to me at all. I don't remember ever being punished for anything although I'm sure I was.

When I was out and on the run I amused myself by acquiring a large number of self-inflicted tattoos all over the back of my hands, down my thumbs and on the knuckles. This was done by first writing or drawing the tattoo on the skin with a pen. Then I punctured my skin along the lines with a needle so that it would draw blood. These hundreds of pin pricks were then stained with paint or indian ink. They were still very dark, swollen and red around the edges when my mother spotted them.

'What the hell is all that writing on your hands? Get upstairs and wash it all off,' she said to me.

'I can't,' I answered and just looked at her.

'What do you mean you can't?' she said, half smiling.

'They are tattoos.' I started walking away from her. 'I can't get them off.' My mother went berserk.

'You little bastard!' she shouted, horrified. 'There is something wrong with you. For Christ's sake, you didn't even put them where you could hide them.' I quickly left the house with her still shouting after me, 'Get back here, this isn't the end of it.'

During my time in this school I also had to see a child psychiatrist once a week. My parents were with me sometimes, and other times they would see her on their own. I didn't want them to talk about me, I felt they had no right. I don't know if they were helped by it in any way themselves; I certainly wasn't. I would say nothing at all during these sessions because I didn't trust her, and the psychiatrist said practically nothing to me. She would have me fill in masses of questionnaires and do inane exercises, such as matching up knives and forks, salt and pepper shakers. I couldn't see the sense of it at all.

The psychiatrist wrote a report about me which ended up in my medical files. Recently I asked to see my medical records, which dated back over twenty years. It was an eye-opener to see what had been written about me at various times in my life. This particular psychiatrist described me as a very aggressive, uncommunicative and extremely paranoid child 'who hates her mother and father and won't join in any family activities. She is a very selfish person who won't listen to anyone or do anything she is asked.' The report went on to say that I differed from my sister in appearance as well as attitude and behaviour, and that I tended to lean towards the masculine. A note at the bottom suggested, 'This could be looked into.' But nobody ever bothered to look into it.

I stayed in this school for about a year. Towards the end it was suggested that I should go back to the comprehensive for just one afternoon a week, to see if the teacher could cope with me, but nothing came of it. I don't remember ever going back.

In the meantime my sister didn't have an easy time of it in the comprehensive. My parents' fears for her were being realized. My mother made a lot of effort to encourage Anna since she had been unable to do anything to encourage me. Anna was excellent at cookery yet her school reports were always mediocre. My mother soon got suspicious, since Anna had the same teacher as I had had. Anna was very quiet and reserved and certainly didn't want to cause any trouble for anyone and my mother had to prise the truth out of her. She finally confessed, 'The teacher doesn't like me, Mam.'

A couple of years earlier, when she first joined the class, they had had a lesson in dental hygiene.

'I haven't lost any of my teeth yet,' Anna piped up in the class.

The teacher turned around to her and sneered, 'Well now, aren't you lucky . . . Lucky that your sister didn't punch a few out for you.' Anna had been keeping this and other incidents to herself, putting up with them and bottling them up, somehow in order to protect me. On hearing all this my mother marched straight to the school to see the headmaster.

'I've had a gutful of this. You've already done it to one of my children. I know she was a bit of a troublemaker but I know that you blamed her for a lot more than she really did. But I will not allow you to victimize my other daughter. Any more of it and I'll be taking it to a higher authority.'

It was a good thing that I knew nothing of this at the time. Not only did I never lay a finger on my sister, but I would have wanted to kill anyone who tried to hurt her in any way. My mother's outburst must have made an impression. In her next school report, Anna excelled in cookery.

Anna was very withdrawn and stuck closely to my mother. She reflected my mother's feelings in everything. Because my mother and I didn't get on, my relationship with Anna was not at all good either. When my parents argued about whose fault it was that I was going off the rails, and they did argue fiercely about it, Anna always took my mother's side. This caused Anna to become alienated from my father for a time.

A couple of years later, when I was no longer living in the area, my mother met the deputy headmistress of the comprehensive school in the street, and they got talking about me. She was one of the teachers who had spoken out against me in court. Now she told my mother that I wasn't a stupid child and could have done well if I had only tried. She enquired as to what I was doing now and my mother told her that I wasn't living at home any more and she didn't know what I was doing. The deputy headmistress already knew this and confessed that she'd seen me in Cardiff.

'Maybe we were wrong in our assessment of her,' she said to my mother. 'It is possible that her problems run a lot deeper than we understood. Maybe now it is time to start building bridges.' This conversation seemed to lay all the blame on my parents when really these teachers had indirectly helped to bring the bridges down. But, then again, so had I.

As I was getting on in adolescence, the feelings of discomfort intensified. Because my body was becoming more and more alien to me as I developed, there was an urge to rip off my own skin, for lack of a better description. The frustration and anxiety were tearing me to bits. I couldn't stand what was happening to me. Fortunately I was very slow to develop and not much was happening in the chest department, nothing that I couldn't hide with reasonable success. The other aspect of puberty, the word for which I cannot bear to mention in relation to myself, also started. I coped with it by blocking it off in my mind, and dealing with it in a mechanical, unconscious way. I had blocked off so much of myself, I had had plenty of practice. I remember my mother trying to talk to me about this aspect of female puberty once. As soon as she mentioned the word, I got up and walked away. Strangely enough, as much as these changes in my body made me uncomfortable in the extreme and very embarrassed, I didn't feel they were a reflection on my maleness. I felt I wasn't responsible for them. I wasn't even supposed to be there, in that body, so it wasn't my fault.

Because of the way my peers perceived me, as lesbian mainly, there were never any sexual threats or challenges. I had no problems asserting myself; in fact, there was no need to. Most people knew not to give me any hassle. If I told someone to leave me alone, they would. I wasn't really interested in sex anyway, although I did mess around with girls a few times, in a very innocent sort of way.

There was one girl I liked quite a bit. Once, when we were down on the canal bank, drinking flagons, she let me kiss her. But even though we were kissing and having some physical contact, I felt at the same time that she was inwardly laughing at me. Not long after, she confirmed to me that she did find it all laughable. I had started to pad my trousers out a little bit in the front – to make me feel more a boy – not a lot, because I didn't want to draw attention to myself, but she spotted it and laughed, thought it really funny. I had that feeling in the pit of my stomach when you wish the earth would open up and you could drop down and be swallowed up.

'Shut the fuck up!' was all I could think of to say, but I didn't show her how hurt and humiliated I felt.

Even though sex didn't seem very important at the time, I gradually became more aware of my physical handicaps. I couldn't have done much more with a girl even if I had wanted to. As I grew older I became more aware of my limitations. There wasn't going to be a miracle. I still believed in God, but I knew he wasn't going to do anything for me. Because I was drinking more and spending time in the company of a crowd of acquaintances, most of them older and none really a personal friend, I was getting lost to myself. I was losing my imaginary world and my capacity for isolation which I had relied on until now. Instead I was 'going off my head', drinking and causing trouble. I was desperately unhappy during this period of my life.

There were times when I had a clearer, more removed perspective on my own behaviour, and could see that my aggressive behaviour was causing myself and others harm. This happened once when I was attending the September Fair in my home town. I used to go to the fair every year, usually very drunk, doing reckless things on the rides like standing up, jumping off and on, provoking or arguing with people around me, generally going over the top.

I was on the bumper cars, bumping into everyone, being a real nuisance. I got into an argument with a girl in the car behind me so I jammed the car against the side and jumped out and went for this girl and her friend. Suddenly two women grabbed me each by a shoulder and said, 'What do you think you are doing? You shouldn't be hitting girls. Boys don't hit girls.' A friend of mine heard this and laughed, 'He's not a boy.' But I stopped dead in my tracks. What was I doing? Suddenly I saw clearly how I must look to others. I didn't want to be a bully but I used my hostility to keep people at arm's length. I thought my whole person gave off an aura of oddness and, yes, I was paranoid. If anyone so much as looked at me I immediately went on the offensive, thinking that they were 'seeing' my oddness, probably laughing at it. It hadn't occurred to me that people looked at people just for the sake of looking.

I was heading towards more serious trouble. I seemed to have an urge to be destructive, and I didn't care if I destroyed myself in the process. An incident in a Chinese restaurant really escalated things in the wrong direction.

Paula, Katrina and I were eating in this restaurant, all of us very drunk, when a dispute erupted between us and the owner. Paula sometimes worked in the restaurant and the dispute was about some money that the owner still owed her. I remember Paula throwing me a knife and fork from the cutlery tray and saying to me, 'Fucking go for it!' We went berserk, throwing all the tables and chairs around, throwing bottles of sauce everywhere, going absolutely mad. The owner had phoned the police and they were on their way. We managed to cause quite a bit of damage by the time the police came and dragged us out. We were not about to be removed from there lightly, hanging on to everything, with our feet against the door frames, and so on.

Having been let off with a warning, an hour later we were

back at the restaurant again to continue the dispute. By this time there were quite a few customers, so we went into the kitchen and began performing there, shouting abuse and smashing things up. On our way out Paula noticed that the cash till was open and she dived for it, stuck her hand in and grabbed all the notes; I dived in after her and got what was left and we ran out. Next, we wanted to see what would happen so we hid in the telephone boxes opposite the police station. Soon the police cars started pulling out to go looking for us. We ran around the streets, ducking, trying to get somewhere safe. Outside the church wall we could hear the police cars coming close, screeching around the corners, so Paula said, 'Jump. Quick, jump over the wall if you can.' She wasn't able to get up and over so she hid the money in some ivy growing on the wall and just ran off.

In the meantime I had climbed up on some bins and took a blind leap over the wall, but there was a hell of a drop on the other side. It was twice as high as it was on the front and I landed on a pile of glass and broken window frames. It was quite a fall but amazingly I wasn't hurt. After waiting for what seemed a reasonable interval, I walked up a lot of steps to get back to street level and I started walking away from there as fast as I could. Paula was nowhere in sight.

Suddenly the police cars came around the corner, and I threw myself to the ground behind some parked cars, feeling sure they hadn't seen me. The next thing I knew there was a tap on my shoulder, and someone said, 'Up!' My position was a bit embarrassing, and I got up and was locked in the back of the police car.

The Chinese restaurant owner decided not to press charges against us, so long as he got some of the money back. I was brought home at three o'clock in the morning. My parents were fuming. 'What do you think the neighbours will think, you being brought home in police cars all hours of the morning?' they shouted at me. I was beyond caring.

I and a few others were known as real troublemakers by now. Three of us went on a rampage in a pub at about this time. We had gone in to have a drink and they had served us a few pints, but then abruptly they called last orders.

'Drink up, it's time to leave,' we were told.

We didn't want to rush our pints that we had just ordered, but as the barman kept insisting, we quickly drank as much as we could and then threw the glasses across the bar where they smashed into the glasses and bottles. We managed to smash a few more things before we went out. We also broke into a clothes shop one night and helped ourselves. All I kept in the end was a pair of pinstripe trousers. I was wearing them when the police came into a derelict house where I was kipping the night on an old mattress. It was just one of the many times that I was in trouble with the law.

Soon I was to commit a crime that was way beyond adolescent lawlessness, and which finally got me into very serious trouble. I had been in the Scrumpy House early, drinking pints of cider, which were sold at the very reasonable price of twelve pence. Paula walked in – she knew where to find me. She worked in a cigar factory but had taken the day off because she had a cold. Brandy was the remedy for colds, so she started ordering them for herself and for me. Soon we were steaming drunk.

Then we went into a café to eat something, and when we had finished we refused to pay; maybe we didn't even have any more money, I can't remember. We grabbed all of the salt and pepper shakers and flung them at the staff as they chased us out. We were running like mad, with total abandon, weaving in and out amongst the cars on the road in the town centre.

There were masses of shoppers around, and as we were running through them Paula spotted a lady about to put her purse into her handbag. Paula just reached down, grabbed the purse and threw it to me: all this whilst running, ducking and diving through the crowds. I ran straight into a woman and, as I was trying to push past her, her shopping bag fell to the ground and the contents went everywhere. In my only gentlemanly action of the day, I picked up what looked like a couple of packets of tights and threw them back towards her.

When we got away from the crowds on to a quieter street we slowed down and Paula asked me for the purse back. 'Fucking hell, how much is there?' The thing was stuffed with money. We counted it out – it was nearly £170, which was a lot of money back then. Our first stop was going to be the tattooist. We ran to his house, which is where he conducted his business. I had been there not so long before and had had a star put on my earlobe for five pence. I asked him to put my birthsign, Libra, on my chest. It is still there today. It's crap, mind, not a professional job at all. Paula was waiting impatiently for me to be finished, since we thought we'd shoot off to Cardiff for the day and find ways of spending the money.

Our exit from the tattooist could not have been more adversely timed. As we came out of the door, three police cars were driving past, and when they spotted us they conveniently pulled in at a bus-stop, right opposite where we were standing, dazed and confused. The owner of the purse was in the back seat of one of the cars. Before we had time even to think we were grabbed. I was pushed up against the wall, and one policeman searched my clothes. He took a pepper shaker out of my pocket and held it in front of my face.

'What's this then?' he asked me. I looked at it in a daze. I was still very drunk.

'Fuck, what the hell is it?' I thought to myself. I had no idea where it came from or why I had it.

I was charged with carrying an offensive weapon. I must have put it in my pocket as we ran out of the restaurant, but the cops thought that it was meant to throw into someone's eyes in order to rob them, or whatever.

What had been an action of impulse, grabbing that lady's purse, came to look like a premeditated robbery. We were even charged with trying to rob the lady whose bags had fallen to the ground.

3

Locked up

Paula and I were separated and I spent all evening in a room at the police station while the cops were trying to locate my parents. Paula's sister came and bailed her out at about half past nine. She was happy because there was still time to go and have a drink before last orders.

My parents were having a meal at a restaurant next door to the police station, and didn't come home until after midnight. By the time they were located and brought in, I was sobering up and feeling very grotty and a bit disorientated. I was sitting in an interview room, half asleep with my head resting in my arms on the table; I woke up a bit stunned when my mother and father walked in.

My mother looked at me. 'My God, this is the last straw. We can't take any more of this. You have really done it this time.'

I looked up in a daze and in an attempt to delay the inevitable confrontation, I said, 'You haven't got a fag have you?'

She gave me a look of utter disgust. 'Is that all you can say for yourself, after all the trouble that you've caused: have I got a fag?' She got out a packet of ten No 10 from her handbag and threw it on the table.

My parents refused to sign bail for me. They had, by now, reached the end of their tether, and decided it was time they washed their hands of me and let me face the consequences of my actions. I remember a woman coming to see me while I was at the police station. She was supposed to foster me and I could have gone to live with her right there and then.

'I am not living with anybody,' I said. 'If you are going to put me away somewhere, then lock me up.' I wasn't about to go from the frying pan into the fire. It would have been the same issues, the same problems, the same upheavals, just another set of adults imposing their own standards and principles on me.

As soon as my parents had been to see me, a policeman and policewoman from a nearby city came to collect me and I was taken to another police station about ten miles away. A policewoman gave me a cheese and onion roll and a cup of tea. 'That's all I can get my hands on at this time of night,' she said in a friendly manner. She locked the cell door behind her and there I spent a fitful night. Because it was a weekend, a private court was hastily arranged on the Saturday and it was decided that I should be transferred to a remand centre until my case was heard. We set off from the police station in a police car almost immediately after the court hearing. I was accompanied by the same police officers that had brought me there the night before.

I was just three weeks past my fifteenth birthday when I was taken away from my home town, and started on a whole new chapter of my life. Apart from two very brief visits, I didn't go back there for ten years. I had achieved in part what I so badly craved, to be out of there and out from under the weight of people's expectations of me. In spite of the difficulties I was to encounter, at least this aspect of my life did improve. At last I was free, as free as I had ever been, to enact and portray my real identity as a male. Not that anyone understood what was wrong with me, but it didn't seem to matter much. The people I was to meet and associate with over the next few years were from all walks of life. Individuals like me who refused to or were unable to conform to society's view of 'the right way to live'. With them I was to feel more at home.

The remand centre was near Bristol so we had a long way to drive. I was trying to help with directions, but I got it all wrong and we ended up making quite a detour up a long valley in the opposite direction. The mist was low on the ground and the visibility poor so we were driving very slowly, not knowing where the hell we were. I was sitting in the back looking out of the window at the scenery slowly rolling past me. In the mist I could see sheep wandering around in the fields and in gardens.

My mind drifted back and forth between the past and the future. I had glimpsed my cousin Sheila on the road as we drove past my home town. I turned around and waved to her and she saw me and waved back. She looked shocked and upset to see me there in the police car being taken away. Seeing Sheila got me thinking about my family, my relatives and the good times we had all had together when we were younger. Soon I snapped to: 'I mustn't get sentimental, not now that I am leaving, not now.' I decided to try and stay focused on the journey and the place ahead. Things were going to be different for me, I was leaving my family and my friends, and I did not want to go back. My destination was forward, into the unknown.

We found our way at last. The journey ended up taking most of the day. When we finally arrived at the remand centre in the evening, I and my few belongings were handed over and I was put through reception. I was handed a blue towelling dressing-gown and placed in a box, a tiny cubicle, so tiny your elbows hit the sides if you tried to move your arms. I was asked to strip and hand out all my clothes. I was to sit in there on a small seat and wait while all my clothes and belongings were being checked, for drugs and weapons I presumed. I felt vulnerable and very uneasy sitting there waiting. I had never been this undressed before without being in charge of the lock. I felt a mess anyway, still suffering the effects of a hangover. My eyes were bloodshot and I was cold to the bone. I longed for a bath. Twenty minutes must have passed, as I sat listening to the sounds of keys rattling and metal doors clanging open and shut. Finally there was a key at my door.

I was then subjected to a personal check, for fleas, scabies or contagious diseases. I was scrutinized everywhere, in my ears, my hair; they checked under my feet; and I was also asked to bend over. I felt apprehensive and tried to object: 'Have I got to? What do you want me to do that for?' I kept objecting: I didn't want to bend over with several people in the room. They finally produced a kind of screen, behind which I bent over quickly in the presence of only one prison officer. Thankfully I wasn't asked to do it again.

Finally I was to have a bath and was handed a set of clothes from my bag, and they provided me with some prison-issue shampoo and soap. Water hadn't touched me, in fact I hadn't been out of my clothes for two days. That bath was an enjoyable experience. It warmed me up and made me feel refreshed.

Next I was taken to my cell. The door clanged shut behind me. It was a big heavy iron door with a little spyhole in it. And there I was. The first thing that struck me was that the cell was freezing cold. The window had been left open. It had a somewhat chilling effect on me, internally as well as externally. I felt very alone and there was an uneasy feeling in the pit of my stomach. At the same time there was a definite feeling of relief, the feeling of having achieved a way out of my former predicament. I didn't grasp that being incarcerated was perhaps an equally daunting situation. I had felt desperately frustrated and unhappy, so I didn't care what happened and where I went, so long as it wasn't back. The offence that I had committed had gone right out of my mind, it seemed to have happened in another time and another life altogether. Everything seemed so utterly unfamiliar.

The cell was sparsely furnished: an iron bed, a wooden cabinet with a work surface between it and the wall, and a chair. There was a bucket of water and a bowl to wash in, and a piss-pot. Someone brought me a meal on a plastic tray with a plastic plate and a plastic knife and fork. I had already been told that it was too late to get a proper meal. The only thing on the plastic plate appeared to be a large square of fried sausage meat. I had never seen anything like it and at first glance wondered what the hell it was, but I was hungry and when I got stuck in I really enjoyed it.

I hadn't seen any inmates but I could hear women shouting messages to each other through the windows and all around me: 'How are you doing?', 'See you in the morning', and that sort of thing. I lay on the bed most of the night thinking, wondering what was going to happen to me from here on. I thought that if I didn't get involved, didn't say much to anyone and didn't let anyone take advantage of me, I would surely be OK.

'If I don't divulge too much of my past, hopefully I will forget it and then slowly but surely I will find myself,' I thought. I felt that for the first time in my life I was truly responsible for myself and answerable only to myself. The direction in which my life had been heading, the way I had behaved, could never be just my own problem if I remained at home; it had become my entire family's problem, and my humiliation about myself had become their humiliation also. I didn't want to have the responsibility of other people's grief on my shoulders. So long as I only had myself to look after, the consequences of my actions would only be mine to suffer. Nevertheless, on that first evening of my confinement, everything seemed utterly foreign and, in spite of my relief, I was a bit apprehensive about what lay in store for me.

The morning of my second day I was shown the routine. Slopping out was first on the agenda. It meant that the inmates all crowded around a basin to empty their buckets of water for washing and their piss-pots from the night before, and to fill up their buckets with clean water. Back in my cell one of the inmates came and said hello and asked me what my name was and I replied, 'Joe.' This is a masculine version of my name by birth and I was to be known by this name for a long time. The girl then asked me if I had any cigarettes. I didn't, so she gave me two roll-ups. It was nice that someone would go to the trouble to make me feel more at home. I was to meet this girl a few times in later years and similar circumstances.

After breakfast I was let out in the yard for exercise, and I walked around the perimeter feeling a bit awkward. A few inmates were coming up to me and saying hello. They were women of all ages. Some were quite friendly and told me about what I could expect and how the system worked. Nobody pried or asked what I was in for. Seeing all these girls and women brought it home to me that I was in the wrong place. I did not belong in a women's prison, and yet, in this alien body of mine, I think I would have felt vulnerable wherever I was imprisoned. Here at least, in my jeans and T-shirt, I looked and felt quite inconspicuous; it felt all right.

A girl came up to me in the yard, a Cockney from London. Her name was Gina.

'There is going to be a film on tonight and perhaps something is going to happen during the film,' she told me. I didn't think to ask what she meant.

That evening the whole place, all four wings of the remand centre, was going to watch a film, *The Magnificent Seven*. We were all down in the main hall sitting closely packed together in rows, watching the film. The whole hall was full of chairs with just a narrow aisle going down one side. The Cockney girl came up to me and whispered, 'There is going to be a riot, are you going to help out?' I had no idea what the motive for the riot was, and I didn't think to ask. 'Yeah, OK, I'll help.'

'Your job,' she said, 'is to make it difficult for the screws to get to the aggro bell.'

Tea and rock cakes were being brought for us to eat, and just then a couple of girls started a fight. Several screws came rushing to break it up and then everybody jumped on the screws, as seemed to be the plan. There was a lot of scuffling and struggling, with chairs flying about all over the place. I had rushed up to guard the bell, but wasn't able to for long. Anyway, there were other bells, and more screws had been alerted. The male screws from the male section of the remand centre were on their way over to help break it up. I remember seeing the television which was up on a stand, rocking back and forth, about to topple. I found myself caught up in the fight and one of the screws went for me. She was a strong and nimble woman and as I was blindly swinging my fists about, she ducked, and I accidentally hit another inmate and gave her a black eye.

Gradually, one by one, the screws had managed to get most of the people out of the hall. The six of us that were left were locked in the hall while the screws went after the two girls believed to be the main instigators of the riot. Soon we observed, through the small window in the hall door, two male screws leading one of the girls, Irena, down the corridor. We shouted to her, asking if she was all right. 'Yeah,' she shouted back, 'take care!'

It was my second day of imprisonment and I was still slightly dazed by it all. I knew nothing about the reason for the riot, nor had I been part of the planning of it. I had just sided with the inmates against the screws as it seemed the logical and natural thing to do. Without having meant to be, I was in trouble from the start.

Later I found out that it wasn't supposed to have been a riot really, but to create a distraction so that Irena could get the keys to the medicine cabinet in order to get hold of drugs. She did get as far as the cabinet but, predictably, she was caught and she got locked up for much longer than the rest of us. I didn't know it then, but Irena was to become a very important person in my life for many years to come.

A VC (visiting court) was held for Irena and another girl, and the rest of us were put on two weeks of 'lock-up' (solitary confinement) plus loss of privileges and loss of pay. Pay was 53 pence a week and would buy half an ounce of tobacco, a packet of cigarette papers and a box of matches. During lock-up you spend the entire time in your cell, meals are brought to you, and for half an hour morning and afternoon you are allowed out in the yard for exercise. It didn't particularly bother me to be locked up like that, although it was excruciatingly boring most of the time. If there were other people on lock-up, we would talk to each other through the window. You couldn't see who you were talking to but you could hear each other's voices. Mostly we would stay awake talking or singing through the night and then sleep through the day, although sleeping in the day didn't really work very well. I did write a couple of letters to a friend back home, Katrina. She had been one of my best friends, we were always steaming drunk together, falling around everywhere. If I was kipping rough, she would stay with me sometimes. She was one of the few people, if not the only one, that I was able to tell about girls that I had crushes on.

When I finally got out of lock-up I had to attend magistrate's court again for bail, while waiting to be called to Crown Court. For this I was brought back to the city near my home town.

My parents were there, sitting in the back of the courtroom, and had by this time decided that they would stand bail for me. To me the entire proceedings were meaningless; I had no intention of going back home on bail; it was the last thing I wanted. I was mesmerized by the judge, who looked exactly like the Queen of Hearts in *Alice's Adventures in Wonderland*. I chuckled unintentionally. My parents were not impressed, of course, and were probably horrified that I refused the bail when it was offered to me.

My partner in crime, Paula, who was in the dock with me, turned to me in amazement:

'What do you mean, you don't want bail?'

'I don't want to come back here. I'm staying put,' I replied.

'You're mental, we could be out of here now in five minutes. We could be over at the pub having a beer.' She thought I was mad. Paula was granted bail and I was shipped back to the remand centre.

Time passed. We spent part of the day in a class or workshop if there were enough screws to supervise us. If there weren't enough screws on duty, we were often confined to our cells for twenty-three hours a day, allowing for two half hours of outdoor exercise. For this reason the workshops were a welcome distraction. Not that we wanted to spend our time unpicking stitching off patchwork quilts, but it was a way of being together and having company.

One day, when a few of us were in the workshop, Irena was looking at me and, after a few moments, said to me, 'You like girls, don't you?'

It wasn't said with any prejudice or to show me up, but I was unable to answer because there was not any one simple answer to the question. I was paralysed and speechless on this subject anyway. The whole question of my sexuality made me withdraw into myself. I couldn't explain to anyone that I wasn't gay, but a guy. I didn't cope very well with this confrontation, particularly with this girl, whom I secretly found very attractive. I just had that sinking feeling in my stomach, which was partly fear, partly dread. In an attempt to hide my humiliation I just looked straight at her without saying a word until she became flustered and changed the subject.

I realized that she hadn't meant to embarrass me. She must have known that I was attracted to her and had caught me looking at her and perhaps wanted some kind of response from me.

Some of the inmates were gay, as in all prisons, male or female. Even though nobody had a clue about my real condition, perhaps there was an assumption that I was gay too. It didn't seem important. Most of those I made friends with accepted me exactly the way I was. This is how it was anyway, live and let live. We all had our crosses to bear, and we were all different. We didn't pry into each other's business. Unless somebody wanted to tell you what was going on for them, or what their lives had been like on the outside, you didn't ask because it had nothing to do with you. But because it was totally acceptable to be yourself, exactly the way you were, I was in my element. The only obvious thing we had in common was that we had all had our freedom taken away from us. Some of the women had committed the crime they were locked up for, others had not. Some had committed petty crimes, some more serious ones and some had taken the blame for a friend or had been wrongly committed.

One woman had been sentenced to twelve months for nicking a bottle of milk, and she had even left the money for it in its place. Another one had nicked some flowers. One had taken the blame on behalf of a lover on a drugs charge. Some were just down on their luck and had done nothing worse than most people would do in a pinch. Of course, there were those who had committed very serious crimes, but at close hand I could only see them as people in their own right, not evil but human, coping the best they could with their own problems. Despite the background of some of the inmates, most treated one another with respect. I was expecting to keep myself to myself, but there was not much need for caution. Arguments and fights did break out on occasions, which was to be expected living in such close proximity to one another, but these were usually cleared up pretty quickly. Most of us understood that we had to live together in some sort of harmony whether we liked each other or not.

Twice a day we went out in the yard for our half-hour exercise. Some of us would walk round in circles or do a few press-ups, others would have a fag and stand around and talk. For fun, Gina would sometimes practise her pickpocketing skills on us. She could get anything out of a person's pocket without them noticing.

Since the riot they had decided to change the rules and would allow only half of the inmates to go for 'association' each evening (association meant mixing with each other, watching television or having a game of table tennis and that sort of thing) and this meant that every day the other half of the inmates were confined to their cells. This was worse on days when workshops were not being held for lack of screws to supervise them, because this meant that everyone in the remand centre was locked up for the best part of the week, bar exercise, which is every prisoner's legal right. All of us were frustrated and pissed off at having to be locked up for most of the time.

Two inmates and I decided that we should protest, and breaking the monotony of it all at the same time would be a bonus. I had been remanded for two more months and was due to appear in Crown Court for sentencing. I said to my two friends, 'If I get sentenced to Borstal, when I come back here to wait for my allocation, we'll do it then, we'll barricade my cell to protest against the cut in association.' I felt that if I was going to get locked up and put away for a time I might as well get some mileage out of it. Being fifteen, this was my logic at the time.

When finally my court date came up I was brought back to the city near my home town for the hearing. My parents were not in the courtroom. It was huge, and there was hardly anyone in there. I turned around a few times from where I was sitting in the front to see if I could spot my parents, but they never came. In a way I was glad they didn't. I didn't cope very well with forever having to see them upset on account of me. I was a little bit disappointed, I suppose, but at the same time, deep down inside, I knew that I was never going to come back to them and it was easier not to have emotions shaken up, for my parents as well as for myself. Later I was informed that my parents had not received a letter about my court date, so they didn't even know that I was just a few miles from home.

Because of my age the consensus was that it would be better for me to go to a hostel instead of Borstal. However, there was no hostel that would accept me, and they weren't about to let me loose, so there was no alternative: I was sentenced to six months to two years in Borstal.

Personally, I couldn't care less where I was being sent. On the way back to the remand centre in the car, I was singing at the top of my voice. I was quite immature, none of this had any impact on me. To me it was just a road to discovery.

About a week later, one afternoon after collecting my dinner, I found one of my friends hiding in my wardrobe and another under my bed. I was a bit startled to find them in my cell.

'How did you manage to get up here?' I asked them.

'We snuck out through the crowd getting their meals.'

I said, 'Shall we do it now?' and we all agreed.

'It's as good a time as any. Let's go for it,' was their reply.

We grabbed the bed, which was metal, and threw it up against the door.

'What the hell are you doing?' a screw shouted through the door.

'What the fuck does it look like we are doing?'

She turned the key and locked the door, which was an advantage for us because we could ram the door tight with the bed, and there would be no leverage on the other side. Behind the bed we rammed the table and put the chair on top. The door was wedged firmly shut, no one could get it open. We went crazy in there, trying to demolish the place. I ripped all the skirting boards off, being as destructive as I could. Screws were gathering in the corridor and outside in the yard, male as well as female. We took a couple of plastic bottles of talcum powder and topped them up with water. Shaking this up until it became a mush, we stuck the bottles through a row of holes over the door and squirted this mixture over the screws as they tried to get the door open.

In order to keep the screws from coming near the window we mixed all the food from my tray together into a slop in a bowl and pelted anyone who was trying to get near it. They were trying to keep us away from the window by shoving broomsticks at us. Their idea was to get a steel bar in through the window and under the bed in order to lift it, so that they could push the door open. I tried to grab the broom away from one of them and eventually I managed to get it, and was now using it to keep them away from the window.

The situation was nearing a conclusion when the male screws

decided to flush us out once and for all. They came running across the yard with the fire hose and pointed it through the window at us. The screws seemed to be getting something out of it as well, they were laughing and sniggering.

'Right, what would you prefer, hot or cold?'

'Oh, go on, luke warm will do,' I said, and they turned the water on. The pressure of the water was so great it had me splattered to the wall. Everything got completely soaked. Blue dye from some piece of clothing of mine was all over the place.

I could hear Irena screaming at us, 'Fucking let them in, you bastards.' Everybody was locked in their rooms on account of us. 'Let them in, we want to go on association.'

'Fuck off!' we shouted back. 'We're in here until they get us out.'

By this point our only objective was to hold out as long as we could. We were going to stay in there until the bitter end but, in fact, we were aggravating the very situation we were protesting against. The screws were still trying to lever the bed up with the steel bar, and we were diving on the bed to keep it down. In the end the bed just collapsed, caved in. It was several hours before they were able to force the door open and drag us out.

They more or less had to carry me to another cell, I was punching and kicking for all I was worth, trying to get my arms and legs free. They threw me on the floor in the cell. I grabbed the bucket and bowl beside me on the floor and hurled them at the screws before they slammed the door shut and locked me in.

I was before the VC a week later. That morning I had another confrontation with the screws. They were dragging Gina down to the strip cell in the middle of the night. I woke up to the sound of shouting outside my cell and, recognizing Gina's voice, I got up to look through my spyhole. I could see her being dragged by her hair and her arms; her nightie was almost around her neck. I had no idea what she was supposed to have done, but their brutal treatment of her made me furious and I shouted through the door, 'I'll have you bastards when you unlock me in the morning.'

When they opened my door in the morning to bring me my breakfast I threw the tray back at them. I was still outraged at the way they had treated Gina. One of them was holding a cup of tea and when the breakfast was coming towards her, in shock, she jumped back and threw her hands in the air and the tea went all over me. One side of my head was totally wet and sticky and my jumper was covered in tea, and this is how I looked when I went in front of the VC.

I was marched in through a side door and their side-view of me was probably quite clean and respectable, but when I was turned around to face the court, the other side of me came into view. When she saw the mess I was in, the chief screw grinned and just lowered her head. I could see what she was thinking: 'Now, what the hell has this one been up to?' I was sentenced to twenty-eight days of lock-up and loss of privileges.

I don't want to give the impression that all these screws were bastards. They had a job to do, and it was far from an easy one. I didn't trust most of them, but the chief was fair. Being the person in charge of the remand centre she was very stern. She didn't stint on punishment when it was deserved, but she had a sense of humour and you could see by the glint in her eye how far you could go with her. If you had been accused of something she would actually listen to what you had to say for yourself and wouldn't just take a screw's story as gospel truth. She would take any other factors into consideration too, such as if you had been upset about a letter from home, or whatever. At the same time she would think nothing of running at you and bringing you to the ground with a rugby tackle if you were in any way being physically obstructive.

Once she asked me to do something for her, empty some bins I think it was.

'What's it worth?' I ventured. 'Do I get a cigarette or something, maybe?'

She gave me a stern look and wagged her finger at me. 'You watch it, don't be cheeky with me.' But then in the evening after being locked in my cell, two cigarettes – regular ones, not the roll-ups we inmates smoked – fell through the hole in the top of the door.

'Ah, nice one – nice one!' I shouted after her.

After I had pulled the stunt of barricading my cell, and I was in solitary confinement, my mother travelled all the way to see me. It was a 'closed' visit, because of my confinement – just me and my mother and a screw.

Seeing me there was too much for my mother, and she started to cry. It upset me a lot to see her cry, but as usual I reacted in the only way I knew how:

'If you don't stop crying this minute I'm going to end the visit. I'm already in solitary confinement. Isn't that enough? Do you have to come here upsetting me as well?'

The last thing I wanted was to have to feel responsible for upsetting my mother yet again. I had enough of my own problems to deal with.

I gave the impression that I couldn't give a fuck about anyone else, but this was mainly due to my feelings being locked somewhere deep down inside me. If I were to be more in touch with my feelings I would be too vulnerable, and this I could not afford. Even so, seeing my mother so upset did affect me, and I felt a tight knot in my stomach. I had not been able to get on with my parents at all, and I felt they were not even really friends of mine, since we couldn't have a conversation about anything, especially about me. So it was very difficult to connect with my mother, particularly in this setting. We really didn't have very much to say to each other at all. I knew that she had travelled a long distance to see me and that she cared but, seeing the distress I was causing her, I really did wish I had come into this world on my own, without parents, so that I wasn't the cause of such grief.

I also felt bitter about my parents' total lack of understanding of my predicament. I felt continually bombarded by how everybody else was feeling, and how unhappy I was making everybody. But what about me? What about the way I felt? All our interactions seemed to be about how I made everybody else feel. I did feel upset for her. The feeling of hopelessness and being out of control was only too familiar to me.

I never got out of lock-up: they came to get me directly for transfer to Borstal. The last thing I did was to hide my blanket out of the window so that my friend next door, Gina, could retrieve it for a bit of comfort. The journey from the remand centre to Borstal was quite a long one, and it involved a stopover at Holloway prison for dinner.

Initially, when I walked in through the Borstal gates to the courtyard, and the sombre buildings towered over me, I felt unsettled and intimidated by it all. I was put through reception and placed in an induction unit where they try to ascertain which house you should go to. There were four houses in all. One of them was specifically for drug rehabilitation, and another was for girls with psychiatric problems.

The houses were placed in a square, forming a large courtyard in the centre. Surrounding the houses were a few acres of land fenced in with barbed wire. Surrounding the fences was Epping Forest. Behind one of the houses there was a swimming pool. Underneath another building was the punishment block, with its own little courtyard. There was also a factory in the grounds, where the inmates had a variety of jobs. In each house there were about twelve double cells on the ground floor and perhaps thirty single cells on the first floor. If you wanted to be bunked up with a friend, you could request it. Each house also had an association room and a dining area.

It didn't take long to settle in, although Borstal was a different experience from the remand centre. There was more of a routine than I had been used to. We were out of our cells most of the day, working or doing other things. Every night there was association and we were able to bath every night, instead of once a week. All through the day there was music from the radio playing through loudspeakers, and there was a record player and loads of good records for the evening. We were mostly under eighteen in Borstal, whereas in the remand centre they detained women of all ages.

It was at the beginning of my time in Borstal that I had my first sexual experience. A girl was very friendly towards me when I first arrived, and a few days later, when we were alone in the dormitory, it just happened. She was more experienced than I was and guided me to what she liked. She didn't question me about myself – and that made a world of difference to me. It felt very good to be able to express intimacy and for it to be unconditionally accepted. It was also a new experience to find out about a woman's shape and form, how she responded, what she liked, what turned her on.

My sexual experiences were one-sided, and for many years they had to be. While my body was the way it was, there was no way that anyone would be allowed to see or touch the parts of it that didn't belong to me. I had rejected them myself so long ago, and had learned to close off from my mind the fact that they were there. I never looked at the parts of my body which were wrong – it was hard enough to wash them. The only physical affection that I could be on the receiving end of, was being kissed and held by a woman. I always slept in my underpants, and the women that I became involved with respected this – they had little choice. The older I got, the more I perfected my detachment from my body. My body didn't exist in the way it was born; for me it only existed in my inner identity as a male. Having a woman touch me sexually would not only have seemed perverse to me, but also it would have broken my detachment, which I needed to maintain in order to keep my sanity.

Apart from my long-term relationships, where I did talk more about myself and my needs, as you do in a relationship, I have never felt the need to explain to any woman I have been involved with why I had this need for privacy, both within the sexual relationship and outside of it. No woman ever questioned it.

Two or three months after I arrived at Borstal, Irena was sent there as well. Initially she was put in the same house, along with another girl I knew. Soon, however, they realized that the three of us had been in the riot together, and Irena was already classed as trouble with a capital T. She also had a drug problem. She had broken into a chemist's in order to get hold of drugs, and this was the charge she was on. Within two days of arriving she was transferred to the drug rehabilitation unit and we were separated.

A relationship between us had already begun, however. I had got the courage up to ask her to 'go out' with me. She answered, 'OK, if it makes you happy.' I didn't have a clue what it was going to mean or how we would conduct a relationship, and I had no idea of what to expect from her or what she could expect from me. I was very attracted to her from the first time I had set eyes on her, back at the remand centre. She was different from every other girl I had met so far. She was very fair so I was surprised when I discovered that her mother was African and her father Dutch. She told me that she had eleven brothers and sisters. Some of them looked like the mother and some like the father. She herself had pale skin and green eyes, and her hair was long and brown. She looked so unusual. Her posture was very straight; I thought she walked with a lot of elegance. She wore her hair frizzy from plaiting it and tied it with a head band. Mostly she was dressed in jumpers down to her knees and desert boots. She was a couple of years older than me and she was very articulate and intelligent. She had done well in school and had several O levels, and yet she was as reckless as I was. I was intrigued by her.

Our relationship for the time being consisted mainly of letters, but it was a relationship nevertheless. She seemed to take it very seriously and gave a lot of thought to how things were going to be between us when we both got out.

I could see her through my window, since her house was opposite mine and the exercise yard was in front of her house. When I was on exercise in this yard, she would hang out of the window so that we could talk. On one occasion she lost quite a lot of pay for talking to me out of the window. I could hear them shouting to her, 'That's ten pence you've lost. Talk out that window again and you'll lose another ten.' The screws realized that there was something happening between us and sometimes they had the decency to let us stop and talk in the corridors. We talked a lot about meeting up on the outside, and I promised that I would come and see her as soon as I could, providing she was out as well. It didn't make an awful lot of difference that we were not in the same house because I spent a lot of time in the detention block on solitary confinement for various offences.

'What the hell am I doing down here again?' I would think as I walked round the exercise yard in my shoes without laces, right away from everywhere and everyone.

Because of my age there were lessons that I should have been attending, but anything connected to schoolwork I rejected out of hand. I plain refused to go. However, we were all expected to work in some capacity. I didn't mind this because it was a way to spend time talking to friends and having a laugh. There was a factory, where I worked for a while, where we made Thermos flasks and lampshades. I was on a production line, operating a machine which stamped out the plastic bases of the Thermos flasks. In my breaks I would go over to where they were making the lampshades in order to get a little whiff of the glue they were using. It had been ages since I had been high on anything and it was a great feeling. One day I got hold of a small bottle and filled it up with glue to take back to the wing. We had a good time with this for a couple of days, hiding it in our cell until one girl broke out in spots around her nose. It was becoming a bit dodgy.

We also used to nick string from the factory. Because there was only a communal pilot light for us to light our cigarettes on during the day – matches were not allowed – we needed the string to light our fags at night. Some of us would light the ends of a few pieces of string last thing before we were due to go to bed and sneak them back to the cells. We had to hang them out of the window to avoid detection, since they produced a lot of smoke. They would keep burning for hours. If anyone in another cell needed a light we would hang a bedspread out of the window with a water jug and the burning string tied to the end and then swing it over to the next window. They in turn would swing it over to the next window in the row. A lot of things were passed around in this fashion.

In spite of all the things that were going on, and the fact that I was often in trouble, I did feel good. I was away from all that had caused me so much distress, my family, school.

My parents came to visit me once. My mother's heart sank when she saw me. I had had my hair cropped very short and I was wearing a pair of jeans and a shirt. As usual it was awkward, and there was very little to say. I really wanted to say something to my father to explain things, so I thought I would tell him that I was having a relationship with a girl.

'I've got something to tell you,' I began.

My father looked at me for a moment. 'You don't have to tell me, I already know.'

I tried to explain about the girl, but my mother overheard this and quickly cut in: 'What are you on about – what are you on about?' She just didn't want us to talk about it, and I don't think my father knew what I was trying to tell him.

The inmates accepted one another exactly the way they were, so the way we looked, dressed or behaved was never an issue. Some of the inmates dressed and behaved in quite a masculine way and some wore rags in their hair and jeans rolled up to their knees. You dressed as you felt. None of the other inmates pried into my private life or asked me any intimate questions. I felt very relaxed from this point of view and I made quite a few friends. There were some individuals in there that would try to throw their weight around, and you had to learn to stand your ground.

In spite of having my freedom taken away from me, I still felt freer in other ways, and on the whole I felt the place was all right. You soon get absorbed in the routine and the business of just getting by. It becomes your own little world, being shut off from the outside. You play cards and table tennis and talk a lot, and no doubt speculate on what life is going to be like once you get out. Having said that, there were people who got very depressed, even suicidal, and couldn't cope with being locked up. Of course I was frustrated and there was a lot of boredom, but I was never depressed.

My life was regulated by meals; everyone seemed to time the day by breakfast, dinner and tea. Although time seemed to stand still in some ways, things were also in constant flux and changing, like friends coming and leaving. It was hard to lose some of these friends. You say 'Ta-ra' and wish them all the best, and try not to show too much emotion about it. But the thought goes through your head, 'Oh well, I won't ever see her again', although I did, in fact, meet up with some of them in later years.

I wasn't that desperate to get out but once I thought I might escape by making a hole in the wall of my cell. Every night I would scrape away at the brickwork, and in the day I covered it with a poster. I was sure I would get out through this hole eventually – probably a week before I was due out, knowing my luck. Had I succeeded in getting through the wall I would have had to tackle the screws outside with their guard dogs, and then get over the fence. I was just fifteen years old, after all, and my head was still in the clouds. As it was, I was transferred to another cell, and didn't bother to start scraping my way to freedom all over again.

Once I made a more realistic attempt to abscond. It was during one of the times I was allowed out for 'mixed exercise', meaning all the houses were out. It was a rare occasion, perhaps once a month, that all houses were allowed out into the grounds at the same time. Previously I had always been on lock-up or the punishment block when mixed exercise took place.

A few of us decided on the spur of the moment to run for the fence and try to climb over it. The idea was that if we all made a dash for it at the same time it would create confusion and distract the guards, and hopefully one or two of us would get over. Apparently it had been done before, a year earlier, and three people got over the fence and out.

I was clambering up the fence for all I was worth when I was grabbed from behind and dragged down and sent straight back to the punishment block. Nobody made it to freedom.

I got twenty-one days 'behind the door' (solitary) for that, followed by a week's 'lock-up on the house', which meant you were back in your cell but not allowed out for association in the evening. You were not allowed to eat with the other inmates either, so my meals were brought to my cell. During the day I had to work on the wing, mopping the floors, while everyone was working elsewhere.

After a day or two of mopping floors on my own, a screw's lighter went missing. I didn't even know anything about it until one evening in my cell when I was talking to a friend in the next cell through the heating pipes (talking close to the pipes would echo the words clearly in the pipes of the next cell, if the receiver had her ear pressed to them). I commented on how many screws there were around on the wing at the time. What I didn't realize was that they were coming for me, believing that I had stolen the lighter.

Suddenly they opened my door and said, 'Are you going to walk down, or are you going to cause a fuss?'

'No, I'll walk,' I said. But as soon as I stepped outside the door they jumped on me anyway.

'I said I'd fucking walk!' I shouted at them. Struggling to get free I shook them off and ran. The screws had already locked everyone up and left all the doors in the corridors open so they could drag me through the building unhindered. My cell was on the second landing so the only way I could get away was to go down. I was heading towards the staircase when I saw a guy waiting for me on the landing, he was the head cook, by coincidence named Mr Thompson. He grabbed me and we scuffled and ended up rolling down the cast iron stairs together. I managed to get up first and made a dash for the fire extinguisher before he scrambled to his feet.

'Don't one of you bastards move, or I am going to let it off!' I shouted. The screws were all approaching me in a semicircle. I put one foot forward and before I knew it I was on the floor with all of them pushing me down. As they tried to get me to my feet their hold on me loosened and I managed to get away again by the skin of my teeth. I didn't know where the hell I was going anyway, there was nowhere to run and they would inevitably catch me, but I was driven by a gut reaction to get away from them. I didn't know why they had come for me or what I was supposed to have done wrong. When they finally did catch me, they dragged me down the stairs backwards, bumping the small of my back on every step. My back was in agony and I was wild.

'I'm going to fucking kill you bastards, you've hurt my back!' I was shouting and swearing and fighting all the way to the punishment block, where I got pushed into my cell.

The screws use a mattress to get you into the cell if you are struggling. They take a run at you, holding the mattress as a shield and push you through the door and throw the mattress on top of you. Before you've fought off the mattress they've slammed the door and locked it. It is a way of avoiding additional unpleasant and damaging contact with the inmate.

I soon found out what the charge was all about, but because I wasn't brought before the governor in the morning I assumed they had searched my cell and not found the lighter. In fact they came to collect me to take me back to my house. I was still on lock-up for trying to abscond with four days left to go.

That evening a meal was brought to me in my cell, and when I went to take the tray from the screw I saw that the food was covered in greenfly. They were even floating in the gravy. I couldn't believe that the screw was handing me this and I knew that the cook, Mr Thompson, must have had something to do with it.

'Can't you see the flies on this food?' I asked her, incredulous. 'You don't expect me to eat this shit, do you?' In anger I threw the plate out of the door and it splattered on the landing. I was hauled straight back to the punishment block where yet again I was walking around with no laces in my shoes.

I felt sadness and longing for my freedom to be in the countryside and to walk around on the hills which I loved so much. Obviously we weren't free to go outside the fences, which I regretted because Borstal was in the middle of a lovely forest and its sounds and smells were vivid, particularly at night. There were numerous creatures around – squirrels running along the fences and birds singing, and in the evenings there were a lot of bats. But there was still a feeling of life being a big adventure, even though it was happening behind bars. In spite of my confinement I felt freer than ever to explore my own inner world.

I would have liked to take advantage of the nicer jobs available, such as working on the farm within the prison, but it would have meant working out of doors, and they wouldn't let me because of my attempt to escape. I wasn't very good at keeping out of trouble and making life more pleasant for myself.

As part of the routine I was required to see a psychiatrist once a week. I felt that this guy, Dr C, really wanted to get into my head, but he could get nothing out of me. Our sessions consisted of me looking around the room, and him looking at me, pipe in hand, feet up on the table. He had a lot of drawings and paintings on the walls of his office which made it easy to focus my eyes on something, but when I got used to him I would stare back at him.

'What the fuck are you looking at all the time?' I said to him once.

'Oh well, that wasn't too difficult now, was it?' I don't know what he was trying to do, or how he figured it would help me. I found it impossible to express anything at all, even if I'd wanted to. I don't think it occurred to me that he could help me, and I was on the defensive with anyone in authority. Also I sensed that the sessions had little to do with my thoughts and feelings and what I could have said to him. It was more to do with what he wanted to say to me, what label he would stick on me, and what he would do with the information once he was in possession of it.

Revealing to a stranger something that causes you extreme humiliation makes you very vulnerable. I couldn't take any risks and I kept believing that my silence was my strength.

Dr C did me one favour. His little sideline was removing tattoos. The tattoos that I had on my hands and my neck were quite primitive, not very handsome. They had stretched and blurred and I agreed initially to let him remove the ones on my hands. He did my hands one at a time, with an interval, so that I would not be too incapacitated. After injecting the hand with Novocaine, he cut away the tattoo with a small round-headed scalpel, pulled the skin together and stitched the edges up. When I went the second time, he refused to do my other hand unless I let him tackle the cross and chain around my neck first, and the two stars on either side of my neck. It was probably well meant, he may have thought my neck decorations would stand in the way of a brilliant future. I didn't really care what he thought, but he was giving me the opportunity to get rid of them so I thought, why not?

'Go on then, you can do my neck,' I said at last, although I didn't fancy having my neck injected in spite of having stuck needles into it a hundred times myself. As it was, he gave me fourteen needles to numb my neck.

The scars were painful and did cause me some grief. When I went back for my check-up, Dr C grabbed me by my hair and yanked my head back. 'Let's look how they're doing then.'

'Hey, that fucking hurt!' I shouted.

'Oh come on,' he said sarcastically, 'that didn't hurt.'

'It's my fucking neck, I should know.'

Later, a large scar on my right hand split open. It got very infected, becoming a large oozing hole in my hand. I went to see the nurse about it and she cleaned it up.

'Right, we'll stitch these edges back together now,' she said.

'No way,' I said, and got the hell out of there. The wound slowly healed up on its own.

Irena had served her sentence and was let out about a month before I was. Dr C got Irena and me in together before she was due to leave. He had found out about our relationship and our intention to get together once we got out and wanted us to talk about it. She was a lot more relaxed and felt easy in this situation, perhaps because she had attended quite a lot of group therapy and sessions with Dr C to do with her drug abuse. Dr C wanted me to tell her what I thought of her, and her to tell me how she felt about me. She did have a few things to say. She wanted to explain about her family to me, about her mother and her brothers and sisters. Her mother had eleven children and her husband had taken off, and as mother and daughter they weren't getting on too well.

'That doesn't bother me,' I said. 'I don't care about that, I'm not coming to live with your mother.' She told me what she felt for me, but when it was my turn, I was tongue-tied, I simply couldn't speak. It wasn't that I didn't have strong feelings for Irena, I really did, but I had such difficulty in expressing that sort of sentiment. All I had ever told her about my past was that I didn't get on with my family and that I didn't want to go back home or back to school.

My whole life, my condition, my family and their feelings about me all amounted to a state of humiliation, and I remained quiet. I had to keep all that to myself and not to let myself be opened up like a can of worms. I still felt the same way about my inner world, it was pure and true, so long as nobody came into it and tried to shatter the flow of it. Because of my emotional introversion I was very immature in many ways. Coupled with the fact that I had not read anything or learned anything in school, it all added up to a deep sense of inadequacy. I tried to make up for it with my rough exterior and my reckless and fearless stance towards the world.

For reasons that I am not sure of, Dr C strongly recommended to Irena that she end her relationship with me. It certainly could not have been on account of me being a bad influence on her, since she was as much trouble as I was.

After almost a year, counting the two and a half months on remand, they decided to release me on condition that I went home and back to school. I agreed to do this and was informed that I had about a month to go. But I said it only in order to get out. They finally let me work on the farm a few weeks before I was due to leave. I helped with the cows, cut grass and generally kept the area clean.

On the day that Irena was leaving, I was out doing some clearing near the road. The van that was taking her away drove past me. She saw me and rolled down the window and threw me all the tobacco and cigarettes that she had on her, and called out, 'Don't forget, you take the M4 to Newport.'

As the time drew nearer to my release, I was impatient to get out, feeling very frustrated and oppressed. I complained that I had not been allowed out anywhere. Consequently I was let out for a day to assist with Meals on Wheels, taking food around to elderly people. I was dying to see some traffic, walk on roads and past shop windows. A few days later I was taken by truck to one end of the grounds outside the perimeter fence, and left there to pick up all the sticks and branches on the ground and tidy the place up. I was only yards from the road with nothing to stop me from walking away, but when the screws came back a couple of hours later I was sitting on a pile of sticks, waiting for them.

'We didn't think we were going to find you here.'

'I'd be a damned fool to run now, wouldn't I, when I only have a couple of weeks left.'

Soon it became my time to leave Borstal. I was put on a two

year 'licence', which is similar to probation. It means complying with certain rules and regulations, including staying put in one place, attending school and regular meetings with a probation officer, and so on.

When I left Borstal I had no idea what the future would hold, but the idea of returning home and going back to school seemed laughable and unreal. Nevertheless, I couldn't think what else to do so, in the first instance, home I went.

4
I Abandon All Former Names

I walked home from the station and had a strained reunion with my parents. Making an effort to make me feel at home, my mother asked me what I would like to eat.

'Just a huge plate of chips,' I said, 'with loads of tomato sauce,' something I hadn't eaten for a very long time.

That night I went out drinking, meeting up with all my old friends. Unbeknown to me, they had all come to the train station to meet me that afternoon. They had made a huge banner out of a roll of wallpaper with Welcome Home written on it. But I had missed that train and missed the home-coming reception. I wonder how I would have felt if I'd had such a welcome. It was very disorientating to come back, even though only a year had passed since I'd left. But I had changed and grown up in so many ways, I felt like a stranger in my own home and in my own town. Nothing seemed to have changed there at all.

In the last year I had come to realize that the world was full of different people with different outlooks and opinions. Although I felt I could never make peace with my own body and the way I was born, at least my self-esteem had been boosted a notch from knowing that, as far as human peculiarities were concerned, I was far from being alone.

Everyone kept buying drinks for me at the pub, and the table was full of pints. They really tried to make me feel welcome. I had a couple, but the feeling of not belonging was quite overwhelming. I felt that even my old friends were people I hardly knew, and the things they talked about seemed distant and I felt detached from it all. Perhaps I put up resistance, wanting to back off from all that reminded me of the past. I didn't want to be sucked back into this world which I had gone to such lengths to be exiled from.

After a short while I felt I had to get out of there. I asked Katrina, my friend that I had written to, to come to the chippy with me to get some fish and chips. On the way out of the chippy we met the local tramp.

'Give me a chip, will you?' he asked me, tottering, drunk as always.

'Here,' I said, 'have them all, mate.' Everything about the place was making me feel uneasy. I turned to Katrina and said, 'If you want to see me again, meet up with me tomorrow for a drink in town. I am leaving for good this time.'

My parents were resigned to having me home again and were fully expecting me to stay, but I knew that I couldn't. I hadn't even unpacked my bag from Borstal. I didn't mean to hurt them, but I knew that I would be causing them more grief if I did stay. I was doing both them and myself a favour by moving on.

The following day I took my bag and walked out of the house. My parents were at work and I left a note to them saying that I was going to sleep over at a friend's. It would have been more decent to tell them the truth and say goodbye, but I knew that there would be one hell of a performance if I did and the parting would be even more bitter.

I walked into town and found Katrina and we had a drink in a pub. Katrina came with me when I went to meet my probation officer as I was supposed to. On the way we bumped into a distant uncle of mine.

'Where are you off to?' he asked me.

'I'm leaving, I can't stay here no more.' I felt OK about telling him, he was a decent sort of person. 'I'm running away, and I'm off for good and I'm not coming back ever again,' I said to him. Without asking me any further questions he gave me a tenner to help me on my way. I already had £14 in my pocket, so it amounted to a tidy sum – in those days anyway.

The probation officer was a new woman assigned to me, I had never met her before. I told her straight away that I was leaving. 'You can't do that. These are the conditions of your licence, you must live here and you must go to school.'

'Well, I'm not going to,' I said. 'In fact, I am leaving now, this afternoon.' I showed her my bag. 'I've got all my things with me, and I'm all ready to go.'

'You leave this place,' she said in a menacing tone of voice, 'and I'll have a warrant out for your arrest in three weeks.'

'You'll have to do that then, because I'm fucking going.'

Her mentioning the warrant made me realize that there was nothing she could do right there and then to stop me leaving.

The truth is that as soon as I set foot on the platform the day before, I knew that I would be leaving. It was the whole atmosphere of the place, and every moment that had passed confirmed my need to leave. I had to get rid of and move on from my past.

Katrina was waiting for me when I came out – she was a good friend – and I said to her, 'Come on, let's have a drink before I go to the station.' We went to our local and had a pint of cider.

'Will I ever see you again?' she asked me.

'Yes, you will, but the next time I sit in this pub I'll have a moustache,' I said to her without thinking. I don't know why I said it, but I felt convinced that I would be more able to be myself in the future.

When the train pulled out I felt a sense of great relief similar to the last time I had left town. Two hours later I was in Newport. Consciously or not, my purpose all along since leaving Borstal had been to find Irena and be with her. We had written to each other and she had sent me a couple of addresses where I might find her. I decided I would try her sister's house first. When I finally found it and knocked on the door, a girl came and opened it. Behind the glass door she looked so much like Irena that initially I thought it was her.

'She's not here but try her brother's, where she is staying at the moment.' So I trudged over to the other address. Irena's sister-in-law met me at the door.

'She's not here for the moment, she has gone to Cardiff for the day, but she is expected back tonight.' I started to walk away but she called me back. 'Hang on a minute, what's your name?' I told her.

'Oh Joe, Joe from Borstal? Irena said that you might come to see her. Come in and wait for her if you want.'

Finally she arrived, and she was very excited to see me; I was just as excited of course.

'I'm glad you found the M4 and didn't lose your way,' she teased me. I never left that house. We stayed there, and slowly got our relationship working. For all her tough exterior and her quick tongue, Irena was quite shy with me and wasn't as experienced in relationships as I had thought. And that made two of us. It took a while to get our sexual relationship functioning. We were both in love for the first time, and we had a lot to learn. No matter how close we were, I was just as adamant about my privacy and not being touched. Yet, for the first time, I had strong sexual feelings and I was able to get pleasure and satisfaction from lying on top of her and making love to her as the man I knew myself to be. Irena wasn't a lesbian, she had never had a relationship with a woman. The word lesbian never entered our conversation and as far as I was concerned we were man and woman. She realized I wasn't happy with my condition but we never really talked too deeply about it at this time. We just got on with our relationship and living from day to day.

Not long after I arrived, Irena's brother, who was a merchant seaman, took his wife with him on an extended tour of Africa, and with no hesitation they left us looking after their house and their four-year-old son, John. Within a week or two, a friend of Irena's was sent to Borstal, also for ripping off a chemist's, and she left her little boy Isaak with us to look after as well.

I couldn't claim dole because of my age, so the four of us lived on £9 a week which was the amount of Irena's social security. Irena's brother and sister-in-law had left us some money for John. It was enough to buy us all a decent amount of food, fags and a bit of booze. Because of the kids we didn't go out much, but we had a drink and a smoke in the house, and it was all right.

When I was in Borstal I had become friendly with a girl called Gail who was from Cardiff. While we were inside we agreed to meet once we were out. She got out six weeks after me and, as agreed, we met for a drink. She introduced me to her brother

Ty. He was to become a good friend, and over the years he helped me in all kinds of situations.

One issue that clouded our time together was that Irena was still struggling to come off hard drugs, and she would often succumb to having a fix if she could get hold of it. She hadn't quite kicked the habit and found it hard to refuse. I couldn't for my life understand what the pleasure was in it, and seeing how it affected her I wasn't tempted to try it myself. Right after shooting up she would be sick, then her skin would start to itch and she would scratch her nose raw. She'd be in a bit of a daze, although it didn't stop her talking to me – she talked for hours sometimes.

We often had words about it because I felt strongly that I didn't want to wake up one morning and find her dead lying next to me. A friend of hers died during this time. This girl was a heavy drinker as it was, but she had gone to have a fix in a toilet after a night of partying and was found there in a coma the next morning. Fourteen days later she died. I always worried that Irena's next dose would be the one that was too much. But at the end of the day it was her choice. I told her I didn't want her to do it, but she did anyway. About a year later, she did finally quit the habit altogether.

Later I did experiment with injectable drugs, once or twice. The rush and the high of heroin or morphine were nice feelings, and I could understand how easy it would be to get hooked. But having seen what they could do to people, I had a healthy respect for them and I didn't find it enjoyable enough to persist.

The drug squad was often sniffing around since they knew about Irena's record. One day they came with a search warrant. They didn't bother knocking at the door but broke into the house, opening the front door through a broken window pane. They stormed the place; a pile of them ran up the stairs. I was lying on the settee in the front room watching television while Irena was drying the kids off in front of the fire, having just got them out of the bath. At first we both thought it was Irena's brother and sister-in-law coming home from their trip.

The cops went on a rampage and ransacked the whole house. They broke up the tape recorder to see inside it and emptied all the jars in the kitchen. Sugar and coffee were everywhere. They threw the beds over and pulled everything out of cupboards and generally made one hell of a mess. They even had the nerve to ask Isaak where the stash was; he was hardly old enough to speak. They asked me who I was, and I made up some name. In the end they had no choice but to leave as there was nothing in the house incriminating in any way. We felt terrible about the damage they had done, particularly to the tape recorder, since we were supposed to be responsible for the house. Irena's brother was very good about it all in the end; he realized it hadn't been our fault.

The next day the cops came back and told me that they knew who I was and that I had just got out of Borstal. They couldn't do anything about it, however. Although my probation officer had said she would have a warrant out for my arrest within three weeks, in fact it took her three months to get it organized. So there was nothing they could do. When finally the warrant was issued, they were really out to get me and they kept coming back to the house looking for me all the time, in the early hours of the morning, or at any time during the day. Each time I saw them coming I was like a lunatic. I would run through the house, dive through the bathroom window and either get up on the roof and lie there flat until the danger had passed or jump over the fence into the neighbours' yard and hide in an old discarded sideboard.

Across the lane was the post sorting office, and everyone sitting in the windows typing away could observe this routine, probably wondering what on earth was the matter with this person, who was forever darting through the window and hopping into this wooden box. When the cops had gone Irena would reach out of the bathroom window, which was right above the neighbours' yard, and tap on the box. 'They've gone. You can come out now.'

The kitchen caught fire once when the cops were harassing Irena at the front door, and I was in one of my usual positions, lying flat on the kitchen roof. The chip pan was on the cooker, and Irena was trying to tell the cops not to come back, that I wasn't living there any more.

'He's fucked off to Birmingham, so there is no point in you lot coming around here any more.'

At the same time little Isaak was tugging at Irena's clothes, saying, 'Irena, Irena, fire, fire.'

And she was saying, not really taking in what he was saying, 'Shush, in a minute, I'll be there in a minute.'

We got the fire out but we had one hell of a job trying to clean up the mess. The whole kitchen was black. We had a good laugh imagining the ceiling caving in and me coming down with it. It would have been just my luck.

The whole situation was starting to get to me. I was sick and tired of running and hiding. I knew that eventually I would be apprehended, but I had wanted to enjoy a little bit of the summer. Finally there was nothing for it but to give myself up and hand myself in. I went down to the pub and got drunk and then swallowed a handful of DF118s (very strong painkillers) to make me thoroughly numb for the unpleasant task ahead.

Then I went to the police station, accompanied by Irena for moral support, and said, 'Here I am. There is a warrant out for my arrest.'

So they started to search for my warrant, flapping around not finding it. During the three hours it took them to find it, we kept reminding them of the hassle they had put us through over the last few weeks.

'We have a good mind to go home,' Irena said to them. 'You have been pestering us all this time, having the cheek coming back and forth to the house all hours of the night, and now we come here and you can't even find his warrant.'

I was sent back to Borstal for four months. It felt like I had never been out of there really, but the excitement had gone out of it. I was somewhat pissed off that I was back there again, back into the same old routine. I had had a real taste of freedom, and I wanted to be out there, so this time I kept my nose clean and didn't get myself into any unnecessary trouble. While I was in there doing my time, I wrote to Irena and asked if she could get a flat for us in Cardiff for when I came out so that we could have a fresh start in a new city, and she managed to find one for us.

Again, like the last time, when I left Borstal I was on licence and I was supposed to go straight home. The intention was that I should sit my O levels, since I was still sixteen. I said to them when I was leaving, 'Yes, I'm really looking forward to going home, and doing my O levels.' Later, I got to see the report that my probation officer had written about this conversation. It stated that she was somewhat dubious about this enthusiasm of mine. 'Seeing is believing,' she commented. A note had been added later at the bottom of the report:

'Suspicions confirmed. She never arrived home.'

I hopped off the train in Cardiff and the first thing I did was to phone my probation officer and say, 'I'm not going home, I'm not going back to school. You either transfer my papers to Cardiff and get me another probation officer here, or you can come and find me and take me back to Borstal.' Then I took a taxi to the flat which was to be home. I was very excited, and felt quite grown up as well, as it was to be my first place of my own. I could tell from a distance exactly where the flat was by the loud music emanating from the windows.

It was great to be free and I was happy to be with Irena again. Loads of people would hang out and crash in the flat, including two girls called Laura and Tracy. Soon I found out that Laura and Tracy were different in some way. There was no way to distinguish them from perfectly born women, but then I was told that they were transsexuals, although I had no idea what that meant. It didn't take very long for me to make the connection between their condition and mine. We were the same, but the other way round. I was both stunned and elated to meet others who felt the same as me and suffered the same condition. At first I was too shy and embarrassed to ask them too many questions, but a couple of days later I was having a chat with Tracy and she talked to me about being a transsexual.

'This is what you are, too,' she said to me.

'So, I am a transsexual!' I thought in amazement. I hadn't known there was such a thing, and much less a label for it, and there was a tremendous sense of relief to know that I was not the only one in the world who had been born into the wrong body. Tracy also mentioned casually that she had seen an ad in a paper a couple of months previously in which a doctor was encouraging transsexuals in need of help to contact him. She and Laura had rung this doctor right away and had been seeing him for a couple of months. I couldn't believe what I was hearing. It sounded too good to be true. Was it possible that there was help for me out there? What form would this help take? She went on to tell me that she had read an article which said that some surgeon was working on ways to construct a penis. She had seen photographs and diagrams of what could be done. Although I was overwhelmed with hope that I could be put right, I never wanted to talk about or read about my condition. All I really wanted was to wake up in the morning and discover that my past had all been a bad dream. In my mind I was not a transsexual, I was a man.

I wasted no time in ringing this doctor myself and was told that I would have to have a referral from my own GP. No problem! I went to see a GP straight away. Dr Popper turned out to be very nice and extremely helpful. He didn't know anything about this man, Dr Randall, a psychiatrist specializing in the treatment of transsexuals at a clinic at the Charing Cross Hospital in London. He couldn't refer me directly to Dr Randall but promised that he would refer me to a psychiatrist who could make a better assessment of my condition. He in turn could make the referral. I was elated and grateful for having met Laura and Tracy. It may have been years before I had discovered these things for myself.

Tracy was an outrageous person, and she dressed in the most extraordinary things. When I first met her, that same evening when I arrived in Cardiff from Borstal, she was waiting for us at the entrance of the Showbizz Club. Her hair was cut into four peaks, one at the front, two on the sides of her head and one at the back. They were all different colours, and she was wearing a gigantic square tunic. One of her eyebrows was straight and the other zigzagged across her forehead. She was hailed by the local newspaper as the most outrageous woman that walked the streets of Cardiff. She was very feminine nevertheless, and on the odd occasion she would actually dress casually. Laura was much more discreet in her way of dressing, just jeans and

T-shirts. Both Tracy and Laura loved dancing. When we went out clubbing they would swing each other around the dance floor all night. They were quite extrovert people, they were what they were, and they didn't care what anyone else thought about it. I wished that I could have had the same laid-back attitude about my own condition. Why couldn't I be that comfortable with it?

Although I was having fun I was starting to wonder what would happen to me, what I would do with my future. Irena noticed that I was a bit more withdrawn, more introspective.

'What the hell is the matter with you? You are not as much fun as you used to be. You've changed since you've come out of Borstal this time.' Our relationship was affected by this, I was more serious, and we started arguing quite a bit.

One evening I was introduced to a girl called Lorretta. Someone had mentioned her to me before. The moment I laid eyes on her, I was instantly attracted to her.

'So you are Lorretta?' I looked her up and down and took the whole of her in. I didn't normally ogle women but I couldn't help myself. She was black, very beautiful, slightly older than me. In a funny way she felt familiar. There was something about her that I thought I had seen or felt before, it was quite uncanny. She noticed the way I was looking at her and seemed embarrassed about it, which was not surprising, since she knew and liked Irena, but I couldn't help myself. Even her embarrassment I found profoundly attractive. It was unusual for me to feel so strongly and instantly drawn to a woman.

Gradually I became quite obsessed with the idea of seeing her about or running into her. Although she was more cool about it, I think she felt the same about me. This was still only in my mind, since I was obviously with Irena. Irena and I were still the best of friends, but what I was beginning to feel for Lorretta came more from the gut. Irena began to notice it. Whenever we went into a pub or a club my eyes would start to roam. I tried not to make it too obvious, but Irena had me sussed. 'Who are you looking for then, Radar?' or: 'Fucking Radar is off again.'

I saw Lorretta frequently as she was friendly with all of us. A few times we were on our own, a couple of hours here and there. One night I met up with her by chance and we got steaming drunk together. After the clubs had closed we wandered down the street and ran into a gang of gypsies. They were drunk as well.

'Come along,' one of them slurred, inviting us to go with them. 'This guy here is going to buy us all a meal.' We staggered along with the rest of them into an all-night café. Everybody piled in around a big table. The guy with the money ordered chicken and chips for everyone. We were having a really good time, talking and laughing with these gypsies. Then someone said, 'Hey, that fucking guy has left, he's gone.' Everyone panicked since nobody had money or was willing to pay the bill. Lorretta and I grabbed handfuls of chicken, stuffing them in our pockets – so did everyone else – and then we all ran like hell out of there. The law was there within minutes, but we got away, just.

It was very late and we took a taxi together. She ended up asking me up to her flat for a cup of coffee. I wanted to be alone with her and to get to know her more intimately, but I didn't feel it was the right time and place. I didn't want to jump at the opportunity because she might think that I was like that with any woman I met. Also, there was Irena.

'Not tonight, maybe some other time,' I said to her.

I know she respected me for it because she remembered it years later. Things went on like this between Lorretta and me, on an even keel. Mainly we were just friends, although there were undercurrents of stronger feelings but we didn't talk about them. I found her a very lovely and sensuous woman whilst I was also slightly wary of her. Although she related to me as woman to man my own restrictions made me feel insecure. But we were just two people very drawn to each other. Lorretta obviously realized that I was a troubled person and that I was fighting for my identity but she was open-minded and was primarily concerned with emotions and instincts, rather than appearances and physical form. This was her attitude towards people in general, and she approached everyone the same way, giving them the benefit of the doubt.

Anyway, we were all friends and it didn't really matter. Irena was quite forgiving of my weaknesses, as I was of hers.

Irena and I acquired a responsibility in the form of a little girl called Kim; she was about three years old. Irena offered to look after her because her mother had difficulties coping with her own life and kept leaving Kim to be looked after by different people. With us she would have a bit more continuity. Irena in particular grew very fond of Kim. We had a lot of fun with her, playing with her and buying her toys. We went wild buying her Christmas presents. She loved dancing and used to perform for us, twirling around the room in her long nightie. Social services used to come and check that the little girl was all right, but they could see that we were taking good care of her. They said that they didn't think it was the ideal environment for her, but that she was obviously doing well. Kim slept in the same room with Irena and me and she often used to have bad dreams. We would take turns waking her up to comfort her, and in time she seemed to be happier and more content.

After a few months, Kim's mother got into trouble and ended up in prison. Kim was removed from our care and placed with her grandparents. We packed her a little bag with her favourite toys to show her grandparents, and we waved goodbye to her and said, 'See you later.' Kim thought that she was going to come back to us, and we didn't have the heart to tell her that this wasn't so. Irena was extremely upset about losing Kim.

'Never again will I look after somebody else's baby,' she said. 'It would have to be my own the next time.'

This started her talking about the idea of us having children. It was way beyond me in every way – I wouldn't even talk about it. I tried always to smother every thought or memory of the gender I was born as, and talking about children brought up yet another one of my limitations. I had trusted this woman with my emotions. She had stood by me in many ways, but this was an issue that dragged up so many of my inadequacies and she wouldn't leave it alone. This didn't help our relationship.

My plea to the authorities to let me stay in Cardiff had been heeded, and I was assigned a new probation officer, Carole. She was very young, and she came to be very helpful to me. Irena always used to come with me if I had to talk to anyone in authority, such as probation officers. I had such difficulty talking about myself that Irena would talk on my behalf. If I was asked a personal question, Irena would look at me first and then say, 'He feels (this way, or that way) about it', just as I used to do for my little sister when I was a young boy.

I didn't have the capacity, or the desire to talk about myself or specifically about my condition. I never described myself or my condition in any way and I could only express myself in monosyllables, never saying a word over and above what was necessary, to anyone. Instead I spent a lot of time crying about it. My feelings would follow a cycle of crying, then trying to hide my upset, which in turn would make me angry. The anger would have no outlet so this would in turn become frustration, and soon I would be crying again. This cycle was exhausting, particularly when it reached a peak, but I had no control over it. I could go months sometimes, able to ignore my discomfort, but it always caught up with me in the end. In private moments with Irena I had started to try to speak to her about my condition a little bit, but mainly my communication about my feelings was expressed in anger. On the whole Irena accepted me totally and understood my condition and my predicament, but not how deeply I was affected by it all.

Soon, however, I was going to have to talk about myself and my condition, in order to ask for the help that I needed. I saw the psychiatrist Dr Popper referred me to. Bringing my feelings to the surface and actually speaking about them always made me feel emotional and vulnerable, but in order to get help, I had to speak. At the end of our consultation he said that he thought I would make a very good subject for Dr Randall, and would happily refer me to him. I was so relieved to hear him say this and I thanked him wholeheartedly and shook him warmly by the hand.

I was waiting to get an appointment with Dr Randall in London and finally I got a letter with the date and time. On the train to London, I felt quite apprehensive about seeing him. Could he really do something to help me?

At the clinic I was asked to sit and wait in the corridor outside Dr Randall's consulting room. To my surprise there were others waiting for him as well. I looked around me discreetly and thought that some of them were there for the opposite condition, women who had been born in men's bodies, although I wasn't sure. Nobody said anything; there was a sense of apprehension all around. I tried to imagine what Dr Randall would look like. Tall and youngish probably.

When it was my turn to go in, I found him to be a short balding man with glasses, somewhere in his mid fifties. For some reason it shocked me a bit that he was so different from my mental image of him. With him in the consulting room was a brain surgeon, a heart surgeon and a medical student. Dr Randall introduced me and told me not to mind these people, that they were there out of professional interest.

'What is that on your hands?' he asked me. I told him that they were scars from tattoo removals, and he showed my hands to the assembled party.

'How do you feel about having them out?'

'Better . . . I wanted them out.'

He was looking at his notes a lot while he was talking to me, but his interest picked up when I was unable to say the name given to me at birth. He had asked me matter-of-factly what this name was, and no matter how I tried to press it out of my lips, I just choked on it. I simply couldn't say it. I was struggling because there seemed to be a reason why I should say it. I finally agreed to write it down. He looked at the piece of paper for a minute and took in the name which I so detested, then looked at me and said, 'You could have fooled me.' I breathed a sigh of relief. Hearing him say that seemed a definite act of recognition. Then he asked me, 'When were your earliest memories?' I told him that I knew I was a boy at the age of five. This seemed to be significant, and he said that I might think those were my earliest memories, but in fact I had always been like this, even between nought and five.

'I suppose you played a lot of football when you were young, did you?'

'No. Not really,' I answered.

'So what did you do then?' he asked.

'I used to find wild creatures and reptiles, keep them for a while and sketch them before I let them go.'

He looked at me quietly for a while and then said, 'Now, what do you want me to do for you?'

'Just help me!' I implored him.

He looked at me more closely and after a while he said, 'Well, I have never had it put to me quite like that before.' He turned to the audience: 'I usually have people coming in here and telling me that they want this done and they want that done.' He turned to me again and said that he would do everything he could to help me. I felt a tremendous sense of reassurance and of hope. He was a stern man, a man who inspired respect, but you knew that you could trust him. I knew he wouldn't bullshit me. But then he told me there was nothing he could do for me until I was twenty-one. My heart sank.

'Twenty-one? Oh, my God.'

'That's it,' he said emphatically. 'Nothing can be done until you're twenty-one. That is when your body stops growing. There is nothing I can do and there is nothing you can do.'

He knew that I had been in Borstal and he told me he wanted reports every three months from my probation officer.

'I can see that you already know who you are,' he said, 'but you must continue living entirely in your identity as a man and become accepted by society as such.' He also told me that I wouldn't be able to change my birth certificate; it was how the law stood presently. He asked me about my relationship with my family, and I had to confess that it was not good at all.

I was still only sixteen but he obviously thought I was an appropriate candidate for treatment. I was too intimidated by the situation and perhaps lacking in common sense to ask him exactly what all this was going to mean. What was the exact procedure in a case like mine? Maybe I didn't really want to know it all, as long as they did for me everything that was possible and as soon as possible. The only information I had taken in was:

'I am going to put you on a course of hormone treatment. It will deepen your voice and prevent menstruation.' Hearing him say that was an immense relief for me. He gave me a letter to give to Dr Popper, my GP, outlining the sort of treatment that he should prescribe for me.

When I got home I made an appointment with Dr Popper right away. I was eager to start the process of my metamorphosis as soon as possible. Dr Popper took out a giant medical dictionary and looked up the hormone treatment I had been prescribed.

'You might gain weight,' he warned me. What did I care? I was too thin anyway. We talked for quite a while and towards the end he said, 'You realize that the further the treatment goes on and the closer you get to your goal, the harder it is going to be for you.'

I looked at him, puzzled. 'How can you say that? It seems to me that the closer I get, the happier I'm going to feel.'

'You'll be under more stress, because your need to get there will be greater as you get older, I can assure you.'

I started the treatment but I didn't notice anything for a couple of months at all. I just carried on with my life, trusting that something about me would change. The first thing that happened was after all of us residents in the flat had gone out for an evening and had had a fair amount to drink and smoke. When I woke up in the morning, Irena asked me if I wanted a cup of tea or coffee.

'Yeah, I'd love a cup of tea, please,' I croaked.

'My God, what's wrong with you? Have you got a cold?' she asked.

'No I don't think so.' I had a sniff and a snort, but my nose wasn't blocked or anything.

'Well your voice sounds different,' she said.

It wasn't until a day or two later that I realized what it was. My voice was breaking. It didn't come as a complete surprise; I had known it was going to happen. My voice went through some funny stages, one moment it would go up a pitch and the next moment it would be hoarse and gravelly; it could be quite embarrassing.

From the time this happened, all my thoughts became focused on this process. I still didn't talk in any depth with anyone, I was just so happy that I had found Dr Randall. I trusted that he was eventually going to help me put my problem right, and rejoiced in the fact that this process was finally under way. All along the way, until I was twenty, I would write to him frequently to tell him how urgent it was for me that he remove the parts that didn't belong to me. I implored him to help me get rid of them, but as he had said, nothing else could be done until I was twenty-one.

The next thing to come along were the hot flushes. At any time in the day or night, the heat would suddenly rise up through my body, and leave my face flaming, with sweat pouring off my forehead.

At this time, aged seventeen, I also decided to change my name. I wanted a whole new life, to be reborn and to wipe out my past. I went along to a solicitor and asked him if it was possible to change my name. Right there and then he had me fill in a form and pay the fee of £11. I happily signed to the effect that I 'truly relinquish and abandon all former names ... to be known in the future as Raymond Thompson.' This to me was my birth certificate. That evening we all had a drink to celebrate it. My friend Ty (the brother of Gail from Borstal) said, 'From now on, nobody is to refer to you as anything other than he.'

This was a turning point in my life. Between my hormone treatment and my name change, I felt that I had taken a giant step towards a new identity. My medical card and my giro cheques had my new name on them. I felt that I was moving towards becoming the man I had always been on the inside, although the process was never ever fast enough for me.

Alongside this, life was lived very much in the fast lane. I wanted to fend for myself. I had chosen this life, this city and these friends, and I chose to fit in with this lifestyle in which we lived hand to mouth, sleeping most of the day, and partying most of the night, just taking each day as it came. Having been locked up for a time, I was really enjoying the kind of careless freedom that I now had, and soon was about to lose again. The little money that we had from social security didn't last long. Things like food, rent and clothes were necessary but usually came last on the list; booze, fags and fun took priority. I certainly had no idea how to go about earning money. Even if someone had told me how to go about getting a job, I had no O levels and no skills and I had a criminal record. I had a small amount of dole money to live on, and if there was a quick and easy way to come by some more money, I went for it; we all did. Whether it was legal or moral didn't come into it much, although the people I knew were far from being hardened criminals. They were young people like myself, fending for themselves in the only way they knew how.

There was certainly no one to turn to, no one to ask for help or to bail you out of a difficult situation. There were no parents to rely on, no meals to come home to. Yet most of us would infinitely rather fend for ourselves than go home and live with our parents, each for our own reasons and we were prepared to take the consequences of our actions. There were times when we were very hard up and starving. Once, we lived on mostly bread and mushrooms for a couple of weeks. We had no money at all and a friend gave us daily rations of mushrooms which she got from a vegetable wholesaler she was friendly with. We were very grateful for them, but it took a while before I could even look at a mushroom again. My diet was a variable affair. Most of the time we ate toasted bread, but occasionally we would go out to buy, or pinch, some different kinds of food. At night, after the clubs closed, a whole bunch of us used to go and buy a curry in an all-night restaurant. We would put it in the middle of the table and all dip into it.

More often than not we had no money to pay the landlord on time. Sometimes he would come to the door, and we would ask him what he wanted, as if we didn't know. There were times when one of us had done a 'job' and were able to give him a whole month's rent. The poor guy would be over the moon: 'Is there anything that needs doing in the flat, any repairs?' He was so stunned to get money off us.

'Repairs? . . . Yeah, well . . .' I had broken the gas meter's coin box one day when we were desperate for some cigarettes. We were not your ideal tenants.

Drugs were easy to come by. Most of them you didn't even need money for. Downers (tranquillizers and sleeping tablets) were given out by anyone who had them. It was different in those days; many doctors would prescribe them when asked. Now there are a lot of restrictions on all prescription drugs and that sort of drug can be expensive on the black market. If we didn't have a lot of money to buy drinks in the clubs, a couple of downers would go a long way to keep you on a high. Dope (cannabis) and acid (LSD) were a different thing, those you had to pay for.

Looking back on this unpredictable lifestyle, I couldn't contemplate ever living like that again. At the time I didn't care, I was young and quite resilient.

Unfortunately, soon I was arrested for a crime which in retrospect I feel very bad about. I had been out for the evening drinking with Lesley. It was late in the night. We were running very short of money and we were high as kites. We ran into Lorretta and a friend, and all of us went into an all-night café for a cup of coffee. We spotted this guy sitting at the next table, waving a wad of cash about. He was quite drunk himself. Since we were desperate for money we decided to follow him out and try to get his money off him. He crossed the street and we followed. We asked him to hand his money over but of course he wasn't about to. Lesley started scuffling with him, he fought back and she hit him. I hit him too. We didn't hit him very hard but, being drunk, he lost his balance and fell backwards. He hit the back of his head on a cast iron railing and cracked his skull open. I had had no intention of hurting him but I was behaving like an animal in a frenzy to get his money off him. It all came down to money, wanting money, and this seemed an opportunity to get some, quickly and easily. My judgement about what I was doing was clouded by being high on downers and very drunk. We all were. I sometimes wonder if I would have gone to those extremes if I hadn't been. It is difficult to know, looking back on it. When you are high you lose your sense of perspective, and the situation got out of hand. We were all involved in robbing this guy, but it was just Lesley and me who had used violence against him. We got his money and ran across the street and hailed a taxi, but someone had witnessed the crime and minutes later our taxi was stopped by the police and we were arrested.

It was each man for himself in the sort of world we lived in and the sort of life we led. You were just as likely to get robbed yourself as you were to rob someone else. Although we all seemed to live by these codes, we never set out to hurt or maim anyone intentionally. I had to live with the realization of what I had done; I knew I was going to have to pay for it.

It was a very difficult time for Lorretta. Up to this point I had not realized that she had a young son, and I felt terribly sorry for her. We all stated that she had not taken part in the robbery, in order to try and get her off the charge. I was asked in court how I could be sure of that. I knew she had been wearing a long white mac, and I said that I saw her up at the other end of the street. But the taxi driver who had been witness to the whole thing gave descriptions of us all, and she was charged with the rest of us. He had seen us running across the road to get away, one black person, three white.

When I was standing in the dock, trying to be convincing about Lorretta not having been involved, I suddenly had a really bad hot flush. I went a deep red in the face and was sweating profusely.

'Look at the defendant, I think the fact that she is blushing beetroot red proves her guilt and that she is lying,' the prosecutor said. I vehemently denied it, but I couldn't explain that I was having a hot flush because of my hormones, and it was all very embarrassing.

The charge was robbery with malicious wounding with intent to do grievous bodily harm. Thankfully the intent was dropped from the charge since it was true that we had not intended to hurt him. I was sentenced to eighteen months in prison, because I was a YP (young prisoner). I had just turned seventeen. One of the girls got nine months, but Lorretta and Leslie got two and a half years each. It was very unfortunate for Lorretta, because she was the one who was least involved in the robbery. Basically she was just present. I can't help but wonder if the colour of her skin had something to do with her getting a long sentence.

I didn't feel very much about this crime at the time. The man we robbed recovered from his injury. Now, however, I feel very bad about it although it's too late to change anything. I was punished and served my time in jail, which gave me time to think about how my life was going to be. When I came out of prison, apart from a couple of minor slip-ups, I did live by the law of the land, although I didn't always agree with it. As I was growing up I gradually saw the difference between right and wrong, and I certainly didn't want my life to continue like this, getting locked up time and time again.

The main thing that changed in me was I started to respect and be sensitive to the rights of others. Just as I desperately wanted and needed respect and sensitivity from society, I also realized I had to show that I lived by these codes myself. I was also beginning to believe that the things you do to others will come back to you in due course. Years later when I was attacked in the street by two men, I had a sharp flashback to the act that landed me in prison. Just as a boot was coming towards my face, I remembered clearly what I had done to the man we robbed.

What helped me on the way to this change of attitude was also the fear of destroying my chances of getting the help I so badly needed.

5
All My Hopes and All My Dreams

I was placed in the remand centre where I had been three years earlier. Lorretta and Lesley were shipped there with me. This time I knew what to expect and felt no anxiety. As before, part of the reception procedure was to look us over for drugs, bugs, lesions and all that.

I did a good job convincing the screws that Lorretta and I should be bunked up together.

'My friend is very upset and distressed,' I told them. 'We're here on the same charge, and we're good friends.' It was no lie, Lorretta was devastated about the fact that she wouldn't see her son or her mother for two and a half years. They were her only close relatives in the world. The screws could see for themselves that Lorretta was in a bit of a state, and they allowed us to share a double cell.

It took some time for Lorretta to come to terms with her loss, and I tried to be as supportive as I could. We slowly got to know each other better and grew close. After all, we spent most of our time for two months locked up together in a cell eight foot by six. Lorretta spoke a lot to me about her mother and son. She was worried about how her mother would cope with a small child. He was just two years old. Her mother had been quite ill recently, but Lorretta didn't know yet that her mother had cancer. She wrote to them frequently and wanted to make a giant stuffed turtle for Jamie, her son. I felt responsible for the way things had turned out and I wanted to make it up to her in some way. There wasn't very much that I could do for her while we were in prison so I told her that I would get the money to buy the materials for the turtle and make sure that it got to Jamie. She spent a long time making the turtle and did a beautiful job of it.

After a while it was inevitable that our relationship would

become a sexual one, seeing how we felt about each other. With Lorretta, making love was a different experience altogether, and I felt much more comfortable with her than anyone else I had known in that way. I still couldn't allow anyone to touch me in a sexual way, nor see the lower part of my body that didn't belong to me. But it was still a tremendous pleasure to hold her and be held by her, and to give her satisfaction. Lying on top of her, the sensations I had were entirely those of being a man. I didn't even have to imagine what it would feel like to be inside her, I felt it totally.

Although I have achieved satisfaction making love to other women, it has never been as blissfully real as it was with Lorretta. She always told me that her body responded to me as a woman with a man. She made me feel so natural, she wiped out my restrictions. We never needed to talk about my condition, she had told me that she felt my maleness on an emotional as well as a physical level. She said she understood how difficult it was for me to survive in unfamiliar surroundings, by which she meant my body. That sort of comment made me realize that she had the ability to put herself in my shoes and had an instinctive understanding of what I was experiencing.

My feelings for Lorretta grew very quickly and we both wanted this relationship to be more than just an affair, but we seldom talked about it because we both felt we were living on borrowed time and were not in a position to make any real plans for the future. We spent practically all our time together because we knew we would soon be separated and moved to different prisons. On association we would go to the gym. I worked on the weights and Lorretta would go straight for the trampoline. She was very good at it. We also played a lot of badminton together. We had two or three hours in the evening to do what we wanted when we would have a smoke and watch television or play table tennis with Lesley.

Much as Lorretta and I were crazy about each other, it was a highly charged relationship. We were very high on each other but we also had some fierce rows. I don't remember what they were all about but Irena's name cropped up a few times. Lorretta couldn't help reminding me that I was still in a relationship with

Irena, that I hadn't actually broken off with her. She would be warm and giving one moment, but then she would pull back. We hadn't made any commitment to each other so I wasn't completely hers after all. For me there were definitely some mixed feelings. I was in love with Lorretta and felt a tremendous passion between us but I still felt a sense of loyalty towards Irena. Our bond of friendship was very strong and it felt as if she was 'family'.

Once when Lorretta and I were having a fierce row about this, I got so incensed that I made the fatal mistake of running up and telling a screw, 'Fucking unbunk me from this woman.' I didn't mean a word of it, of course; it was all said in a rage. Already the next morning the request was granted and a screw came to remove my name card from the door. I couldn't believe that I had been so stupid and brought this on myself.

'I don't want to move,' I tried to tell the screw. She ignored me and whipped my name card out of the door, marched down the corridor to one of the single cells and plopped the card in the slot on the door.

'You've got to go, the order has been put through.'

I went into a frenzy and ran after her, snatched the card out, ran back and put it where it had been.

'Don't start,' Lorretta pleaded. 'You'll get locked up. You've done it. Just leave it, leave it.' She managed to calm me down, and we went down for breakfast.

My new single cell was freezing. There were two small panes missing from the window and the wind howled through them. Missing the warm and cosy cell I shared with Lorretta, I sat shivering in there, feeling gutted about the move. I immediately requested to be rebunked, but nothing happened and I remained where I was. I still managed to see quite a lot of Lorretta but she was quite pissed off with me for having been such an idiot. I was very angry with myself, too, but Lorretta wouldn't allow me to talk about the subject, she didn't want any apologies or complaints. The deed was done, and that was that!

First thing in the morning we would meet in the bathroom and I would grab hold of her and kiss her. We still met in association and in the gym, but it was the end of any further physical intimacy.

Only a couple of weeks after the unbunking episode, Lesley and I were transferred to Styal prison in Cheshire. Although Lorretta's sentence was longer, she was going to be transferred to an open prison which meant a little more freedom of movement.

They came to get me very early in the morning from my cell to take me to reception. I went up to Lorretta's door as I was being led off the wing; she was waiting for me, knowing that I was leaving. We put our hands up against each side of the tiny glass panel in the door, as if to touch, and said our goodbyes while the screws were prompting me to move on. We spoke for a few seconds through the panel. I said I loved her and to take care of herself. We both felt very sad not knowing when or where we would next meet. As I was led away I didn't take my eyes off her until I reached the stairs and she was out of sight.

Three or four of us were going to Styal and soon we were on our way. When we arrived at the prison, we were put through reception which was not a complicated procedure, since we had arrived straight from the remand centre. There was no need for personal checks, they just booked us in, allocated us a house and sorted through our possessions.

My fellow prisoners – Lesley was among them – were put through first, leaving me to last.

'Right, Thompson, you've been allocated to Bleak.'

'Bleak?' I said casually but a bit surprised. 'I thought Bleak was the punishment block.'

'Yes, that's right, that is where I've been told to take you,' said one of the screws, shrugging her shoulders.

'Pick up your bundle,' said another one. 'You're coming with me.' I was marched straight to the punishment block. Soon I was going to know the reason for the name Bleak. I had already heard about it from others who had been there; apparently it had been a stable in the years before the place was turned into a prison.

The frame of mind that I had been in when I arrived, was to keep my nose clean and not get into any trouble. I was going to serve my time and then get out. And here I was being marched to Bleak within minutes of arriving.

'Why? What have I done?' I asked the screw who was escorting me.

She couldn't tell me anything: 'Look, this is where I have been told to take you. That's all I know.'

I thought it might have to do with my appearance – it probably didn't help. By now I had a moustache, my head had been shaved 'to the wood', and I was becoming quite fit and strong from exercise. I thought that maybe I looked like trouble.

We walked from one end of the prison grounds to the other on a wide avenue with massive red brick buildings on either side. The buildings looked like mansions (apart from the metal bars on the windows) and the avenues were lined with trees and there were lawns and flower beds. It looked quite luxurious in comparison to the places I had been locked up in before; it certainly wasn't what I had imagined.

'This doesn't look too bad,' I said to the screw. Later when all the restrictions became obvious, I found I had had a false impression. It was an offence to set foot on the grass, or sit anywhere, or stand and talk to someone on the avenue, or do anything at all. Even though inmates were walking seemingly freely around the grounds, it was in the course of their various jobs. Everyone was closely watched in everything they did.

Bleak was beyond all these houses with their neat gardens, past the boiler house, past the factory. It was an L-shaped building with cells running down one side and the corridor down the other. Very little light got in and it was very gloomy. It was surrounded by its own barbed-wire fence with a heavy iron gate. It was a prison within a prison. The screw opened the gate with her key and we walked up to the building. Once inside, she locked the door and told me to stand where I was and she disappeared. As I stood there waiting I heard steps coming up the corridor and I turned to look. To my amazement it was Rita, the girl that had first spoken to me and given me cigarettes in the remand centre when I was fifteen.

'My God, what are you doing down here?' I exclaimed and smiled. It was nice to see a friendly face. She told me that she had been shipped out from Holloway prison for attacking Myra Hindley (the notorious child-murderess) and breaking her nose.

'Nice one!' I said wholeheartedly. 'How long did you get for it?'

'I've done my time on lock-up, but I decided to ask for Rule 43 and come back down here.' Rule 43 allowed a prisoner to stay in the punishment block if she had a good reason for it, such as feeling under threat from other prisoners. In Rita's case it was different, she had asked for Rule 43 to prevent herself from getting into more trouble, but she was allowed out for association and to work within Bleak, as would any prisoner under Rule 43.

'You don't look to me as if you need looking after,' she said, gazing at me.

'What do you mean?' I asked, a bit puzzled. She told me that Irena had written her a letter telling her that I was coming to Styal and asking Rita to look out for me.

'What have you done to end up down here?'

'Fuck all,' I shrugged. 'I've just arrived. I've done nothing.'

'Strange,' she commented. 'Anyway, listen, quickly, the screws are coming, I'll sort you out with a few smokes later.'

I picked up my bundle and the screws escorted me to my cell.

'My God, is this it?' I thought looking around my dismal surroundings. 'This is going to be a long and boring eighteen months.' I was certain that they intended me to spend my whole sentence in solitary confinement. My cell was larger than any other cell I had been in previously, but it was empty except for an iron bed, a metallic mirror, a bible and a piss-pot. It had very high ceilings and a huge window with a wide sill, which made for a good place to sit and daydream, and it had a view over the exercise yard, which was surrounded by a high brick wall.

After four days in Bleak the governor sent for me. I had to stand in front of her surrounded by four screws. She was a very large woman and she had this tiny dog on her lap. Later I noticed that this little creature went everywhere with her.

'The records of your behaviour on remand and in Borstal leave a lot to be desired,' she told me sternly. 'Don't think you can do what you want around here: I won't tolerate any trouble from you. If it was up to me, and if there was nothing better for you to do here, you would spend your full eighteen months on the punishment block.' Next came the good news.

'I'm allocating you to the painting party, but if you get into any bother I won't hesitate to keep you down here for the length of your sentence.' What could I say? I was relieved that I was mistaken about my confinement. Nevertheless I was paying for the riot, barricading my cell, and trying to abscond. These past transgressions had left a blemish on my good name, such as it was.

I was moved to one of the houses, Fox House, which was full of pregnant women. I was quite shocked to see them all when I walked in there for the first time. Why was I there? It seemed a most incongruous place for me, of all people, to be. There must have been a purpose to it, and I couldn't help wondering if they put me there to make me feel uncomfortable and out of place. On the contrary, I was made to feel very much at home and the women looked after me well. They got extra rations of milk and eggs, which they were happy to share with me. They washed my working clothes for me and made me coffee.

There was only one woman there who wasn't pregnant. She and I were sitting watching television one night when she turned to me and said, 'God, you don't half remind me of my husband.'

'Oh, do I?' I said, turning back towards the television. I didn't know her at all.

'Yeah, you do,' she said and went on to tell me she was in prison for murdering her husband.

'And I remind you of him, do I?' I asked, smiling cautiously.

'Oh, I didn't mean anything by it,' she reassured me. 'It was just something about your mannerisms.' She told me her husband had sexually abused her children and had had numerous affairs. When she was sentenced for the murder, the judge took into consideration all the mitigating factors and gave her only two years.

A few days after I had started working on the painting party, I came back to the house in the evening and found two screws in my cell, going through my locker. They had laid everything that I owned out on my bed. They took my Y-front underwear and told me I was not allowed to wear male underwear, and that I was to wear prison-issue underwear.

'I came through reception with these. Why are you coming here now to take them off me?' I wanted to know. Without answering my question they took me down to the office and laid two different types of women's underwear out on a desk.

'This is what you have to wear, one or the other,' I was told.

'I am not wearing either. There is no way that you are getting me into underwear like that. I never wore them before I came to prison and I am not wearing them just because I'm in here.' I had just one pair of my own that didn't have a Y-front, which I insisted on keeping. I said to them, 'Look, if I've got to wear this one pair for the next fucking eighteen months, that's what I'm going to do.' I pointed at the desk with the underwear display and said in no uncertain terms, 'There is no fucking way that you're going to get me to wear either of those.'

The force of my insistence won out. I was allowed to keep that one pair. As soon as I could, I wrote to Irena and asked her to send me some more men's underwear without Y-fronts.

After a few weeks the assistant governor came to inspect Fox House. She turned out to be one of the very few persons in authority who was fair with me during my sentence. She spotted me in a queue to hand in our tobacco tins for the night. Turning to the screw, she said in my presence, 'I think a house change is in order here, don't you?' I didn't mind being in Fox House, and I was well looked after, but I would have preferred to be in another house and leave the ladies to get on with their pregnancies. So I was glad to be moved.

I am pretty sure it was my male appearance and my sexual orientation that made the screws wary, and often prejudiced against me. There were a few, in particular, who persisted in making my life difficult even after the change of house. If I stopped to have a chat with someone on the avenue or in a corridor – everyone did it and mostly it was overlooked – the screws would very quickly come up to me, saying, 'If you don't move on to where you're supposed to be going, you'll be on report.'

'What is the matter with you, for Christ's sake, haven't you got anything better to do?' I would ask, exasperated. 'What do you think I'm going to do? Is that how your old man behaves when he is out on the street, homing in on every female he lays eyes on? That's what you think I'm doing, isn't it?'

It irritated me that they stereotyped me in this way and made assumptions about me. I often heard them talking about me, referring to me as a chauvinist pig, and such like, knowing full well that I was listening. It used to amuse me that they wanted me to overhear this but it didn't bother me. I suppose they didn't know what to make of me and didn't trust me. By now it was clear to anyone that I didn't really belong in a women's prison.

Each house accommodated about thirty inmates. It had a dining room and a recreation room with a television. You were not allowed upstairs in the dormitories during the day, only at bedtime. Every week a van would come by and deliver all the food rations for each house in big boxes. Each house was allocated a set quantity of food for the week, and we had to make it last. Most of the vegetables were grown in the prison grounds: Brussels sprouts, cabbages, lettuce, carrots, runner beans, et cetera. Two inmates in each house cooked for everyone in the house. It was their full-time job, and no one else was allowed into the kitchen. They cooked three meals a day, but the washing-up was shared amongst the rest of us on a rota basis. So was peeling potatoes.

Some of the women would offer to relieve me of these duties. They obviously didn't think of me as one of them. Maybe some of them had an old-fashioned attitude and thought these chores were women's work. The washing-up didn't bother me at all, but I confess that I jumped at the chance of getting out of these dreary but necessary chores if I could.

We were woken up at half past six. We had to present ourselves downstairs, washed and dressed before seven o'clock, to sign the book — if you weren't on time you would be put on report and then sent to Bleak. Without so much as a cup of tea, which I found difficult to go without, we were expected to do our morning jobs. We all had different tasks to keep the house clean and in working order. My job was to sweep the stone paths around the house and clean the drains with caustic soda. After this was done, we had our breakfast and then went off to work.

We went back to the house for our cooked midday meal, then back to work until teatime. We were paid £1.02 a week for working on the painting party which, along with the gardening party, was the highest paid job in the prison. This particular job lasted for about eight months. There were six of us on it. We painted a large part of the prison, the stores, the administration block and most houses. Some of the houses we painted were just outside the prison gates, housing screws and some civilians that worked within the prison.

There was nothing really to do in the evenings, just watch television or listen to the radio – there was no such thing as table tennis or a gym as there was in the remand centre; there were no sports at all in fact. Nevertheless, between working hard all day and diligently doing my push-ups, sit-ups and pull-ups on the shower curtain rail, I was getting into very good shape.

It was while doing my sweeping job that one morning I had a few minutes to sit down on the steps to enjoy the sunshine. I was leaning back, smoking a roll-up and thinking about my family, my life and my predicament. I watched the priest of the prison walk down the avenue in his black robe. It made me remember the black-robed priest from my grandfather's funeral who came to give a service at the house to comfort my grandmother, who was a Catholic. Perhaps this man could do the same for me now. He was a man of God and that was enough for me. On a whim I shouted to him, 'Hey, Father, how come none of my hopes and none of my dreams come true?' He turned and walked up to me.

'What do you mean by that?' he asked.

'Just that,' I said. 'None of my dreams and none of my hopes ever seem to materialize.'

'Maybe God doesn't think it is the right time yet,' he answered.

Just that one sentence stuck in my mind. Even now I get some consolation from it. I saw in a flash that all things don't happen straight away, just because you want them to or need them to.

Maybe the time will come when my hopes and dreams will be fulfilled. Maybe God wants me to experience all this, so that when I do get to where I am going, I will fully appreciate and understand where I have been. My meeting with the priest gave me food for thought for a long time. I had always believed in God, one God, the creator of the universe, but I couldn't relate it to any particular religion. On my prison card it said Church of England, but I thought nothing of asking a Catholic priest for some spiritual clarification.

However, bit by bit, some of my hopes were being realized. The hormones were slowly taking effect and my body was changing imperceptibly with each month that passed. Before I was sentenced I had been extremely worried that, once I was imprisoned, the prison medical officer would not allow me to continue with my hormone treatment. Dr Popper had written to the prison to explain the treatment I was having and the vital importance of keeping it up for the duration of my sentence. I was very relieved that they took Dr Popper's word on this.

With the treatment I had gradually become more muscular; I had always had dark hair on my upper lip, but it had thickened into a respectable moustache and hairs were starting to grow along my jaw. For years I had two strands of hair growing out of my chest, and I was really fond and proud of these two hairs. Soon these were being joined by others, and before long there was quite a crop of them.

A less pleasant side-effect was that I started to come out in a massive amount of spots, a really bad case of acne. I was glad that it happened while I was locked up because I looked a mess. Not that it would have made any difference really, because it was a necessary process that I needed to go through. All of these changes kept coming one after another – it was the same as going through puberty. To me it felt like a natural progression from boyhood to manhood. I was eventually prescribed penicillin to combat the eruptions on my face, neck and back, and thankfully they started to settle down. The other side-effects were headaches, which got me down a bit, and I often had dizzy spells.

In the beginning most of my fellow prisoners assumed that I

was one of the civilian guys who came in to do jobs and to teach the inmates different skills. With my deep voice and moustache and dungarees they had no reason to think any differently. Soon of course they realized that I was also an inmate.

On the whole I enjoyed my painting job. I was the one that carried everything we needed: a long ladder on each shoulder, hooks on them for the tins of paint, and all the brushes. Apart from painting practically the whole prison, we also painted all the bars in the prison. I often joked about it: 'It's not good enough to keep us locked behind bars, but they have us painting them as well.' Some of the jobs were quite difficult and I was frequently painting high up on scaffolding, trussed up in a safety harness. My eyes were often red and burning from painting white on white all day in brilliant sunshine, but it didn't stop me enjoying it. There was plenty of variety and we had some good laughs.

I got to know the others in the painting party quite well. Two of them were lifers (they had life sentences). One had been notorious years ago for murdering two children when she was only ten years old herself. Having been told all about her in advance, I was amazed when I did meet her how young she was, I had expected someone much older. We ended up being quite friendly, as you did when you worked closely together day after day, but we never talked about her crime. She didn't work every day like the rest of us because she attended classes to continue her education. She had spent practically her whole life in prison, but she had done a couple of Open University degrees. A couple of times she said to me, 'I wake up every morning and I am no closer to getting out. At least you've got a date and you know that each day gets you closer to that date.'

'I know exactly how you feel,' I would say, but I couldn't explain how close this feeling was to my own heart. Sure I had a date for getting out of this prison, but I didn't know the date of my true release, the surgery that would free me from my own physical prison.

The other lifer was often difficult to get along with, although she and I got on fairly well. I felt very sorry for her. She was in her late forties, she had killed her husband and almost killed his mistress. She had been in the middle of carving the Sunday roast, and her husband had brought the other woman home and taken her up to their bedroom. She went berserk and went for them with the knife. It was quite surprising that she got life for this, it being very much a crime of passion. She was very emotionally unstable. Once I said something to her, and she picked up a boiling hot teapot to throw at me.

'Yeah, you throw that at me and you are looking for trouble,' I said to her.

'Oh God, I'm sorry. You know how it is.' She would quickly come to her senses. She had nothing against me; I used to keep her smiling in fact. I used to sing all the old songs with her while we were painting, and it used to cheer her up. You still had to be careful around her; she could blow up like a torch even though she didn't really mean any harm.

I did make a few friends in my house, although mostly I kept myself to myself and spent most of my free time reading and listening to the radio with my earphones on. There weren't a lot of books available, but I enjoyed a couple of Harold Robbins books, *A Stone for Danny Fisher* and *The Carpetbaggers* in particular. Any thriller or suspense novel kept my mind occupied.

I still didn't talk to anyone about my condition or try to explain anything to anyone. I never took on board what other people thought about me. Perhaps it was just youthful innocence coupled with the fact that no one ever confronted me or asked me what I was all about, whether I was lesbian or whatever. They may well have discussed me behind my back, but I was oblivious to it. Most of them knew that I was having male hormone treatment and probably guessed the outcome I obviously hoped for.

There were a few civilians who came in to teach inmates new skills. I became quite friendly with one of them, a nice guy named Frankie, who taught me quite a lot, such as how to lay lino, how to hang wallpaper, sideways as well as up and down and painting and decorating generally. He was a perfectionist and was concerned that I learn things properly. I had to sand down woodwork thoroughly, then give it two coats of undercoat, which also had to be sanded properly after each coat, before finally painting on the gloss. There was no cutting corners with Frankie.

When I was on the painting party we used to have our breaks in a huge Victorian building housing a swimming pool. It was completely derelict and full of piles of rubble and broken tiles. It must have dated back to a very long time ago when the prison had been a children's home and, later, a refugee camp. We kept all the paints and materials in it. It had an eerie feel to it: it had a very high ceiling and tiny rooms off to the sides, which were all pitch black, and it was quite cold in there. But it was a good private place to sit and have a fag and shelter from the rain.

We were in there one day – Frankie as well – just having a smoke and a chat, and one of the inmates asked him quite casually if he thought that once she had served her sentence she would be back behind bars again.

'Yes, without a doubt,' he answered.

'What do you reckon on me?' I asked him. 'Do you think I'll be back in here?'

He looked at me for a moment. 'I don't know. I'm not so sure.'

'Well, I can tell you I am certainly never coming back here,' and I meant it.

One day at work Frankie was telling us about this carnival that was being held in his home town, near the prison. He decided that he was going to build a float for a charity.

'Do you fancy giving me a hand building this float?' he asked me.

'Oh sure, I don't mind doing that.' It would be a break in the monotony of painting every day.

It was to be a massive boat, made out of plywood. I learned a lot from this job, using various kinds of tools and cutting with jigsaws. It was quite creative too, using all sorts of materials and colours to make it as boat-like as we could. It took us a couple of weeks to finish, and it was nice to see the finished product brought along the avenues of the prison for everyone to see before it was taken out to the carnival.

One day we had been painting one of the screws' houses. It

was one of the houses outside the prison gates. On two occasions within the space of two months I had my photograph taken at the gate before I went out.

'Your appearance keeps changing so much from day to day; if you ran off we wouldn't have anything to identify you by,' I was told. We painted that house from top to bottom. I got totally lost in the job, painting non-stop. It was summer and the sun was shining and we had the radio going. Apart from nicking loads of strawberries from the garden, we had really gotten down to the job. After it was all finished and we were cleaning up, the screw whose house it was, came to take a look.

'How about a chocolate cake then, for doing such an all right job?' I ventured – I had chocolate cake on the brain. The next day, to our amazement, she brought one in for us to share.

After a few months on the painting party I got fed up painting all day, every day. I asked if I could transfer to another job and get experience in doing something else. I fancied working on the gardens. It was a nice outdoor job as well, and involved using different machinery and equipment. Every time there was a hearing about job changes, my request was brought up, but it was never granted. It seemed totally unreasonable to deny it, again and again. I said to the screw who was in charge of the painting party, whom I did get on with reasonably well, 'The only reason you keep me on the painting party is because if it wasn't for me you wouldn't have a fucking painting party. I'm like the donkey around here, carrying all the ladders and all the paints, doing all the difficult jobs. That's why you won't give me a job change.'

The screw laughed. 'What can I do? Your request was heard and not granted. They obviously think you need close supervision.' It was my turn to smile.

'Come off it, you had something to do with it. You objected to my request.'

'No I didn't. Now come on . . . no time for talking, get on with the job,' she said, quickly changing the subject.

One day Lesley came running to me, shouting, 'Lorretta is here, Lorretta is here!'

'Where – here? What is she doing here?' I asked excitedly.

I ran over towards reception and saw her.

'My God, how did you manage to get here? How come you are here?'

'I've come to be with you,' she said simply.

I put my arms around her. 'Love, you shouldn't have come here. You would have been better off going to an open prison. We are not going to be allowed to be with each other.'

'I'm here now,' she said with a smile. I promised I would do all I could to get into the same house as her.

I really appreciated that she had done this only in order to be with me. It was of no advantage to her at all, requesting to come to this extremely restricted prison rather than going to an open one. We had not been allowed to write to each other – correspondence was restricted between prisoners and wasn't usually allowed – so I had no idea that she had been planning a request to be transferred here, but I had missed her such a lot and was over the moon to see her again.

We didn't get to meet that often, however. She was placed in another house, and there was very little opportunity for us to talk, let alone have any privacy. The inmates of different houses never have a chance to meet except while working during the day. Lorretta and I tried to meet on the avenue in the mornings, stopping to have a few moments together. She was in the house opposite mine. Before breakfast, while I was doing my morning sweeping job, was always an opportunity to spend a few minutes talking. If I didn't see her then, I had an excuse to go out later because I had to get my hormone tablets from the prison doctor every morning and sometimes I ran into her. Still, it was hard knowing she was right there, and not being able to be together. In the evenings we were reduced to shouting to each other from the windows. It was difficult since the avenue was very wide and thick with trees. It was also a punishable offence. We enrolled in guitar classes in order to see each other. We didn't learn a thing about playing guitar; all we cared about at the time was laying eyes on each other.

In my spare time I made her a cross out of matches I had collected over time. It was literally hundreds of matches laminated together, which I then shaped and sanded down with a matchbox. It was about six inches high on a base of three steps and had inscribed on it: Love, Peace, Happiness, Togetherness and Tranquillity. She was surprised and delighted with my gift and said she would treasure it and keep it forever.

I felt it was up to me to arrange that we could be able to be together, since she had gone to such lengths to be with me. Unfortunately it was not in my power to do anything about it, except to request a transfer to her house, which I thought they would never agree to.

I had suspected the screws wanted to give me a hard time from the very beginning when they took my underwear from me (that situation had been resolved because Irena had sent me a whole box of acceptable underpants). There was a definite sense that they were cooking things up, one after another, to rile me. Out of the blue I was not allowed to write or receive any letters from anyone. When I asked why not, I was told that they felt I was being 'influenced from outside', whatever that meant. Regulations were that I should have the right to write home. Home for me was Irena's and my flat in Cardiff, but they didn't seem to think so.

A couple of times they called me to the office. The screw would be sitting behind her desk and waving a letter in her hand.

'You've got a letter here,' she would open a drawer and stick the letter inside it, 'but you can't have it.' I would do my utmost not to get worked up over it.

'What's the point of telling me then?' In my mind I would say, 'Fuck you', and just walk out of there. They weren't doing that to make me feel good, were they?

I applied to the governor for permission to contact a solicitor in order to prepare a letter of complaint, but she turned me down.

'I'm entitled to a solicitor's letter,' I argued with her.

'You are not going to get it,' she said. 'We are concerned about your welfare. The Home Office seems to believe that you are being influenced from outside.' This sounded crazy and farfetched to me and I thought she was just making it up as she went along.

'You're concerned about my welfare, but you won't allow me to write home. How will I know if I even have a home to go to?' It made no difference what I said, my application was rejected.

One evening, while on association watching television with the other inmates, a screw came to tell me that the governor wanted to see me. When I got to her office she told me that she thought I ought to shave.

'No way, I am not prepared to do that.' I felt very strongly about it and was adamant. 'I have waited too long to get my facial hair and I am not about to shave it off just because I'm in here. For the same reason that I'm not giving up my underwear.'

I kept trying to get into the same house as Lorretta and at the same time I was encouraging Lorretta to try and get transferred to the painting party. I thought, if one or the other of our requests were granted, at least we would be together part of the time. Although we longed to be together, making love was not the most important objective. Just spending time in each other's company and being able to put our arms around each other from time to time would be enough.

After about six weeks of making these requests things happened all at once. I was granted a transfer to her house, and she was granted a transfer to the painting party. The problem was, the next day I was transferred from the painting party to work on the gardens. What an odd coincidence. I was supposed to be invaluable to the painting party. At least it appeared that we would be together in the same house and we were both very happy about it. The screws knew about our relationship, and we were a bit suspicious at first, but as time passed we started to relax and stopped worrying about what could be in store. I should have known it was too good to be true. It was a set-up from the start.

There were a few petty incidents with the screws which I ignored. One screw had me up for calling her 'a fucking old cunt' for not letting me have a newspaper. It was completely untrue. I was taken down to Bleak and they insisted that I sign a report stating why I was there and what the charge was. I refused, saying it wasn't true. Then I was taken to see the assistant governor. 'Better her than the governor,' I thought, since she had been quite fair with me.

There were four screws around me as I stood in front of her. After reading the report she asked me what I had to say about it. I pointed at the screw in question. 'She's a fucking liar.' The screw turned beetroot red. 'She is. I wouldn't lie about it, I would admit it if it was true,' I said. 'I have not read a newspaper since I have been in here. You can verify that. I didn't have any reason to ask her for a newspaper or any reason to call her a fucking old cunt.'

I was let off with a caution, but as I was walking out I could hear raised voices coming from the room. 'Don't ever try that again,' I heard her say. Somebody was on my side.

Later that day, when I got back from work, a pile of screws were going through my locker and all my stuff. They were obviously looking for something else to get me into trouble. I panicked inside. On my pin-board above my bed were hidden a gold ring and a gold chain that I had been given by two other inmates. They were behind a photograph. It was an offence to have these objects, and it could land you extra time in prison.

'What the hell are you doing?' I demanded.

One of the screws was sitting on a chair with her feet up on my bed. This screw was always walking around the place shouting about hygiene, the importance of hygiene.

'You have a cheek to lecture us about hygiene and then sit with your shoes on my clean sheets,' I said to her. My comment was ignored.

'You've got too many photographs here,' said another screw and went for my pin-board.

Quick-thinking as I can be sometimes, I jumped on the bed and said, 'Oh, you want my photographs, do you?' I started ripping them off the board in a frenzy, throwing them and shouting, 'Here, here, take them all,' avoiding the one that concealed my treasures. I hopped off the bed and picked up my shoes and started throwing them out of the door, plus my clothes, anything I could lay my hands on.

'You better leave me my tobacco!' I shouted. 'I worked all fucking week for it, but take the rest by all means.'

The screws fell for it and were distracted by my performance. They trooped out, snarling, 'Pick up this mess and put it away.'

Within just a couple of days the next thing came along, although this one was partially due to my own stupidity. I had been working hard all day and had got back to the house late. My supper was on the table waiting for me – Lorretta had put it out for me. As I sat down to eat, the weekly fire drill was starting. Everyone in the house walked out but I thought, 'To hell with it.' I was sitting there enjoying my supper when a screw came in.

'There is a fire drill, what do you think you are doing?'

I explained my case: 'I've just come in from work and my food is getting cold. I know there isn't a fire.' I thought that was the end of that, but she reported me.

Again I was brought up before the screws.

'Why didn't you report to the fire drill?'

I explained.

'How did you know there wasn't a real fire?'

'My own common sense tells me that you'd do more than blow a whistle if there was a real fire. I would be the first one out of the door if there was a real fire.'

'You did it to get at us, didn't you?'

'What do you mean?'

'You did it to get at us.' The conversation was irritating me.

'Listen,' I snapped, 'you mean nothing to me. You are nothing but a bunch of keys that lock me up at night and unlock me in the morning. Other than that I don't give you lot a second thought. As for me sitting around scheming things to wind you up, I wouldn't waste my time.' Again I thought that was the end of it. Not so. The next morning I was carted off to Bleak. In addition I got three days added to my prison sentence and loss of a week's pay.

As in all groups of human beings there are good screws and bad ones. The screws were in a position of authority which gives them complete control over prisoners and some took advantage of this, justly or unjustly. But there were some screws who were more fair and mature and really believed that being locked up was punishment enough in itself. They knew that their job was to contain and maintain, not to punish or provoke. For some reason I seemed to attract the worst of them.

Some eight to ten weeks had passed since Lorretta and I had been together in the house. It had been wonderful because there were plenty of opportunities to have some privacy together. We slept in dormitories. After we were supposed to be tucked in and going to sleep, we would get out of bed for some private association. In fact most inmates would get up and have a smoke or a cup of cocoa. The water from the tap was practically boiling, so it was easy to make a hot drink. Our tins of tobacco were confiscated at night; no problem, we smuggled some in.

Every four hours the screws would come around with torches to make sure we were all in our right beds. They would sneak up on us really quietly. On the odd occasion we would have a bit of cannabis to smoke, talking and not listening carefully enough. All of a sudden someone would whisper, 'SOS' (screws on stairs). There would be one hell of a scramble, people bumping into each other trying to get to their beds, hissing 'SOS' to each other.

On this particular night Lorretta and I had availed ourselves of the cooks' dorm, which had only two beds in it, while the occupants were off elsewhere talking. Suddenly there was one hell of a commotion, and I heard a screw shout, 'Where is Thompson? Where is McCarthy?' They ordered everybody else back to bed. Lorretta and I just looked at each other – there was nowhere to run. I was wearing nothing but pyjama bottoms and Lorretta was stark naked. Lorretta dived under the bed but I walked out of the room with as much dignity as I could.

'What the fuck do you lot want?' I asked them. About eight more of them had piled out of the bathroom which was the size of a stamp and stood waiting on the stairs. They had all been snuggled up in the bathroom, hiding and waiting for us to slip into the cooks' dorm. There were about twelve screws in all.

'All you guys just for me?' I goaded them. 'Surely I don't need all of you?'

'Get your fucking clothes on,' one of them said to me. All the lights had come on, and the place was lit up like Blackpool.

'If you are going to take me somewhere you take me the way I am,' I said, standing there in my pyjama bottoms. In the end I put a shirt on and shoes, but no socks. I was in a rage, mainly at ourselves, for being so stupid and dropping our guard. I should have known this was coming.

A few of them took me down the stairs while the rest were around Lorretta on the landing. They walked me out, past all the houses, past Bleak.

'What's going to happen to Lorretta?' I asked. 'And where are you taking me?'

They took me towards an old derelict building that had just two cells in it. It was called Brown House and was an overflow for when Bleak was full.

All of a sudden, as we were walking across the prison grounds, I could hear Lorretta shouting my name, 'Ray! Ray!' She was crying and sounded desperate. It was dark outside and I couldn't make out where her voice was coming from. Then I spotted her. There were screws all around her, about eight of them. They had her arms pushed up behind her back and her head pushed forward and down, which is the usual method of restraining an aggressive or uncooperative prisoner. I broke away from the four screws that were escorting me and ran for all I was worth towards Lorretta. That was my woman and she needed me. The screws surrounding her all got into position to tackle me. I went in there punching in all directions, trying to get to her. One of them went flying and landed with her arm in a funny angle. I had also broken her nose. Little did I know she was the nice one who baked us the chocolate cake.

I ran up to Lorretta and grabbed hold of her, while all the screws descended on us. I was in a frenzy and shouted, 'You lay one fucking finger on her or pump her full of drugs and I'll smash this prison wide open.'

Meanwhile inmates were gathering in the windows of the houses. 'Leave them alone, you bastards!' they were screaming. They were rattling the bars and banging their plastic cups; the whole place was in uproar.

Holding Lorretta I calmed down a bit. 'All right, all right . . . but don't hurt her in any way,' I pleaded with them.

'We won't hurt her,' they reassured me and I let them pull us apart.

My clothes were in shreds, my sleeves flapping under my arms. Two of the screws jumped on me, but I shrugged them off and said, 'I'm quite capable of walking on my own, I don't need your help.'

I couldn't bear to be separated from Lorretta. One moment we were together, lying with our arms around each other, fantasizing about another life in another world, and the next moment we are wrenched apart and carted off. We knew that was the end, we would not be allowed to be together again. I was gutted.

All the screws, including the male screws who had been called down from the gate to subdue me, were lined up in a sort of corridor for me to walk through, into my cell. At the very end stood the screw whose nose I had broken. She was covered with blood. I stopped and looked at her for a moment. She was a nice woman, and it was unfortunate that she had been right there as I was swinging my fists about. There was nothing to say.

'I have done it now,' I thought. All the times that they had tried to wind me up previously, I had managed to keep my cool, and now I had played right into their hands.

I had to spend four days in Brown House before a cell became available in Bleak. I was in quite a state. This was it, I wasn't going to be able to see Lorretta any more. We would be kept apart at all cost. I was venomous towards the screws. When they came to give me my mattress each night, I would throw it back at them.

'I don't want your fucking mattress. I don't want anything from you.'

There was dust and rubble on the floor in my cell and when they put me in there they had left a piss-pot in the corner, full of shit. It seemed to have been there for some time. The first morning, the prison doctor stuck his head in the cell and said, 'Are you all right?' and before I had a chance to say anything he had slammed the door shut and was gone. I started screaming and shouting, 'Get back here. Get this fucking filth out of my cell. If I need a piss where am I supposed to go?' For four days I had to live with somebody else's shit in my cell.

They kept my light on twenty-four hours a day and when my food tray arrived the screw would put it on the floor and give it a shove through the door, so that half of it spilt on to the floor. I would pick it up and just throw it back: 'I don't want your fucking food.' They never gave me a drop of water to wash in, and I was still in my shredded shirt which was hanging in tatters around me, but I was so furious and depressed that I couldn't give a shit about anything.

The one thing that kept me busy was trying to wedge the window up to get some fresh air. I had managed to keep a plastic knife and fork, and with these I worked the window up through the bars, bit by bit, to about four inches. And each time a screw passed my window on the outside she would slam it down, and I would start all over again.

I was very glad when I finally got to Bleak, it was heaven compared to where I had been. I had a bath and food and didn't refuse the mattress, although it was taken out during the day. It became winter and very cold. At nine o'clock we were let out to go and collect our mattresses from the end of the hall. The only way to keep really warm was to lay the mattress against the heating pipes which ran along the skirting board. First thing in the morning when we went to slop out we also had to take out the mattress.

I settled in to do my time there, waiting to attend court for my crimes. I had lost all privileges including reading materials (except the bible) and tobacco. There was an Irish screw in charge of Bleak at the time. She was in fact a decent person. She would pass me the odd bit of tobacco. Friends would also manage to smuggle some in to me. Whenever she could, Rita, who was still in Bleak by her own choice, would put some rolled-up fags and a couple of matches on the floor and then get down on her hands and knees and blow them under my door. It is an offence to smoke if you have lost the privilege, so it was a tricky business not to get caught. I had to time my smokes carefully, sitting on the wide window-sill and blowing the smoke out of the window. With the cold, opening the window would make the cell freezing within seconds. I would be sitting on the sill, cold to the bone and shivering, thinking, 'Why do I bother? I'm not really enjoying this fag.' The matches we got in prison were safety matches. The heads were soft, and I could split them lengthwise into four with a pin which I kept hidden in the bible. I had to economize and make things last. When you're in lock-up and your only pleasure is a smoke, there is nothing worse than not having a match to light it with. All my goods were stashed behind the plastic skirting board.

The Irish screw told me that she felt like she was an inmate herself, particularly when serving time on Bleak. She thought that some of them were allocated to work in Bleak more often than others and that they were being penalized themselves. A lot of screws didn't enjoy working in this particular prison and would be quite sympathetic to the inmates and give them inside information, such as when a search was being planned.

The screws that had it in for me would sometimes gather outside my door. On purpose they would talk loudly about me saying all sorts of choice things. I tried to keep my cool at all costs. One of them came into my cell once and told me to stand to attention. I ignored her and didn't get up.

'What a pity that they haven't brought back hanging,' she said to me.

'You think I should hang for what I did, do you?'

'You'd better believe that you're going to pay for what you did,' she threatened.

The chief of the prison came down to see me one day. She caught me in a compromising position. I was curled up sleeping, wrapped up in a blanket on the springs of the bed. You are not supposed to have your blanket during the day, but I found a way to hang my blanket out of the window so that I could retrieve it for a bit of comfort and warmth.

'Do you mind me having a few words with you?' she asked. To my surprise she told me that I should not have been taken off my house that fateful night. She said that the offence had not warranted such an action. Lorretta and I should have been told to get back into our own beds and to report to Bleak the following morning for some kind of disciplinary action. If I remember correctly, her husband had been killed in a prison riot, and she was very sensitive about these confrontations. She obviously felt that I had been set up and provoked by the screws, and the incident should never have gone to the extremes that it did. Still, I had broken a screw's nose.

I was charged according to the normal procedures and a VC was arranged to hear my case. The chief did try to stick up for me, which was probably the reason for the relatively mild punishment. I was sentenced to two months in Bleak in solitary confinement plus I had two months added to my prison sentence. The screw with the broken nose was urged by her colleagues to press additional charges against me, in an outside court. They were adamant about it: 'Don't think just of yourself, think of all the other officers that she might hit' was their argument.

If she had decided to go ahead and press charges against me, I might well have been sentenced to another eighteen months in prison, but she refused. Her reasons were the same as the chief's. She knew that the screws who had taken Lorretta and me from the house that night had planned the whole thing in advance. They had put us together, and then wrenched us apart, knowing perfectly well how distressing it would be for both of us. They had purposely created an atmosphere that was bound to blow up. Because she was a decent sort and because she knew me and knew that my aggression had not been directed towards her in particular, she refused to press charges against me.

The only walk I did in two months was down the corridor every morning to empty my bucket and the bowl I had washed in the night before. Apart from that I never left the cell in Bleak, because I refused exercise as well. In order not to become unfit, I did press-ups and sit-ups on the floor. I do remember being glad to go for my bath, which I was entitled to once a week.

When my time in Bleak was finally over I was moved back to my old house where I had been before being with Lorretta. I kept my nose out of trouble and didn't go back to Bleak for the rest of my sentence. I was determined not to let myself be provoked again. Nothing would be gained by it, except more time in prison.

I didn't get to see very much of Lorretta, but we still met at the guitar classes. At Christmas there was a party and I was able to talk to her. It was good to be able to dance really close to each other, but soon enough two screws came up and separated us. We were not permitted to dance even.

I knew I would never allow myself to get back into prison. I felt very determined about it: I had been incarcerated three times in my short life, and I knew that it had to be my last. I would be nineteen years old by the time I got out and I had wasted too much time already. I knew I had to get some stability in my life before surgery, but I didn't know how I was going to do it.

Lorretta and I planned to live together. I told her I would get a job so that we could have money and do something with our lives. My mission to accomplish my own physical transformation never left my mind. Although I was as comfortable as I had ever been in terms of myself in relation to others, nothing was going to stop me from taking it to the bitter end.

My probation officer, Carole, came to see me a few times in prison, and was filling me in about a few things. Irena apparently was often in a pretty bad state and would come to see Carole, all drugged up, asking about me. I worried that she wasn't coping with her life, but there was nothing I could do about it. On one of her visits, Carole told me that Irena was pregnant and asked me how I felt about it. I wasn't in any position to have any rights to feel anything, particularly since my feelings at this time were definitely with Lorretta. Carole knew about Lorretta and was not surprised when I asked her if she could find me another flat for when I got out, since I was planning to live with Lorretta. She told me that Irena had written to the Home Secretary and to Jim Callaghan, who was the Prime Minister at the time, to see if they could reverse the decision about us being able to correspond. Both had replied, politely, but the request was still denied. From what I hear, these days things have changed drastically. Prisoners can even make phone calls to their friends and families.

As time went on the authorities got a bit more relaxed about me writing letters to certain people, and I wrote to Ty and his wife and asked them to visit me. Irena got in to see me pretending to be Ty's wife. She was not really allowed to come and see me for the same reason she wasn't allowed to write to me, because she had been inside herself. I had not had a lot of news about her, and none of the news I had about her was good news, but I still cared. I didn't like what I was hearing about her being out of her head on drugs most of the time.

Her pregnancy was already showing, but I couldn't bring myself to comment on it. I felt it wasn't my business any more, and she could sense the change in me. It was obvious, I couldn't even look her in the eye. She told me she had heard through the grapevine that I was in a relationship with Lorretta.

'Are you going to come home to me when you get out?' she asked me, anyway.

'No, I'm not,' I told her. 'I have arranged with Carole to get me a flat of my own for when I get out.'

'You could just come back, you know,' she said. 'We could give it a try and I could register the baby in your name.'

'No, I don't want you to do that. The baby is not mine.'

It was a weird meeting. I talked mainly with Ty. I still had feelings for Irena, I had definitely loved her and she was my first long-term relationship. She was also the first person who had really truly accepted me exactly the way I was. I felt quite mixed up about seeing her again. Even though I didn't want to continue the relationship I still felt slightly betrayed by her getting pregnant and expecting me to be the father of the baby. The visit lasted two hours and I was taken away and searched, which is normal procedure, and returned to the house.

Lorretta and I managed to grab a few minutes together. She had a sense that Irena had managed to get in to see me and felt anxious about it all. I put my arms around her and told her not to worry, I wasn't going back to Irena.

'You haven't really broken the ties with Irena yet, have you?' she said. 'Maybe some of our plans have been unrealistic under the circumstances. But I want you to know that even if you do decide to go back to her when you get out of here, I'll always feel the same for you. That's not because I'm a stupid woman – I just love you.'

I thought a lot about Irena's pregnancy and the whole business of having children. Because of my sense of inadequacy, I think I started to stereotype all women, and assume that all they wanted in the end was to get married and have children, neither of which would I ever be able to offer a woman.

The time was getting closer to my release, and I began to prepare myself mentally for life on the outside. During one of her visits I asked Carole to contact my parents who had not heard from me for about four years. I wanted her to try to explain to them that I was a transsexual and what this meant for me, the treatment I was on, and the surgery I was hoping for. She was always very helpful.

Back in Cardiff she asked my parents if they would come and have a meeting with her, which they agreed to. She had them in her office for four hours trying to put all this across to them. My mother could not handle it at all and would not accept any of it. In contrast, my father was quite open about it and told Carole that he had always known and this came as no surprise to him. According to Carole he tried to reason with my mother, saying, 'Come on now, we haven't walked around with our eyes closed. We both knew that there was something wrong. Why deny it?' But it was fruitless; my mother was clinging to the idea that this was something I would grow out of. The idea of surgery horrified her completely, and I suppose you cannot blame your mother for that.

I continued working in the gardens until the end of my sentence, and I enjoyed most aspects of it including erecting 'tunnels', large plastic greenhouses. In the winter it was a different story, picking frost-covered sprouts in all weathers. I suffered from a lot of earache which was aggravated by the cold. I learned a lot from this job, too. I was taught to operate various kinds of farm machinery. One of the civilians who came in to teach us used to take me aside every morning and open up the lid of the tractor engine. He quizzed me about the names of each part and what they did. Finally I knew everything about a tractor engine, although now I would be totally clueless if I saw one. One day, when I was going to fetch some petrol for a mower I was using to cut the lawns, this guy told me to get in the tractor seat and drive it to the stores while he was standing on the outside step. It was one of those giant tractors with huge back wheels and a bucket on the front. I was really chuffed about the chance to drive this great big vehicle, and I thought I did really well.

I was counting the days as my release approached, but it didn't feel right to leave Lorretta behind, so I advised her to apply to go back to open prison so that the time for us leaving Styal would more or less coincide. As at our last farewell, I wasn't able to say goodbye to her privately, which was awful for both of us. It was a very emotional parting; I felt devastated about leaving her there.

On the day of my release I was asked to go to reception at 8.30 in the morning. I was handed the rest of my belongings and £14 to get me home. Then I walked through the prison gates, out to freedom. It was an amazing feeling to be free after fifteen months of imprisonment, and yet I felt very sad. I made it to the nearest town and went into a supermarket to buy a bottle of vodka. It was still early and they had just opened. Next, I went upstairs to the café and ordered a glass of orange juice. After tossing back three-quarters of it, I opened my bottle of vodka and topped the glass up. 'Let's get a head-on,' I thought and tossed it back. What looked like the manager marched over to my table.

'If you don't remove yourself from the premises immediately, I'm phoning the police,' he said. I looked at him for a moment, and thought, 'God, I've only been out of prison for an hour and a half, and here is someone already threatening to get the police on to me.' That would be the last thing I needed now. I got up, put my vodka into my bag and left.

On the train I met a girl called Goldie. We both had to change trains at Manchester, and while waiting we went to a pub for a drink. I was drunk out of my mind by this time, and all my money was gone. Goldie was good as gold, and had paid half the cost of a donkey jacket for me, because I had no jacket and it was cold.

I missed my connection. I was too drunk to notice. Finally I got on the right train, and sitting in an aisle seat I promptly fell asleep with my head lolling about and hanging out into the aisle.

Once in a while I could hear a voice in the background. It was a mother cautioning her little boy, who was running up and down the aisle, 'For God's sake, watch the man's head.'

6
A Sober and Industrious Life

I arrived back in Cardiff on the train in quite a state. My plastic bag containing my few possessions had ripped and some stuff had fallen out. I had two pairs of shoes, and one of each pair had disappeared. The £14 was spent. I had celebrated my freedom, and how!

I was supposed to have arrived in Cardiff hours earlier, and had an appointment with Carole. As luck would have it I ran into her and her boyfriend in the street near the station. They were just coming out of a pub.

'Where on earth have you been?' she said to me. 'What the hell happened to you? You should have been here to see me at two o'clock. I was waiting for you for ages.'

'Ah, lend me a couple of quid, will you, for a taxi to the flat,' was all I could say for myself.

'What happened to your money?'

'Can't you tell?' I said feebly. I was still steaming drunk.

'I want to see you in my office tomorrow,' she said, not amused, and handed me some money.

I went back to the flat I had shared with Irena and the others. Irena had just given birth to a little boy, and was still in hospital. One of the girls, Doreen, took me to see her and the baby the following day. I went there with the intention of telling Irena that our relationship was definitely over, but when I got there I couldn't bring myself to do it. The setting didn't seem right somehow, and she was so happy to see me. I decided to wait. She wanted me to see the baby who was in a cot beside the bed and I looked at him briefly, but I felt uncomfortable with this scene and quickly changed the topic of conversation. When I said goodbye, Irena walked me to the lift and told me she still loved me. I didn't know what to say. Later Doreen gave me some money that Irena had slipped her to give to me, so I had a few quid to live on, which was nice of her.

Three days later Irena came home from the hospital and then I said to her, 'Look, I still care for you but I don't love you any more. I have made up my mind to live with Lorretta when she comes out.' Irena didn't take this very well. She kept saying things like: 'I hung on as long as I could, so that you could be there at the birth.'

It was a difficult situation to be in. I couldn't be out-and-out cold towards her, particularly in the vulnerable state she was in. Also, she had stood by me through many difficult times, and we went back a long way together.

Finally, after a few days, she started to take on board what I was trying to tell her and she decided to go back to Newport with the baby and stay with her mother. She was getting organized to go and then said, 'Right. I'll ring the baby's father to pick us up and move our stuff to Newport then, shall I?'

'Yeah, you do that,' I said. Although we hadn't really rowed or had harsh words, the atmosphere in the flat was tense. In many ways I felt relieved to see her go.

That day I went to see my friend Ty. He had got a crate of Bacardi to celebrate my coming out of prison, but since I hadn't come around straight away, he'd started without me and was three days into celebrating.

'Where the hell have you been? I thought you'd have been over here sooner. Come on, get stuck in.' He was really happy to see me. We drank and drank, and talked and laughed. Another few people came as well. There was a girl there by the name of Marcy, she was a 'working woman'. After a time, Ty took me aside and said, 'That girl, Marcy, she likes you a lot. She'd be willing to give you the money you need to live on and get a flat. Go on.' He nudged me. 'Why don't you "go out" with her.'

Money? She would give me money – just like that! Money was foremost in my mind so, whatever else I thought of the proposition, I accepted it.

It was a strange relationship. Marcy was a nice girl and I liked her as a friend but I wasn't interested in any relationship with her beyond her giving me money. At first we didn't live together. After a few weeks we went for Sunday lunch at the house of a couple of friends. Well, we never left, we ended up living in this house for quite a while, a few months at least. Even though we were now living together, Marcy and I didn't really spend any time together at all. She would go out working in the evenings, and I would go my own way. In fact, sometimes I wasn't very good to her. If a friend came around and asked Marcy to do her hair, she would look at me and I would say, 'What time is it?'

'Half past six.'

'Well, are you sure you've got enough time? You've got to be out there by seven. Go on then, but be quick.' She had a good sense of humour and would laugh at my obsession with money. She would have given her earnings to whomever she was with and I took advantage of this, and sometimes went over the top. I used to see her in the street at night and would grab her.

'Where is the fucking money?' and she would give it all to me. I'm sure she kept some to herself because sometimes she gave me £30 or £40, but I often had up to £80 a night.

We had very little physical intimacy. If I was around I might give her a kiss before she went out. Once or twice it went further than that but it wasn't really what I wanted. Occasionally I took her out and we had a couple of drinks or I agreed to meet her in a club later in the evening. She was twenty-seven, eight years older than me, and she had been living this life for some time. I had no prejudice about what she was doing; I was in no position to judge anybody. I did have respect for her as a person. This may sound incongruous, considering our association, but I didn't have much respect for our relationship, although that was the way a lot of people related in the world that I lived in.

Soon enough Irena came back from Newport. Things had not worked out very well at her mother's house. Our old flat had in the meantime been vacated by our friends, who had stayed on there. Notice had been served on them since the house was to be sold. They had all moved into a house across the road and now lived in the attic flat three floors up. Irena moved in with them as their 'guest' instead of the other way around. Even though I had told her that our relationship was over, I still wanted to see her as a friend.

She complained that it was impossible to live with her mother, and things weren't any easier in the new flat, with the usual partying and comings and goings. The environment wasn't very suitable for a baby. I couldn't help but feel sorry for her. I felt angry too. The girls didn't make her feel very welcome which didn't impress me, seeing that they had gladly accepted our hospitality in the past. The landlord wasn't easy to get along with either. He complained about the noise constantly and often just locked the front door in the evenings.

On top of Irena's concerns about her baby's welfare, she got into trouble. I didn't know anything about it when a neighbour came over to the house where I was living with Marcy, and told me that three girls had stabbed a taxi driver the night before. None of us thought much about it, it was a common occurrence in this part of the city.

I ran into Irena later that day at Ty's house, and was pretty shocked to discover that she was one of the three girls. She had just been let out on bail. She told me what had happened. Irena and Lynn had been in the back of the taxi, and Diana was in the front. They had asked the driver to make a detour to get a bag of chips, and he got stroppy about it and refused. Lynn got pissed off and punched him from the back, and he turned around and started to fight back. Diana had a knife with a seven-inch blade on her, which she pulled out and stabbed him. The blade pierced his kidney.

'That's a pretty crazy thing to do,' I said to Irena. 'Remember when you are in prison, it was all for a bag of chips.'

But I hadn't heard the whole story. They had all piled out of the taxi, but Irena and Lynn had no idea that Diana had been carrying a knife and had stabbed the driver. When he shouted, 'I've been stabbed', Irena said to him, 'Don't be so stupid, you haven't been stabbed.' Later, when they were all arrested, they couldn't believe that Diana had done it.

Months later, when it went to trial, Irena and Lynn were let off the charge with a £40 fine for disturbing the peace, but

Diana, who was out on parole after serving four years for another stabbing, got six years.

The girls were on a curfew as part of bail, so they were stuck in the flat. Since I wasn't short of money, I would go up there sometimes and bring them some fags. Irena was finding it hard to be stuck there with the baby. The more I saw of this baby, the more I grew fond of him. I enjoyed playing with him and rocking him in the bouncy chair, and I loved making him laugh, tickling his feet and bouncing him on my knee.

One night after the court hearing the girls agreed to look after the baby so that I could take Irena out for a drink. When we got back, the landlord had locked the door and there was no way for Irena to get in. It was late and we were freezing. I suggested we broke in to our old flat across the road and at least have shelter until the morning. We got in but there was no electricity or gas and no blankets. Irena was cold and miserable and fretting about the baby. We could see the light on in the girls' flat, and I finally decided to take charge of the situation.

'You wait in here,' I said to her. 'I'll try and get their attention somehow.'

If I hadn't had a few beers in me, I would never have attempted that climb. It was a hell of a height. I climbed up the drainpipe all the way to the top of the building, and grasped the window-sill of the attic flat for dear life. Looking down I realized that I would never be able to climb down. A nasty few moments followed. I managed to push the window open and shouted to get the girls' attention. They were really shocked to see me hanging there from the window-sill.

'What the fuck are you doing all the way up here?'

'Never mind, just pull me in,' I gasped.

So, Irena was reunited with her baby and I stayed the night on the sofa bed in their flat.

The following morning I woke up early and remembered that I had seen a pile of letters addressed to me at the old flat. I hopped out of bed and went back across the road. The door to the flat was broken where I had kicked off the lock the night before. I was rummaging through the letters on the floor, and suddenly there was a knock on the front door.

'That's strange,' I thought. 'It's an empty house.'

I decided to go and open the door, and there stood a guy.

'Eh . . . Raymond Thompson . . . does he live here?'

'Yeah . . . that's me.'

'Right, I am from the social security.'

'Come in,' I told him and took him up to a room that was completely bare except for a bed with a mattress and a chair. He sat on the bed and I sat on the chair. He glanced around the room and at the broken door.

'So you live here, do you?' he said in disbelief.

'Yeah . . . I know I haven't got much . . .'

It was a lucky stroke, a chance in a million. He was coming to check that I was living at this address, since they were still giving me money for rent. After this incident I stopped claiming the dole; living with Marcy, I didn't need the money.

Ty had bought a four-storey house and thought he would try and turn it into flats. It was next to a derelict hotel and it was in pretty bad shape. He had bought the house for a pittance from someone who had gambling debts. Ty's brother and I helped him clean it out, taking vans full of rubbish out and trying to get it into shape to move some tenants in. Irena would occasionally come over to see me, telling me of her difficulties in the flat. She simply wasn't happy living there. I said to her, 'If you ask him, I'm sure Ty will give you a room in his house to live in.' I wanted to help her out, but only as a friend. Of course, seeing more of Irena, I couldn't avoid seeing quite a bit of the baby, and I was getting attached to him.

Things felt somewhat messy. I was living with Marcy, and I was still supposed to live with Lorretta when she came out, and here I was getting involved with Irena and the baby. I couldn't sort my feelings out and felt confused. I wanted to make a life with Lorretta but being apart from her made it all seem unrealistic and remote. It felt as if I couldn't make anything concrete or solid in my life. I had not long been out of prison and I was still into drinking, smoking and partying but in the back of my mind were all the niggling thoughts about what I should be doing. I shouldn't be pimping off Marcy, and I should be thinking of how to earn some money. I had promised Lorretta I would try to find work to support us but my confidence was low and I didn't rate my chances very highly. I had picked up some skills in prison but I couldn't imagine that someone would hire me, as I was basically unskilled with no work experience, no O levels and a criminal record. It all added up to a feeling of drifting and being at a loose end. How was I going to be able to explain all this to Lorretta?

I decided to go and visit her at the open prison, and tell her everything that was going on in my life. I certainly missed her a lot and knew that she was counting the days to get out to start a new life with me. I was glad to be admitted in to see her when I got there. The rule was that former prisoners were not allowed to visit.

Lorretta was over the moon to see me, and we had a long talk about her coming out and what we were going to do. Seeing her and talking to her made me feel reassured about our love and our commitment. I told her I had bought a three-piece suite for when we got our own place, and was saving as much as I could. That, of course, led me to tell her how it was that I was able to save money. Lorretta wasn't exactly impressed with my source of funds, but decided to accept what I was doing.

When we were sitting talking at the table, a screw approached us. I recognized her from somewhere else I had been detained and she must have remembered me.

'You know you're not supposed to be here, you were lucky to get past the gate,' she said sternly. 'I'll let you go on with the visit, but you won't get in here again.'

'Fair enough,' I thought and we thanked her. She had the authority to stop the visit right there and then and tell me to leave.

After a few months the situation with Marcy came to a head. Irena had moved into Ty's house. One day I was visiting her – we were sitting talking – when Marcy came in, and, seeing us, ran up the stairs to the lounge, shouting and being abusive. She started shouting at Ty and telling him about all the money she had given me, and how this was all she got in return. I lost my cool and ran up the stairs; just to shut her up I took a swing at her with a bottle. It is fortunate that I only hit her in the chest.

She got even more furious and stormed out of the house, screaming that she would have me locked up for living off immoral earnings. I was quite upset about having stooped to that. Ty urged me to run after her to calm her down. If she really made true her threat I could be in a lot of trouble.

'If she goes to the police and makes a statement she would have a good case,' said Ty. 'How are you going to explain where your money comes from?' I decided not to run after her and trusted her good nature not to get me into trouble.

Our relationship, as it was, came to an end but Marcy and I continued being friends and I remained quite fond of her. She had been good to me and had looked after me well and we'd had a few laughs together. We were both at fault for that final incident. She never gave me any more money but she told me she would buy me clothes if I needed them. However, that was the end of my living off immoral earnings.

Not long after this things looked up a bit. Carole arranged an apprenticeship for me with a mosaic and tile manufacturer. It meant working on building sites laying tiles in bathrooms, verandas and such like.

It was summer and very hot. I enjoyed the job and the company of the other men but a couple of factors made my life miserable. Since having started to live and work entirely in my male identity I constantly had to disguise my body. I was overly paranoid about it and all the layers of clothes I wore to hide my body made my working day a misery. No matter how hot I was I couldn't afford to take anything off. The other guys all had their tops off and were getting brown in the sun.

'Come on, man, take some of those clothes off,' they all said. 'What's the matter with you?'

They were mystified about my stubbornness, seeing me there with sweat pouring off my face.

'I don't like the sun too much,' I would say but, of course, this wasn't true. Sometimes I relented and took my jacket off. When I got home after work I would rip off all the layers of clothes in a frenzy and cry with frustration and helplessness. I always felt angry about it too. Why did I have to feel like a fraud? Why did I have to suffer this torture?

My other torment was the toilet situation. All the men on the job would pee anywhere on the ground since there were no toilets on the building sites. For me it was an ordeal every time I needed a pee. I would make sure that I drank only a bare minimum of liquid. Nevertheless, sooner or later I had to make an excuse that I needed to pick something up from a shop. It was often impossible to find somewhere where I could pee in privacy. Sometimes public toilets have only urinals and no cubicles, and shops and pubs don't like you wandering in just to use their facilities. I often ran around the streets in a desperate need, in pain, wondering what the hell I was going to do, thinking, 'I can't go through this all my life. I can't spend the rest of my working days running around the fucking streets looking for a loo.'

I was quickly discovering how difficult it was going to be for me to live and survive emotionally in the workplace. I was getting paranoid about people finding out about me. The fear of discovery and the subsequent humiliation would shoot through my mind unexpectedly at any time during the day, but I didn't want to be treated any differently from the way I felt and looked. 'What if?' questions were always rearing their ugly heads. I could never have proper peace of mind just to get on with the job.

'How long can I put up with this pressure?' I used to ask myself. This whole situation had a devastating effect on my morale and emotions. Although the job itself was great, my concentration was poor. My mind was constantly elsewhere, worrying about the next time I needed a pee, panicking about being discovered. Some days I felt I just couldn't cope with it, I didn't want to be there at all. After a few weeks my torment reached a peak and I quit.

My confidence was wiped out by this first attempt to hold down a normal job. All my restrictions were magnified and I felt frustrated and despondent about my inability to carry on with the job. It had been a really good opportunity since it would have led to a trade. It was a small, friendly firm that paid very decent wages, and I could have been happy working there for some time. But once again I was drifting away from any opportunity of normality. In this mood I received and used a stolen credit card. I wasn't very clever about it and was caught using it to buy jewellery to sell and obtain money. The shop assistant took the card and told me to wait for a moment. In a back room he must have phoned through and was told that the card was stolen. He pressed a button that locked all the doors and the police were there in minutes.

I was arrested and taken to a cell in the police station. The last thing I wanted was for the police to realize that I wasn't just a man, but a transsexual man. I knew only too well the kind of sick curiosity this tends to generate. I told them my name was Malcolm Thompson. I knew that when it came to court they would know about me, but as long as I was in this police station I was going to try and keep a low profile and get out as soon as possible. But a friend rang up to enquire about me, asking for Raymond Thompson. They checked the records and found Raymond Thompson, alias the name given to me by my parents.

All of a sudden the cell was full of coppers. One was arguing in the corridor: 'Well, I searched him, but how was I to know?' So, they had found out about me. My cell was full of people, at least half a dozen policemen, two policewomen and a doctor. They told me to pull my trousers down. I argued and shouted and called them every name under the sun. They had no right to do this to me. Why should I have to submit to such a humiliation just for them to satisfy their curiosity? To an ordinary man or woman it would be bad enough, but for me it was an atrocity. In the end I had no choice.

Looking at me, they couldn't comprehend what kind of human being I was and still believed that I was a naturally formed man, and that I had my penis pulled back between my legs. They then asked me to bend over. I protested even more wildly: 'Fucking bastards! You have no right!' I shouted.

'It's all above board,' one copper shouted back, 'because the doctor is present.'

Even though I appeared to be exploding with rage and outrage I was, in fact, feeling extremely vulnerable and frightened. A part of my mind retreated into a childlike prayer: 'If there is anyone up there, please do it now. Please make me into the man I am. Please make my private parts the way they are supposed to be. Please take away this humiliation.' I looked at all these people. If they could see inside me, they wouldn't subject me to this degradation. As viciously angry as I felt towards them, I felt equally angry with myself. I had promised myself never to get into trouble and put myself in this situation ever again.

Finally I had to do what they asked me, for fear that they might bend me over by force. It was only the doctor who had a closer look at me, but the others didn't leave the cell, they all stood there in a row observing the proceedings. Finally satisfied as to the nature of my identity they left, but every once in a while the spyhole on the door would go up and I could hear them whispering and talking outside. Sometimes there would be laughter. Occasionally some of them would come into the cell and tell me to stand up. They would look me over and then leave.

Marcy, faithful friend as ever, came and bailed me out. I was grateful and very relieved to be out of there. There was going to be quite a long wait for my court date and I worried a lot about what would happen. I felt sure I would end up back inside prison because I was still on licence.

Between failing to keep the job going, and my slip-up with the law, I was anxious about how it was going to affect the process of my transformation. I had not seen Dr Randall since coming out of prison, but I was notified that he wanted regular reports from my probation officer regarding my behaviour. Carole had taken it upon herself to write to Dr Randall to enquire if there was any other way to treat my condition, avoiding surgery, perhaps through therapy or the like. She later told me that Dr Randall had responded to her letter, saying, 'In this case, no, there is no other way. The only way to help Raymond would be to take him forward.'

My first appointment was coming up, and I went to London to see him. Carole accompanied me for support and out of professional interest. I was anxious about how he was going to react to the credit card story.

He wiped the floor with me.

'This just is not good enough,' he growled. 'You've been to Borstal twice, you have just been in prison, and now this.'

He warned me that if he was to help me any further, I had to prove to him that I could lead 'a sober and industrious life' from now on.

'If you don't, you are wasting your own time and you're wasting mine. For me to do all this for you, and you ending up back in prison, is a complete waste of time.'

This conversation made a profound and lasting impression on me. I understood the devastating implications of what he was saying. If I didn't pull my socks up now I would lose my chance of having the surgery that was going to save my life. Dr Randall also took me off the hormone tablets that I was on, telling me matter-of-factly that prolonged use would eat holes in my liver. But he told me not to worry. If any damage had occurred, my liver would heal itself. He explained to me that they were a synthetic hormone, and that he thought it would be better for me to be on a natural hormone, which he then prescribed. I didn't take in properly what was being said until a bit later. Perhaps I felt tense and anxious and wasn't able to concentrate properly. On the train back from London, his words came back to me.

'My God . . . eating holes in my liver.' In my mind's eye I saw a great big cheese with holes in it. I felt that familiar feeling of bitterness about my condition creeping back. So now I might suffer all kinds of health problems as well, in addition to my psychological traumas. I didn't really know anything about the internal effects of the hormone treatment, and yet I had no choice but to continue. I needed it in order to become myself.

I had been thinking quite a bit about my parents and I felt now that I ought to go and see them. I was afraid that when I did go to court about the credit card I would get another prison sentence and there wouldn't be an opportunity to see them, perhaps for quite some time.

I wanted them to understand that I didn't hate them or dislike them at all and that I didn't hold them responsible for anything.

I wanted to make some kind of peace with them. I hadn't written to them or seen them for four and a half years.

I had been out from prison for four months when I decided to go, and wrote them a letter saying that I would be coming. With the letter I sent along a photograph of myself. They had not seen me for such a long time I thought it would ease the shock when they saw me in person. Not that I had changed that much in appearance, but now there was no question of me being a man. In fact when I saw my father I realized how much I looked like him.

A few days later I took the train to my home town and went straight to my parents' house. I didn't know what to expect and I felt quite nervous. Even the town itself had a claustrophobic effect on me. I didn't want to run into anyone I knew from the past; I felt as if I didn't have a past.

My mother opened the door.

'I don't want to see you,' she said and without any further explanation she tried to push me out by closing the door against me. I stood fast like a brick wall and she couldn't get the door closed.

'Didn't you get my letter?' I asked, bewildered.

'Yes,' she said curtly. 'Your sister recognized your handwriting and opened the letter. I found her crying and looking at your photo, so I took it from her and ripped it up.

'Do you enjoy upsetting us like this?' she added. I felt hurt and taken aback by her reaction, but I suppose it was to be expected.

'So where is Anna now?' I asked my mother.

'Your sister is at work,' she answered sharply.

'Look, I've not come to see you,' I said, smarting from the rejection. 'I've come to see my father.'

'Your father is in bed. I want you to go – just leave.'

I ignored her words, pushed the door open and marched past her and up the stairs. My father, who worked shifts, was fast asleep so I shook him to wake him up.

'Do *you* want to see me? Can *you* understand me? Or do you not want to see me either? Just tell me if you don't.'

The poor guy was trying to come to his senses and was quite stunned to see me there, ranting at him.

'What's the matter, what are you talking about?'

'My mother doesn't want me here, she just tried to push me out of the door. Now, do you want to see me or don't you?'

'Don't be silly,' he tried to cover up for her. 'You know what your mother is like.'

We sat there on his bed and talked for a while. My father was really trying to understand what I was telling him about myself.

'All I have ever known in my life,' he explained, 'is that I fancy women. I don't really know about or understand any of the other ways to be.'

'Can't you understand that women are all I fancy too?' I knew he understood because Carole had told me that he did, but it was still quite bewildering for him. There I was, looking and sounding very much like a man. I was still his child. 'But I need to become whole, and I need to feel comfortable in myself. I have to have surgery,' I told him.

He looked at me with compassion. 'Your life is going to be difficult,' he said, as he had said so many times when I was younger.

I soon felt I ought to leave. I was aware of my mother downstairs wanting to see the back of me. When I got down we had a showdown about the prospect of my surgery, which Carole had already explained to them. My mother tried to tell me that I was not to have it. She threatened that if I did go through with surgery, I would no longer be part of the family. I would be excluded from all weddings, all funerals and I wouldn't be left anything in their will.

'None of that is important to me, but a little bit of understanding wouldn't go amiss,' I said to her. But she couldn't accept it.

'Please, just continue being the way you are, don't change anything,' she pleaded.

I think she still fundamentally believed that I was gay.

'How can I be the way I really am unless I change something? How can I be myself unless I change the parts that are wrong? I will never be all right in myself unless I have surgery.' I tried to explain to her that I was not a lesbian, that this condition had nothing to do with sexual orientation, but with my very identity as a person, and that I couldn't ever be happy in this body as it was.

'I am not prepared to live a life for you or anyone else,' I said. 'You have had your life, now this is my life, and I want to live it my own way. I cannot do or be what you are asking me to.'

My mother was in a state and we weren't getting anywhere at all. She couldn't comprehend what I was telling her, so I said, 'I have to go now, but before I go I want to see my grandmother.' I hadn't seen her for almost five years.

My mother was outraged. 'Your grandmother is getting old. You cannot let her see you looking like that.'

'Why not? What's the matter with me? It's not as if I have two heads or anything.'

To my surprise my mother relented and took the car to go and fetch my grandmother. I was standing waiting by the gate. The old lady got out of the car and came towards me with outstretched arms. 'Oh, you look lovely, my handsome boy.'

Those familiar words instantly brought back vivid memories of my childhood, the happy aspects of it with her and my grandfather. I was really pleased to see her. She sensed that the atmosphere was strained and she tried to ask me what was the matter.

'I've only come for a very short visit, and I must go back now.'

My mother's last words to me were to say that she would do everything she could to stop me from having surgery, including going to London to talk to Dr Randall himself.

She did, in fact, go and see my GP in Cardiff. Dr Popper told me later that she had been in tears and that she was very upset about my plans to have surgery. I do believe that she genuinely feared for me. In any event, she had a bit of a phobia about hospitals and surgery. I can imagine how queasy she must have felt at the idea of what I was planning. Dr Popper was quite blunt with her: 'There is nothing you can do to stop him. Ray is over eighteen years old, and he has a right to go ahead with this if that is what he wants to do.'

I did feel for my mother, coming all the way on the train on her own to try and save her child from the worst possible fate. I knew she cared for me to go to those lengths, and it made me really sad. On a few occasions, when I thought about what I put my mother through, my insides would turn with anguish for her. In spite of our very difficult relationship I realized how deeply I cared for her. But this is why I had left it so long before I allowed my parents to know about the treatment I was having. If my mother had known that I was on hormone tablets at sixteen, in all likelihood she would have gone to great lengths to stop it, and possibly she might have had some recourse. Now it was too late, and she had to accept that she no longer had any control, moral or legal, over what I did with my body and my life.

I had been helping Ty fixing up his house. Irena was the first resident, but she didn't like being there on her own.

'I'll move in to keep you company,' I told her. Soon we were all living there, a whole bunch of us, including Marcy. Irena, her baby and I shared a room. The three of us did everything in that room, cooked, slept, ate.

Gail was in our room one day and suddenly she said, 'For God's sake, why don't the two of you just get back together?' That was what eventually took place – Irena and I gradually found ourselves together again. I have a feeling that Irena made more of a conscious choice about it than I did. I was crazy about the baby and I liked and cared for Irena, but I was not in love with her. It was Lorretta I really wanted.

There was another factor that brought about my reconciliation with Irena. My confidence and self-esteem were very low, and I had been getting worried about the prospect of living with Lorretta. She was a few years older than me, and I wondered if I could really ever be enough for her. I was so attracted to her and in awe of her, I thought she could have any man she liked; why would I be the one, how could I be enough? I felt that she would soon tire of me or be disappointed in me. I had broached this with her in prison on a few occasions, but she would laugh it off and say, 'What do you mean? Of course you are enough, you are all I want and need.' What I didn't realize at the time was that Lorretta was a lot more grown up than I was, and she took our future together very seriously.

One day a friend came over to the house to tell me that Lorretta was in town on home-leave from prison. I immediately made my way to her friend's house, where she was staying. The minute we laid eyes on each other we just grabbed each other and hugged for ages. Seeing her face brought back all the hopes and dreams I had had for us both. Everything that had happened to me since we were in prison together seemed unreal.

Lorretta had heard through the grapevine that I was living with Irena, and she asked me if it was true. I was abruptly brought back to the reality of the situation and felt gutted. Lorretta was scrutinizing my face for any expression and after a long silence I just nodded. I had fucked up and felt embarrassed and pathetic. I couldn't provide what I had promised Lorretta and that made me feel profoundly sad.

'I knew it,' she said emphatically. 'When I was packing up my stuff this morning, the cross that you made me snapped in half.' She told me that when she saw the broken cross, she felt a surge of sadness and knew that the promises that we'd made had also been broken.

I spent the night with her. It wasn't unusual for me to be gone the whole night – if I had been out somewhere I would end up dossing at someone's house – so Irena knew nothing of it.

A couple of nights later Irena and I were in bed asleep when, in the early hours of the morning, people piled into the house to have a party upstairs. There was a large room on the first floor with a music system and some settees, which we often used for after-hour parties. I was half awake when there was a knock on our bedroom door. Lorretta stuck her head in and said, 'Can I have a word with you?'

I got out of bed and went out on the landing. She wanted some answers and tried to confront me and ask me what the hell I was doing. Was this the end of our relationship, or what? I was dodging her questions, trying to tell her that I didn't know what was going to happen. I didn't expect anything to last, since I thought I'd soon be back in prison.

Soon enough Irena came out and the two of them started shouting at each other. I grabbed Irena and pushed her back into the bedroom and closed the door. Lorretta, turning to me, looked me in the eye and said, 'I want you to tell me that you don't love me. Look me in the face and just tell me that.'

I couldn't tell her that I didn't love her, because I did. I had got myself too ensnared in the situation with Irena and wasn't brave enough to let go. It was too complicated for my already complicated existence.

Lorretta came back in the morning with all her things packed and knocked on my door again.

'At least take me to the train station,' she said. She was due back in prison later that day.

'OK. Give me a moment to get dressed.'

Irena woke up as I was leaving and said, 'Where are you going?' Lorretta seemed more important in my mind at this time and I just told Irena the truth.

We sat for a long time at the station, talking and drinking coffee. Again, she asked me what was happening between us.

'Why are you with her again?'

'Better the devil I know than the devil I don't,' I answered feebly, knowing it wasn't good enough. It was true nevertheless. I had known Irena so well and for such a long time, I felt less insecure about her. Also I had grown very attached to the baby. It was a very emotional couple of hours. I loved and wanted this woman, and yet, here I was telling her I couldn't cope with a relationship between us.

When she came out of prison for good, I went to see her again – I couldn't stay away – and we spent the night together at her mother's house. The following day I needed to pick up some money from the house and, unwisely, I took Lorretta with me. While we were there Irena saw us just as we were leaving the house and she shouted to me from the top of the stairs, 'Don't go. Please don't leave.'

I felt a twinge of remorse but I had no choice, I had to go with Lorretta. I needed to be with her. Predictably I wasn't going to get away with it scot-free. When I came back home all my clothes and the television had gone.

'I have given all your clothes to my brothers, and I've sold the TV to Ty,' Irena told me.

'I don't believe you've given my clothes away. Where the hell are they? Just tell me where they are.'

No luck. I ran upstairs to Ty, to see if he knew where they were. In the meantime Irena, who had packed my clothes in black bin-liners, snuck them out the front door for the rubbish collectors to take. I saw the bin-liners there several times that day, but it never occurred to me that they contained my clothes. It was three o'clock in morning when I finally coaxed the truth out of her, and ran out to rescue my wardrobe.

We made up. 'Why did you do it?' she asked me.

'I needed to be with her.' It was the simple truth. Even though I was trying to make a go of my relationship with Irena, I knew in my heart that I would have a hard time trying to stay away from Lorretta.

One day I heard from a friend that Lorretta's mother had died. I knew how close she was to her mother and how devastated she must have been, so I immediately ran to see her at her flat.

'She is not living here any more,' her friend told me. 'But you have just missed her, she called in earlier.' I'll always regret not having gone to find her, but I assumed that she would have been surrounded by her relatives and I didn't want to intrude. In fact, she had no support from anyone. She was totally alone with her son and it wasn't until much later I found out what a difficult time this had been for her. Not only had she counted on coming out of prison to start a life with me, and then lost her mother who was the only person she was really close to, apart from her son, but also her son had been diagnosed epileptic. She went through a terrible crisis at the time, and I should have been there for her.

After the fiasco with the credit card and my conversation with Dr Randall, I realized that in order to get on with my life and not jeopardize my chances for further help, I would have to change my life quite drastically. Living off crime had got me nowhere, and I had never given myself an opportunity to develop and grow as a person. Coping with my condition had always been foremost in my mind and had not allowed me to explore my potential. For this, I desperately needed continuity and stability in my life. I would have to try, yet again, to do something honest for a living. Also, when my court case came up, at least they would know that I was doing my best to straighten myself out. I needed a job, but this meant facing the same difficulties I had in the previous one. I would have to learn to deal with these in some way. But how? The workplace was a minefield for a person like me, practically and emotionally. My detachment would have to be built like a fortress around me in order to keep me safe.

I landed a job with the council, rubbish collecting. Well, it wasn't as easy as all that. I went down to the council office three times to apply for a job, and each time I was told there was no work. The third time I went, the guy at the counter said, 'I told you there isn't any work available – now, piss off.'

'I know there are jobs, and I want an application form.'

As it happened, some other man with obvious authority overheard this and asked me what it was I wanted.

'I just want an application form,' I said, 'for a job.'

'What sort of job?' he asked me.

'On the bins, or sweeping the roads, anything, I don't care what it is.'

'Give him an application form, what's the matter with you?' So I had the job. 'You can start on Monday,' he said. It was my first ever real job, and I didn't mind it at all even though I had to be out of bed at five in the morning.

When the date for my court appearance arrived, I was very despondent and had little hope of getting off the charge. I had violated the conditions of my two-year licence and was fully expecting to go back to prison. They obviously wanted me back in prison, but my probation officer, Carole, who was with me in court, argued strongly in my favour. She told them that the longest that I had been out of detention in three years had been six months, that I hadn't had enough time to get to grips with my life and that since the offence had been committed I had been able to secure employment. In addition she spoke about my treatment with Dr Randall in London, how this process had been stressful for me and how I needed time to adjust to many new aspects of my life.

The policeman made a mockery out of me and thoroughly humiliated me by insisting on calling me by my birth name. He was standing to the right of the judge, and he refused point blank to call me by my real name. I sat with my head in my hands and wanted to sink through the floor. I felt like the main attraction in a freak show. Carole shouted that it was illegal to refer to the defendant by anything other than his real name.

'The defendant has had his name changed by deed poll, and the court must refer to him by his legal name.'

I was impressed with how assertive she was, but the copper persisted. In the end, the judge had had enough. He just stood up, looked at the copper and said slowly and emphatically: 'Will you *please* . . . refer to the defendant . . . by his *name* . . . which is Raymond Thompson.'

I was so happy coming out of there. My licence was extended for a further two years and I had a £100 fine, but I was free to go. Little did I know what was coming.

When I went to work the following morning, I was asked to fill in for a chap who was off sick at another, small, depot, where there were only about five men working. Normally I would have been in the main depot with about forty other guys, where they all used to swap newspapers in the morning. I hadn't looked at the papers yet. When I got home Irena asked me, 'Have you read the newspapers today?' She showed me one and there it was, a big headline: Hundred Pound Fine For Sex-Change Man, followed by my name (the one I was given as a child), the exact department where I worked, and all the other details that they had been able to lay their hands on.

I couldn't face going back to work. Not because I thought they would confront me with all this, but because I knew they would treat me differently. Up to this point in my life I had never really been confronted with the full impact of what the average person feels about transsexuals or 'sex-changes', as they are called in the tabloids. Although I knew that people find it bizarre and often they haven't a clue what it really means, most people that I had associated with didn't think anything of it. Certainly I had come across a lot of prejudice and curiosity, but amongst my friends it was all right to be of any creed, colour or sexual orientation. My problems as a transsexual had been mainly my own difficulty in living with myself and having to exist in the wrong body. I had never read anything in the newspapers or elsewhere about transsexualism and I wasn't yet aware of the sensationalist value of the condition.

It didn't help me to have this additional realization. When it dawned on me that the world sees people like me as aberrations of nature, as mutations, freaks, perverts or deviants, I felt even more alienated from myself and increasingly anxious about people finding out about me. At the same time I felt I had a right to a life, and fuck 'em all.

Now I had to face my present situation without a job and with many people knowing my circumstances. Irena said, 'Why don't we move back to Newport?' It seemed like the best solution not only to what had just happened, but also to our housing problem.

A couple of weeks earlier we had moved into the house of another friend, Amanda. The main reason was that Ty's house was being overrun by rats. Swarms of them were coming up from the river, through the derelict hotel next door and into the house. They were eating all our food, breaking the eggs and eating them, and getting into the bread bin and eating through the loaves. They were eating holes through the walls and getting in everywhere. When I was getting up at half past five in the morning to get ready for work, I heard them scarpering wherever I went in the house.

Irena was frightened for the baby. She had read in the paper about a baby who had had its face chewed by rats who smelled the milk on its face, and she was convinced that she had found a rat flea on the baby's head. She scrubbed our room down with bleach and disinfectant. Ty had the rat people come to lay traps and poison, but it didn't do any good.

Irena's mother came to visit us. She was horrified about the condition of the place and the rats. She sat on the stairs and cried about Irena and the baby living in this awful room, as she described it. She decided to take the baby with her back to Newport until we had sorted ourselves out in some way. Irena herself couldn't take these living conditions any more, so when

Amanda offered to put us up in her house for a while, we accepted the invitation and moved.

We couldn't stay with Amanda for ever either, so moving to Newport seemed a way out. Another factor, which Irena maintained, was that, with our lifestyle in Cardiff, it was easier to get into trouble. 'You'll just end up back in prison if we stay here,' she kept telling me.

We packed our belongings and moved them to Newport in a couple of taxis.

7
Removing Everything That Didn't Belong

Once we arrived in Newport Irena asked around the members of her large family if anyone knew of a vacant flat. Her sister-in-law had the key to a friend's flat, so we went to check it out. It looked OK: a bedroom, living-room and kitchen. As the whole house was empty we checked the place. On the first floor there was another, apparently much bigger, flat. We thought it would be nice if Carl, Irena's son, could have a room of his own. The top window was open and we climbed in to have a look at it. It was a dream compared to where we had come from: fitted carpets and wardrobes; a fridge, cooker and breakfast bar in the kitchen. We found the rental agent's address and Irena went to see her. We thought it better that Irena, as a single woman with a child, approached the agent. I had saved £250, which meant I had more than enough to pay the bond. To be truthful, the agent hadn't much choice: we had already moved our stuff in, since we had nowhere else to go.

We were supposed to start a new life but I was feeling very rough; things were not the way I wanted them to be. Everything had happened so fast, and the shock reaction from what had transpired in the last few days was just setting in: the court case, the newspaper article, quitting my job and now I found myself in this flat in another city with a ready-made family. You could have dropped me on the moon, it would have been no different.

I knew Irena's family and most of them were all right, but Cleo, Irena's mother, didn't approve of me as a partner for her daughter and there was a lot of conflict between us. Some little dig or comment always had to be slipped in by Cleo. In that sense she was similar to my own mother. Having said that, she also spoiled me sometimes. If she went to the market early in the morning, she would bring fish for Irena to cook and would occasionally buy a bag of sprats, which she knew I liked. She'd lumber into the flat and gruffly throw the bag in my lap. Little gestures like that showed me that deep down somewhere there must have been a hint of a soft spot. She was a short African woman with a very strong personality. With eleven children she had to be strong. She wasn't naïve about life, having experienced it fully, and had faced a lot of hardship.

I started to look for work, but with all that had happened in Cardiff my confidence had been severely damaged and was at rock bottom. It was quite an agonizing time. I used to wake up in the middle of the night with attacks of anxiety and panic, a sudden fear of the hopelessness of my predicament. I didn't know how to get rid of the panic and the fear. I would try and wrap myself up into a tight ball, squeezing my knees into my chest. It never helped much and, in anger, I would bash my head against the wall, or plunge my head into buckets of ice-cold water. I'd be shaking from head to foot and sobbing in sheer frustration. I felt so bitter at not being able to solve my situation single-handed. I had abilities, hopes and needs, but I couldn't assert myself as a man because of the complications of being shrouded by this fragmented body that hid me, embarrassed and restricted me. During these nights I often still asked God to indulge me, to give me the pleasure of being able to embrace my body, for my body to wrap me up, keep me warm and protect me.

'God, where are you?' I would implore, at the same time thinking that I was going crazy talking to someone who either wasn't there, or if he was, wasn't listening.

Sometimes I could sit for hours watching the blank television screen, my mind far off in another world. During these times it was difficult even to get my arms and legs to work for me.

Irena dealt with most things that involved communicating with the outside world. At times I couldn't bring myself to open the front door if someone came to visit. But we were desperate for money, and I simply had to do something. I was apathetic and listless on one hand, and frightened of exposing myself to the outside world on the other. I couldn't cope with continually being undermined by the fear of people finding out about me.

But Dr Randall's words kept echoing through my mind: '... must lead a sober and industrious life...'

There was always the danger that if I didn't get some work and lack of money became a real problem, I might turn to crime. I knew that there was no way I could afford to let that happen. Eventually I pulled myself together as best I could and faced the outside world in search of work. I got the odd temporary job. Sometimes I'd get a morning or a day's work unloading a lorry and the driver would give me a fiver.

I did finally get a proper job in a cold storage depot. In the first week, all I did was unload fifty-six-pound boxes of butter. It was very hard going. I could tell apart the guys that had worked there a while: they had it down to a fine art. They were going like mad, hurling these boxes through the air, and at first it seemed easy, but as you get three-quarters down into the load you start noticing it. My arms were hanging off my shoulders. It did give me a boost though, my efforts had paid off and I had got a job, and the money was going to mean a lot to us.

After a week there I was on the bus going to work and I could hear someone at the front of the bus talking about a fire. I didn't think anything of it, got off the bus and walked towards the ... well, there was nothing there, the building had burned to the ground. The trucks in the garages were stuck in about a foot of butter. I was standing there, dazed, when someone tapped me on the shoulder. 'Go up to the office and pick up your pay. You're out of a job.'

I went home in a very despondent mood. I couldn't believe my bad luck. Irena was still in bed when I got home. 'What the hell are you doing home?' she said.

'The place has burned down.'

'Come off it. What a load of bullshit – you just don't want to go to work.'

Irena and I were fundamentally good friends, but I couldn't help feeling that our relationship as partners was a mistake – certainly since the baby, Carl, had come into it. At the same time, getting so fond of him was partly what had pulled me back into the relationship with Irena. We argued quite a bit about him or, rather, how he had come about. Irena had changed her story about his conception several times. Initially, while I was still in prison, she told me that she had been raped. I knew I should feel sympathy for someone who has been violated in that way, but I never believed her. Then, when she came out of the hospital, she decided to change the story. The new story was that she had gone out deliberately to make a baby for the two of us. Much as I would have liked to, I couldn't bring myself to believe this.

In the beginning, while we were in Ty's house, these different accounts didn't have any impact on me. I didn't much care. I thought I was living with Irena and Carl on borrowed time anyway. I was certain that I was going back to prison and that there was no future for our relationship, whether or not I wanted it. But now, when we found ourselves more on our own, trying to lead some sort of normal family life, these fabrications began to come back to me. I started to ask Irena about what had actually happened.

Little comments made by members of Irena's family were getting through to me. Her sister mentioned that Irena had gone mad when she found out that she was pregnant. She had gone over to see the father and given him hell about it. So that confirmed what I already knew: she didn't get pregnant deliberately for us. So why did she lie? What was the real story? As I felt closer to Carl, these things took on more importance.

Irena's mother would come and visit and was forever praising her sons-in-law and whoever else had employment, how so-and-so wanted for nothing, et cetera. I used to resent her comments, which I felt were deliberate put-downs directed at me. One day I overheard Cleo talking to Irena.

'If you are finding it difficult to make ends meet, why don't you ask Carl's father to start paying maintenance?'

Not only did I resent the idea of this bastard being involved in any way, but all these comments just added to my feelings of inadequacy as a father and provider. Irena always told her mother we would manage, but I could tell that Cleo's words were getting through to her, and this was the cause of a lot of rows between us. Carl certainly never went without anything, we made sure of that. Nevertheless, most of the time we were really short of money.

One morning I woke up to the sound of banging and crashing.

'What the hell is happening?' I thought to myself, Irena was not in the bed beside me. I ran out into the hall and there I found Irena up on a chair with a lump hammer in her hand, trying to smash the electric meter up on the wall to bits.

'I'm not putting no more fucking money into this thing!' she shouted.

'Hell, stop that noise,' I tried to hush her up, but laughing to myself at the same time. 'What do you think you are doing?'

She was so worked up she didn't take any notice of me. Then she got the scissors and cut off the seals around the box. I had to go down to her brother's house and borrow a soldering iron so that I could solder the seals together again.

In the end I found another way of saving money on electricity. I drilled a minute hole in the side of the box, and stuck a copper wire through it. Put in carefully, the wire stopped the wheel that clocks up the electricity from turning round. I built a wooden box around the meter to disguise all the damage inflicted on it, and I painted the skylight in the hall dark green so that daylight wouldn't shine on the damage. Whenever somebody knocked at the door, we would whip the wire out before answering in case it was the electricity board.

Our life together had its moments, and I was able to laugh at things, but I felt very uneasy and the same old feelings were still there. Alongside my fear of being 'found out' I was ever more uneasy with my own body, I couldn't stand the 'bits' that didn't belong to me. I felt as if I was in a prison of flesh and bones. I had withdrawn much more into myself since moving to Newport and I didn't feel comfortable going out. Whenever I did, I felt compelled to wear layers and layers of clothes. Irena had made me a chest strap out of elastic bandages and a vest. I wore it under all my clothes to make sure that my chest was flat. It was uncomfortable and tight, but I felt more secure in it. Over that I would have a T-shirt and then a thick checked shirt, and over this a big bulky crew neck jumper.

The layer which I really needed to take off was what can only be described as a second skin. But no matter how hot or how cold or how uncomfortable it makes you feel, you cannot get it off. I yearned for the pure relief you get from ripping off some really uncomfortable piece of clothing, except I couldn't because that last layer was me. But all this anguish was invisible to others; to the men at work I was just like them.

I had stopped trying to keep fit since I had come out of prison, but I remembered how much more confident I felt when I exercised. Having my body in good condition had boosted my confidence and made me less uncomfortable. Stamina and strength do exert power over the mind too, and helped me feel better. But it had always been difficult to keep this up. Because I rejected my body, most of the time I had no wish to improve it in any way and neglected it. It wasn't even my own, and I didn't want to be reminded of it, so why should I bother?

The only way I could handle any exercise at this time was to do it first thing in the morning, when I started to wake up but before I had become totally conscious. This way I could blot out my body from my mind, and just quickly go through the motions.

'You're fucking nuts,' Irena would say, watching me in amazement as I frantically did my sit-ups and press-ups. More often than not it would give me one hell of a headache. 'What do you expect? Who gets out of bed before they've even opened their eyes, and does fucking press-ups?' was Irena's no-nonsense attitude.

However much I neglected my health, no depression or anxiety state was going to interfere with my motivation and determination to have surgery. Having surgery would help me take charge of my health without any inhibitions. It would enable me to go about like any man and do any male activity. I daydreamed about what it could be like if I could join the army or the navy. That would certainly whip me into shape in a hurry.

I was getting more concerned about my fitness, my agility and my reactions, and since I couldn't join the army or the navy I decided to take up boxing. I had to work really hard to overcome the embarrassment of my body and it was an effort of will to join the boxing club. In the end my paranoia got the better of me and I couldn't bring myself to continue. Getting fit became a fantasy once again.

I had plenty of time to ruminate and daydream when I was sitting in the Job Centre, like a beggar, waiting for anything in the way of work that could give me a couple of quid. Sitting there one day I overheard the lady behind the counter talking to her colleague. 'That boy over there,' she said, pointing discreetly at me, 'might as well bring his bed here. He is always in here first thing in the morning.'

Lorretta was frequently on my mind and I often felt the urge to go to Cardiff to look for her. My situation reminded me of how light-hearted she used to make me feel. She always made me forget the heavy burden of myself. She had always made me feel like me. But I had made my choices and I really wanted to make the best of my relationship with Irena.

Ever since the visit to my parents I knew that it was going to be hard, if not totally impossible, to get their approval and their blessing, but I kept trying. I felt compelled to keep in contact with them. It was very distressing to do this, because every time I phoned and talked to my mother, she would start on me and the conversation would turn disagreeable, to put it mildly. I really only phoned to find out how they were, and I would have been happy just to hear that they were all right, but it never worked out that way. My mother would lose her cool within minutes, saying that on account of me she was on nerve tablets and if anything happened to her it would be my fault, and I was to be held responsible. When we spoke on the phone my mother would often mention the neighbours and what they thought.

'I cannot live my life in such a way that you won't have to worry about what the neighbours think,' I would say to her. Once when she mentioned the neighbours I went through the roof and shouted, 'Put my father on the phone!'

'Hello . . . What's the matter?' my father said.

'Look,' I shouted at him. 'Who means more to you? Me, your own flesh and blood, or the next-door neighbour?'

'Of course there's no choice, you mean more to me than any neighbour. Why on earth do you ask?'

'Because my mother has just told me that it is the next-door neighbour that is more important to her.'

'Well, you know your mother,' he said, resignedly.

When my mother brought up the business of excluding me from all family functions and cutting me out of their will if I went through with surgery, I would say, 'Would you really want me to change who I am, knowing that I would only do so in order not to be excluded from your will? Give it all to my sister, I don't want any of it.'

Other times her approach was slightly less harsh. She would ask me when I was going to come home, and I would say, 'Don't be so daft, I'm not coming home. I can't come home. I must be able to live my life. You are always telling me that you can't hold your head up in the street because of me, and I live nowhere near you. Just imagine, if I did, how embarrassed and uncomfortable you would feel.'

Once I phoned her up to ask how things were going. Again she asked me when I was planning to come home, and I answered as I usually did.

'The only fit place for you,' she shouted down the phone, 'is in a circus, where people can stare at you and laugh at you.'

It was very painful to hear her say such a thing.

'Why, what is the matter with me? Why would people be staring and laughing at me? I don't know how you can say these things to me.' It wasn't until after I had hung up and thought more about her words that I got into an emotional state. These calls would upset me a lot. Irena kept trying to prevent me from going out to the phone box.

'Don't bother to phone,' she said to me. 'You've got your own life now and your own family. Your parents always get you so upset. Why do you bother?' She was right.

Once when I phoned, my father answered. On hearing my voice he sounded unmistakably strained. I demanded to know what was going on and he admitted that there had been quite a few rows between them.

'Is it because of me?' I asked. 'I want to know if it has to do with me. Are you blaming yourselves for my condition?'

'Don't worry yourself about it, it's between me and your mother.'

'I want to know,' I demanded. 'If it affects me or if it's because of me, I want you to tell me. My mother is already telling me that if she drops dead it is my fucking fault, so you might as well tell me.'

'Look,' he said. 'It's like this: your mother wants me to have a vasectomy.'

'Why does she want that?' I didn't understand a thing.

'I have to. Your mother says that she doesn't want me to put a monster like you inside her again.'

'Oh, so is that what you think I am, a fucking monster?'

'I don't think that, I don't think that,' he tried to reassure me, but the damage had been done.

After that I stopped phoning my parents.

A few months later I had a letter from my mother. I don't know how she found my address. It said: 'If you are at all bothered, your father has lost his fingers in an accident at work.' That was all it said, nothing else, no 'Dear Ray . . . Love Mum.' I got on the phone right away and spoke to my father. He told me he had stuck his hand into a machine that appeared to be turned off, in order to retrieve a scrap of metal. As he stuck his hand in, the machine started up. It cut off his index finger first, then miraculously skimmed over the next two fingers, but ended up taking the little finger as well.

There was a seven-foot fence around this machine with a door to get in and out, but my father was in such a state of shock that he forgot about the door and scaled the fence to get out of there.

My father had been in the steel works for thirty-two years, all of his working life. He was a dedicated worker and had spent more time in the steel works than he had with his wife and family.

They offered him a pittance as compensation for the loss of his fingers. To a big business like that, where production and profits come first, an accident like this is probably just a nuisance. After all, to them my father was no more than a cog in the machine.

Nevertheless he chose to continue working when he had recovered sufficiently, although he was in pain for a long time after. He didn't accept the money they offered him and took it to court. His solicitor warned him that he might end up worse off than if he had accepted the original offer. But to my father the money was immaterial at this point, it was the principle involved that mattered to him. He had received very little help and support from his employers and he was very disappointed in their lack of concern. In the end he was awarded quite a bit more, and the case set a record for an injury of that nature. It was still little compared to what he would have got these days, but I suppose nothing could compensate for such a loss.

Life went on and I continued doing the odd job, struggling to keep to Dr Randall's request to lead a sober and industrious life. It was my motto. In spite of my escalating discomfort and my domestic complications I had definitely matured in my outlook and I was starting to feel the importance of not just humouring Dr Randall, but really doing something with my life. So much time had been wasted and I needed to find a purpose apart from my struggle to feel whole. I wanted a way of making a living that was also enjoyable and satisfying to me.

I liked carpentry. There were a few courses going, but they were difficult to get on. On an impulse I phoned my uncle Peter who lived a couple of miles away, who I knew was on all kinds of boards and committees to do with these courses. I thought I could get some advice from him on how to get on one of these courses a bit quicker. On his way to somewhere else he actually stopped at my home in Newport. He was visibly uncomfortable in my presence. 'It's like this,' he said. 'I can't help you, because I think too much of your mother and father.'

'Oh well,' I said to him, 'I'll sort something out.' But I was taken aback by his ridiculous comment. It amazed me that he would take the trouble to come and tell me this, and I didn't believe for a moment that my parents would share that petty attitude. I was sure they would want me to get on with my life and do something constructive with it.

I signed on to do a carpentry course. I waited months to hear that I had been accepted. When finally I was called to start I was over the moon. It was a chance for me to get a trade. I went for my first day full of optimism. It was a thrill to be given an overall and boots and the basics that we needed to start. But it wasn't to be quite so smooth and easy.

Towards the end of the first day we were all called to have a medical check-up. This kind of possibility had always been at the back of my mind while searching for work, but now it became a reality and, of course, it was perfectly logical. Some of the physical requirements of carpentry would demand strength and good health. My heart sank to the very pit of my stomach. My initial reaction was to run, to get out.

'I can't cope with this,' I thought. 'I'm going to have to take my clothes off, and that'll be it.' But I stayed.

I knew that I was going to have to refuse a physical check-up, but I decided to see how far I would get before having to make a quick exit. While I was waiting I went through a whole range of emotions. After the initial shock and the fear of possibly being found out, I became enraged. 'These fucking bastards with their little bits of paper, how dare they, they have no right to put me through this!' All I wanted was to learn a trade so that I could support myself, and here I was, already feeling defeated and like a freak. I was going to lose this opportunity because my body was not quite the same as the other guys.

Before going in to see the doctor, I was interviewed by a nurse.

'Have you got anything wrong with you?'

'No.'

Loads more questions about past ill health.

'No, no, no, no, no.'

She checked me for colour-blindness.

I wasn't colour-blind.

Then she gave me a bottle and told me to go and pee in it, for a urine sample. I was already at breaking point, and this was almost too much. Standing in a little cubicle in the waiting room trying to pee into this bottle without making a mess, while two other guys were waiting outside, I don't know how I kept my composure. I gave the sample to the nurse.

'You're a young man, and you look pretty strong and healthy,' she said. 'I don't think there is any need for you to have the full medical.'

In spite of my relief I felt bitter. 'Why the fuck do I have to continue putting up with these embarrassments? Why does it have to be me?'

Discounting my fear of being found out, I did enjoy the course and I learned a lot. We were taught to do everything connected with the building trade, including a lot of bench work and joinery, roofing, et cetera. I had already picked up quite a variety of skills while I was in prison, and I was starting to feel that, at last, I was gaining confidence in my abilities.

For a short time life didn't seem too bad at all. After being on the course for three months, we moved back to Irena's brother Dave's house, where we had started our live-in relationship five years earlier. Dave and his wife had split up, and he was going back to sea for nine months at the time. The move happened in a flash, although I knew that it was on the cards. I came home from work one day, and the next-door neighbour handed me a note from Irena saying that we had moved, and to go straight to her brother's house.

One day there was a phone call for me at the training centre. It was Irena telling me that my mother had been to the house looking for me, and that she was on her way down to the site to see me. I panicked. What was she doing here? Why did she want to come and see me at the training centre? I had no choice but to go to my instructor to tell him that my mother was coming down, and ask that he was not to let her in. I couldn't risk it. After the things that she had said to me on the phone, how could I be sure she wouldn't say or do something that would jeopardize my male identity?

At least a year, perhaps more, had passed since I last talked to her, and I had no idea what she wanted from me.

'It's all right, don't worry. She won't come through that gate,' the instructor reassured me, a bit puzzled. I felt so bad, almost physically sick, at having to do this to my own mother, but I had no choice. None of the other blokes knew about my background, and it meant a lot to me to keep it that way. My mother was turned away at the gate. I was in no state to continue working and asked if I could take the rest of the day off. The instructor could see that I was upset and preoccupied so he let me go, and off I went in pursuit of my mother.

When I got home, she was on the street corner, waiting for me.

'Do you want to go for a cup of coffee,' I asked her, 'or would you rather go for a beer?' We ended up going to a pub, a quiet place where I didn't normally go.

'What was the matter with you?' she said, referring to her coming to the site. 'I'm only your mother. What did you expect me to do? I've only come to see how you are, since we haven't heard from you at all in so long.'

I went up to the bar to get us some drinks, and when I walked back she said, 'You're too small to be a man anyway.' I knew it. She would have to say something about my condition, she couldn't leave it alone.

'What's height got to do with anything? I work with a guy that is much shorter than me.' I don't know why I bothered to answer. Again, I went through the motions of trying to explain to her how necessary it was for me to become a whole man.

'Sometimes I think you are doing all this just to upset us,' she said.

'You mean to say that you think I'm putting myself through all this just in order to upset you all?' I asked in disbelief.

She changed the subject. 'Well, I want you to know that we don't talk about you any more. Your name isn't even mentioned any more, ever. It's as if you don't exist.'

'That's your fault,' I snapped. 'But you're right, the person that you remember doesn't exist.' As usual the impact of her words didn't hit me right away; that came afterwards, after she had left. By the time her words had made their journey through my head, I was completely devastated by them. I felt bitter. I had never asked to be born. I had never asked to have a condition that made me feel so inadequate and so confused that many times I would gladly have ended my own life.

After we finished our drinks we parted company. I didn't feel like asking her back to the house. She had once gone to see Irena with her sister Kathleen while I was in prison, and there had been a difficult confrontation. My mother had insisted that she knew me better than anyone else and knew what was right for me. Irena had said, 'Listen, nobody knows him like I know him. I sleep with him, I eat with him, I live with him. I'm not having you come in here and shout about him like you are doing.' I didn't want to have to deal with comments about me said by my mother in front of anyone else, including Irena. So I said 'Ta-ra' to her. 'Take care of yourself and try not to worry about me, I'll be fine. Give my love to my sister, my grandmother and my father.'

After the course was finished I got a job with a builder. The job was only for six weeks, but it was a start. It was a small firm, and on the whole I managed quite well in spite of my limitations. The complex we were working on had a pub next door, so toilet facilities were not a problem.

I had turned twenty by this time and I was getting nearer the magic twenty-one when I was supposed to have stopped growing and when I was considered mature enough to consent to surgery. I kept writing letters to Dr Randall pleading with him: 'You've got to help me get an operation to remove the organs that shouldn't be there. I cannot live with this stuff inside me any longer.' I told him that to be able to work amongst other people, I simply had to have some of these things sorted out; it was just too uncomfortable and too risky for me to be out in the workforce as I was now.

He must have realized that it was becoming an urgent problem. Finally he sent me notice of an appointment and I went to London to see him. He could see my distress and desperation and was very sympathetic. He decided to refer me to the surgeon even though I was technically still not old enough. The surgeon was a nice enough man. He agreed to do the internal operation first.

It was some months short of my twenty-first birthday when I got word that the date had been set for my first operation, which was to take place in a couple of weeks. It was to have the 'foreign bodies' inside me removed.

One thing I couldn't handle was to be examined in those places that didn't belong to me. I had never ever allowed anyone to come near me in that way. In prison they checked all the women for disease, pregnancy or whatever, but I never allowed such an examination to take place on my body. When I presented myself for this surgery, it proved to be somewhat tricky. They wanted to take a swab to make sure I didn't have any infection.

'I don't have an infection,' I told them in no uncertain terms. I was simply not prepared to have anything examined, at least not while I was conscious. In fact, nothing or nobody had ever seen, touched or penetrated that area of my body. The surgeon could vouch for that.

I felt a tremendous amount of excitement and expectation about this operation. It was going to liberate me from bits of myself which were a constant discomfort and distress to me. Those organs were alien to me and I couldn't wait to be rid of them. I had not the slightest bit of apprehension about it.

While I was waiting on the operating table, the anaesthetist gave me an epidural injection which, he explained, is supposed to relieve the post-operative pain. It means putting a needle into the spine which numbs you from your feet up to your armpits for quite a number of hours. The anaesthetist then stuck a pin in various places of my body to ascertain that I was completely numb.

Unexpectedly, I started to shake violently. My teeth were chattering and I was shuddering from head to foot. I felt freezing cold. It was a strange sensation, and I felt embarrassed in front of all the nurses milling about, since I seemed to have lost control of my limbs. There was some difficulty in getting the drip into my arm for the general anaesthetic and I said something to the anaesthetist and he answered, 'Yes, yes, yes, no problem, start counting down from ten . . .' and finally, out I went.

Through a thin incision above my pubic hair they took out everything that didn't belong inside me. The morning after the operation I woke up, feeling alert and excited. I had a small room to myself with a toilet and bath. A lady brought me breakfast which I ate with a good appetite. Since there were no nurses around I decided to get out of bed. I had a bath, put my gown back on and slowly walked up the corridor to have a cigarette. When the nurses came to see to me, they were astonished that I had done all this by myself. On account of the epidural I felt no particular pain and I was high on the fact that finally I had been relieved of this burden.

The anaesthetist came to pay me a visit. 'Do you remember the last thing you said to me before going to sleep?' he asked me.

'No, I don't remember a thing,' I said.

'Well, you just gave me one hell of a look and said: "Am I going to go to fucking sleep or what?"' I was glad he wasn't offended and we had a good laugh about it.

The following day I was ready to go home, although I had been told I would be in for about ten days. It was important for me to see Dr Randall and to thank him for getting me in so quickly, but he would not be in until the following day. I decided to stay the extra day in order to see him and say goodbye. Irena had been staying in a bed and breakfast around the corner from the hospital and came to pick me up for the journey back home.

I was in hospital a total of two and a half days. The nurses instructed me about how to remove my own stitches, which I did at home after a week. But I was too smug about the whole thing. A few weeks later I was moving carpets and furniture in the house, and a friend called me outside to give his car a push. I was pushing the car and all of a sudden I felt a rush through my lower body; my legs just went and I collapsed on the road. I realized then that having had this operation, it was no good me running around flinging furniture and carpets about the place or pushing cars around town. Much as I didn't want to acknowledge that an operation also does harm to the body, I had to accept that I wasn't as strong as I thought I was. So I calmed down a bit.

Three months later I was referred by Dr Randall to another surgeon for a consultation regarding my chest. When I saw the surgeon, who also seemed nice enough, he took one look at my chest and said, 'There doesn't seem to be any need to operate.'

Hearing this, I ripped off my layers, including my elastic vest, to show him that there was indeed something that needed to be removed. He still wasn't convinced and he unbuttoned his shirt to show me his own chest.

'Look at mine,' he said. 'They are a lot bigger than yours. What are you worried about?'

'I know that my chest isn't the way it's supposed to be. That's why I wear all this,' I said, gesturing to all the garments I had just taken off. He could see that it was of utmost importance to me, so he agreed to go ahead with it.

This operation was quite painful. Even so, because of my youth and resilience, I felt quite fearless and was not daunted in the least. You'd swear I was off for a week's holiday.

Before going in for the anaesthetic I was looking through the newspaper and saw that a film I liked was on television that night.

'If I have come round by eight o'clock, could you please make sure I see this film?' I said to the nurses. As it happened I woke up at eight and managed to convince them that I should see the film. I was up till the early hours of the morning, playing cards and talking to other patients. I had two bottles draining blood from my chest, which I kept in my pyjama pockets. When I got my pain-killers and sleeping tablets that night, I got up and enjoyed the high, rather than go to sleep.

I was on such a high anyway. The day after the operation I got out a new pack of different coloured T-shirts that I had brought with me and it was a thrill to try them on. The idea of being able to be lightly dressed and feel cool filled me with relief and joy. Very soon after the operation that feeling disappeared. It was as if I had always looked and felt like I was now, as if I had become what I already was. It was like shedding an annoying and uncomfortable garment and being back in my own self.

I quickly forgot that I had had surgery, but not before I thought: 'If I feel like this after this bit of surgery, how much better I am going to feel after the next, and when it is all over . . .' The fantasy of it just filled me with such joy. I could put up with virtually anything to get there. I was well on the way to becoming the man I knew myself to be.

When I saw Dr Randall again after these two operations, he told me that there was nothing more he could do for me for the time being. They were experimenting with surgery, and I was on a waiting list until they had made more advances in this field.

All surgery that had been done in Britain so far had been experimental and a satisfactory way of fashioning the most important part of my malehood was not yet available. It had been done quite a number of times, usually in one single operation, but the failures were as common as the successes, and there were a number of ongoing risks involved.

I didn't care about any of that. I was willing to take any and every risk for the opportunity to be whole. I had been told many times of the risks, but it didn't stop me from asking again and again that they use me as a guinea-pig, that they experiment on me. I was open to anything they might want to try, so long as there was a fifty-fifty chance of success, and anyway I never quite believed that the risks applied to me. Without the necessary surgery I lacked self-expression and therefore had very little quality of life, and I didn't allow myself to contemplate failure and the effect this would have on me, at least not at this stage. I think I still believed that there was a magic miracle cure. Even if he couldn't do anything for me, I used to pray to God, asking for one single day as a whole man, and I would be grateful and not ask for more.

When I was that age, I was a lot braver about it all. I didn't care if I died on the operating table, so long as I died in the attempt to put things right. Without it I felt there was no future for me, so I had nothing to lose at all. If this could not be done, and if I didn't fall into such despair that I wanted to end my own life, I would certainly have become a recluse. The only way that I could have any relief, and not be constantly reminded of my condition, was if I was completely on my own. If I could have lived in my very own inner reality I might have survived without surgery.

After I had recovered sufficiently I did go back and do quite a bit of carpentry, working for a guy I had met casually while I was home between operations. Colin and I soon became very good friends. He was into buying houses, fixing them up and then selling them. He was also a plumber, and when he got work he would hire me as his mate. He invested in a Land Rover and, as luck would have it, there was a very heavy snowfall that winter and all the roads were blocked. Colin rang the council and asked whether they would like to hire his vehicle, since all of theirs were stuck in the depot. They were very glad to.

'Just a minute, me and "my boy" will come with the Land Rover.'

We made quite a bit of money for a few weeks working up to twenty-two hour shifts doing emergency plumbing jobs. Colin's wife took all the private calls. Whereas most private plumbers were charging £30 or £40 for an emergency call-out, Colin put £4 on to his normal £6, and charged £10. He was a decent sort of person; we had more work than we could handle, and a good laugh as well.

The quality of my life improved immeasurably after I recovered from the two operations. Even though it was winter and quite cold, the fact that there was no need for me to be bundled up in my straps and paraphernalia was a total joy. Indoors I could wear T-shirts if I wanted to, feeling completely relaxed and identifying at least with my upper body. Colin knew about my condition, probably from one of Irena's relatives. He had no prejudice against me at all, which made it easy for me to work with him. He understood my need for privacy and toilet cubicles with doors.

As I was living with Irena I had no choice but to participate in parenthood and I enjoyed it. Even though Carl was some other man's child, I was crazy about him. I had known him since he was a little baby. He used to sleep in the pit of my neck and cuddle up to me. I was the one who walked him around the block when he was teething. It was my finger he wanted to chew on. Women would come up to us in town and say, 'You can see whose boy he is,' or say to him, 'You're a real daddy's boy, aren't you?'

Sometimes he was sick all over me, as babies are, but it didn't bother me at all, and soon I got the hang of changing nappies. It was always me he came to if he wasn't well. When he got to be a toddler he followed me around everywhere. If I wanted to sit outside with my shirt off, then he wanted to take his shirt off too. If I was having a sandwich and a bottle of beer, he wanted a sandwich and a bottle of beer. I would do my press-ups on the floor with him lying on my back with his arms wrapped around my neck, or I would run on the spot holding him right out in front of me. Later I would hear pitter-patter, pitter-patter and I would sneak up to see what he was up to, and he would be running on the spot, holding his teddy bear out in the air.

My relationship with Carl reminded me of mine with my grandfather. I would take him to do the things that I had done when I was a child, such as spinning stones on the river bank and looking at things in the countryside. I would sit him on my shoulders and off we would go.

He never wondered why I was wearing my underpants when we were playing in the bath together. 'I'll stamp on your winkie,' he would threaten. 'No you won't, 'cos I'll stamp on yours.' I had such a lot of laughs with him and, with the innocence of a child, he never questioned me or was suspicious of my peculiarities.

I had never thought a lot about the fact that I would never have kids of my own. Having Carl playing on my lap got me thinking about children. Confronted with him, a real baby, I gradually started to feel a sense of loss. I would never be able to produce anybody in my own image, and this feeling began to be like a bereavement.

Before Carl came into my life, I had been in a process of disowning every part of myself. I selectively ignored the things that I felt didn't have anything to do with me. If children were ever mentioned I would think, 'Right, sure, but it's not my department.' Years before, Irena had discussed having children with me once or twice, but I didn't have anything to say on the subject and blanked out the whole issue. I said to her: 'Why get into it? Why even talk about it? I can't produce children, so let's drop it.'

I had already realized that it could well be an issue with every and any relationship in the future. I would never measure up or be quite enough for anyone, and I would always have sadness and regret over this inability. I sensed that the older I got, the more of a problem it would become. It magnified my feelings of inferiority and it made me feel very insecure about everything, my life, my relationships, my future. I tried to reason with myself: 'You're just going to have to face up to it, it is something that you will never be able to do.'

Irena didn't or couldn't understand what the problem was. She wanted to have more children, and her argument would be: 'What do you mean? What's the problem? I can have kids, why should your problem be our problem? There is a guy down the road, him and his wife have six kids, and none of them are his own. What is the matter with you?'

This compounded the difficult feelings that I already had to deal with, because now I was also responsible for depriving this woman of another child, which was her right as a person. Not only because I could not give her one, but because the way in which she proposed to do it was unacceptable to me. To ask me to accept her becoming pregnant by another man, and for me to bring that child up, was asking too much. To her it seemed to be perfectly natural.

Artificial insemination was a possibility that I would have found slightly more acceptable, but Irena wasn't interested in that sort of thing. She thought it was a ludicrous complication, when it was so easy to do it the normal way. And with her record of Borstal and drug abuse and me being a transsexual, she didn't think that we would make desirable candidates for the procedure on the NHS.

I felt, 'You either love me for me, and that is the end of that, and that's enough, or you go out and have your children by whomever you want. But leave me out of it.'

On some level, much as I loved Carl, I also knew that when the chips were down I would have no rights to him at all, as would be the case with any other child born within my relationship with Irena. My relationship with Carl – as father and son – was very tenuous, and that again made me feel extremely vulnerable. I would have wanted nothing more than to be secure in the fact that I could bring him up as my own. But at the end of the day I would be creating illusions for myself. Another thing that lurked at the back of my mind was the fact that on top of not being his genetic father, how would I explain to him when he got older who and what I really was?

I knew that if things were not right between Irena and me, Carl could not keep us together, and it was already evident that things were not going all that well. The issue about having more kids aggravated the situation further, and it was starting to feel as if the end was only a matter of time.

I found it difficult at times to stomach the sort of image that Irena wanted for us: a happy little family, conforming to all the petty rules about what a family should be and how it should behave. I'm not saying that she had changed drastically — she could still be quite bizarre herself — but underneath it all, she did want to conform to the dictates of society. I found it entirely false and was uncomfortable with the whole idea. I was already hostile to the idea of conforming in any way; it was the very thing that I had always had to fight against to maintain any semblance of inner identity.

This was another point which I was starting to resent about Irena. She had accepted me at first exactly the way I was, but now she wanted to slot me into her own concept of how I should be. My needs seemed less and less important to her. I think she basically loved me, but she was quite crafty and manipulative, whereas I could be quite gullible, and Carl was my weak point. It seemed that so long as I went along with her wishes, she was happy and agreeable, but these constraints and conditions were driving me away from her, both physically and emotionally.

We were still friends and I felt there was a lot of mutual loyalty between us; she would stand by me if I had any problems. Although we still had a sexual relationship, the passion had gone out of it. The separation while I was in prison had killed something between us which was never recaptured. I wasn't in love with her, and there was no point in pretending any differently.

We argued a lot about the past: how come she got pregnant, how come I went with Lorretta, and so on. We argued about Carl. I felt that she expected me to be there for him and bring him up but at the same time she did not offer me anything in return in terms of reassurance. I had no control, no rights over him. Perhaps it was my sense of inadequacy, but it felt like she

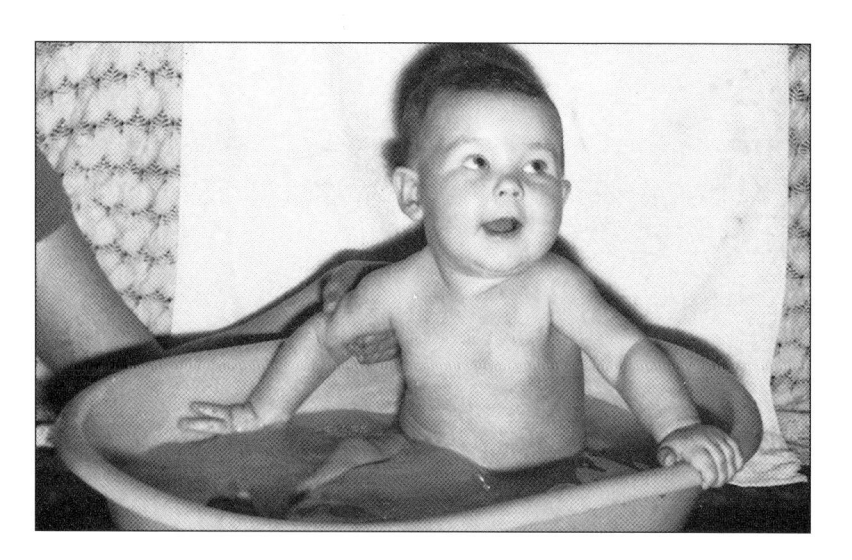

1. *(Above)* In the bath at about one year

2. *(Right)* On the swing, aged 2

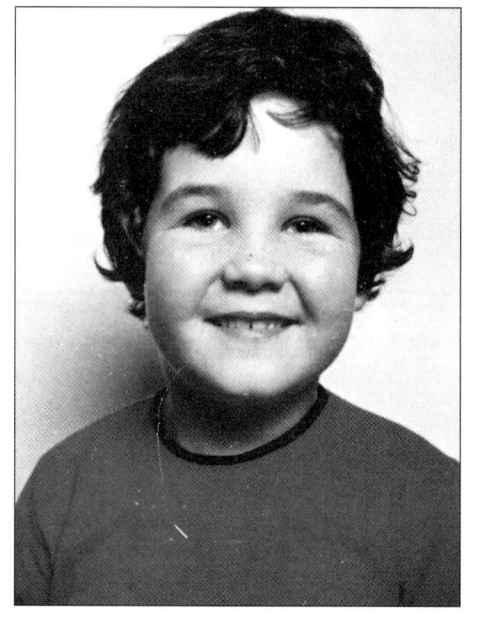

3. *(Top)* Outside at about four years old

4. *(Left)* Ray's grandfather, an enormously important figure in his early life

5. *(Above right)* Having successfully insisted on short hair, aged 6

6. *(Top)* Still pinning hopes on Father Christmas, aged 7

7. *(Right)* Rebel with a cause, aged 13

8. *(Below right)* At 16, a precious picture of early days with Lorretta (aged 21)

9. Ray, aged 19

10. *(Right)* Living alone, struggling to survive, aged 21

11. *(Below)* Ray, aged 23

12. On holiday before starting college, aged 24

13. At home, aged 25

14. (*Right*) Ray with Lorretta, at home, 1994

15. *(Below)* Ray and Kitty Sewell piecing together the story of his life

16. Ray and Lorretta, the end of a journey

was saying to me: 'Beggars can't be choosers, and be happy that you're allowed to be a stepfather.'

Cleo had a lot to answer for. She was always putting me down, reminding me that Carl was not my child and advising Irena to involve his 'real' father.

'What the hell am I doing here? Why am I still here?' I would think more and more frequently. I continued staying there out of my own free will, but at the same time it felt like living a lie. And through all this I couldn't stop myself from growing closer to the little boy, and it was too painful to contemplate life without him. I was being selfish, of course; it had a lot to do with my own needs.

During the years after moving to Newport I hadn't been fully able to let go of Lorretta and a few times I went to Cardiff to look for her. I didn't always find her, but when I did, she always greeted me with her beautiful smile and was really happy to see me. We were just so glad to be together, nothing else seemed to exist in those moments. We did what we always did: make the very most of our time together. Sometimes we made love, sometimes we went out and had fun, sometimes we just talked. She knew that Irena and I were having difficulties, but we didn't discuss it.

While all this was going on with Irena, I was making frequent trips to Cardiff to meet up with her. The same old attraction was as strong as ever. However, the feelings I had around the issue of children would creep into my thoughts in relation to her as well.

Lorretta's son Jamie was two years older than Carl, and I felt pretty certain that she too would want to have more children one day. 'What will I have to contend with, in order not to deprive this woman of her rights?' I thought. At the same time, knowing Lorretta, I thought she was less likely to put me in that position.

Four years had gone by since I had come out of prison and restarted my relationship with Irena. Now, the inevitable gathered momentum and came to a head.

There had obviously been some kind of plan of action on Irena's part. Cleo had thrown Alec, Irena's brother, out of her house and Irena had agreed that he could come to live with us. This was obviously in order to make room for Irena and Carl to move in with Cleo.

Irena left one day and went home to live with her mother but, after a few days, she changed her mind and sent a message to me via her brother Dave, asking me to come and fetch her back. I went over to Cleo's house to talk to her but we ended up in a heated argument. Irena decided this was a good time and place to tell me a few home truths and brought up my refusal to consider her having more children. Seeing that we were on the subject of truths I told her that I was still in love with Lorretta, and had been to Cardiff to see her on many occasions.

That was it. She changed her mind and wasn't coming home any more. Our relationship ended there, for good.

Alec came to live with me in Dave's house. I kept working with Colin whenever there was a job to do. We did everything, building doors and door frames from scratch, fitting skirting boards, damp-proofing, exterior and interior painting and decorating, et cetera. Dave would sometimes send me money to do a few jobs on the house. Alec worked on panel beating and spraying. He could occasionally borrow a car, and we would shoot off to various places. He wasn't supposed to borrow these cars, but we always made sure they were nice and clean when we took them back early the next morning.

Sometimes we went to Cardiff to see some old friends, and I would go looking for Lorretta. For a time I felt quite free.

After the stress of my break-up with Irena, this period was quite a fun and relaxing time for me. Alec and I worked during the day, and at night we would go for a couple of beers and have a few games of pool. We split the chores in the house. I did the cooking and he did the washing. I wanted to prepare Alec for the fact that there was another woman in my life. I told him, 'Wait till you meet Lorretta, she is beautiful and a lovely person, you'll see.' He wasn't too bothered by the fact that my life with his sister was over.

Lorretta started coming to stay for the odd weekend, and I fell in love with her again. Over the last four years I had often spent hours thinking about what we had together, the warmth and love that she gave me during those dreary months in prison. How many times I had berated myself for being so gutless and not having the courage to make a life with her as we had planned. Now I would have liked to give free rein to my feelings for her, but I tried to hold back. There were so many complications in my life and I was worried about dragging her into them.

Not long after I split up with Irena, I wrote her a letter asking her to let me continue seeing Carl. I emphasized how important this was for Carl, that it wasn't just for me. She agreed to it, and at first it worked, so long as it was entirely on her terms. I would go over to Cleo's house to collect him while Irena was off doing her own thing. Within a very short time she got pregnant. Sometimes I was allowed to take Carl to stay the weekend at the house, which was so much more fun and relaxing for both him and me. There was absolutely no other motive for my continuing association with Carl, except a purely emotional one. I loved him and I missed him and I wanted to see him. Irena saw in this situation a means of having some control over me.

After almost a year of living with Alec I asked Lorretta to come and live with me. I had tried to put some time between the end of my relationship with Irena before I tried to restore my relationship with Lorretta. I didn't want her to think that I had come for her just on the rebound. I had already upset her a lot and let her down. This time around I didn't want anything to go wrong.

Lorretta agreed to come. She loved me, that was obvious, but it was still a bit of a gamble and an upheaval for her and her young son. She managed to exchange her council house in Cardiff for a maisonette in Newport.

8
A Man with a Mission

Lorretta and I moved into the maisonette, and we started our life together. With hindsight, it was probably a mistake to ask Alec to come with us. I still felt a kind of responsibility towards him. We had lived together for a year and I didn't want him to think I was shunning him. From Lorretta's point of view, although she never said so, he was my link with Irena and her family. I was aware of this and stopped confiding in him about my feelings for Lorretta. His being there made it difficult for me and Lorretta to have any privacy; nevertheless the three of us did have a few laughs together, and most of the time it worked quite well.

I felt as passionately about Lorretta as ever, and it was obvious that she felt the same about me. I knew that what I got from her was one hundred per cent the truth. She was straight thinking and straight talking, there wasn't a devious bone in her body. And likewise I had no reason ever to lie to her. Lorretta was a very strong and capable woman, and a complete realist. At the same time there was also a childlike innocence about her which I found extremely attractive. Whereas Irena was quite materialistic, Lorretta had more of an inner depth and was in tune with her own feelings and emotions. Possessions and riches didn't mean much to her at all. In this we were similar. I liked the freedom that money brings, but actual possessions seemed meaningless in themselves.

The relationship Lorretta and I had was unique for me. There was friendship, understanding and acceptance and also a strong sexual passion. It was a purely instinctive ardour that came straight from the gut. Our sexual relationship was different from anything I had experienced before, or since. It was so intensely personal, just for us.

Everything about her turned me on. I thought she was

gorgeous. I loved the tone of her skin, which was golden brown, and the softness of it. I enjoyed watching her oil her skin after a bath. She was of medium height, but slim and well proportioned. I thought her lips the most perfect pair of lips I had ever seen. Her nose was beautifully sculpted, her eyes were hazel. She had a most unusual, exotic, tribal-looking face. It was a face that would be hard to forget, not just for me but for anyone. Her hair was short and she liked to wear a beret. She had several in different colours, and occasionally she put a spray of small silver stars into her hair if we were going out for the evening. She had her own style of dressing and would put unusual outfits together; they were always stunning.

For the first few months everything was wonderful between us. My continued relationship with Carl was the only small bone of contention. Not that Lorretta minded it at all, she handled my visits with Carl with a lot of maturity. But she knew as well as I did that the situation was heading nowhere. Although she was a strong and outspoken woman, in this situation all she could do was stand by and watch me get more distraught and more frustrated as my rights to be with Carl were gradually taken away from me. Rightly, she didn't feel it was her business to interfere, so she left me to it.

For a few months we did have some good times with the two boys together. Occasionally we would take them on an outing in my grey Volkswagen Beetle. We often took them rowing on a boating lake, to the park or to the cinema. A couple of times we all went out together, including Alec and his girlfriend. One particularly enjoyable outing was to a river to show the boys the salmon jumping as they swam upstream.

In the evenings we sometimes went to the beer garden at our neighbourhood pub. There was a playground there for Jamie to play in and we could have a drink whilst keeping an eye on him. Unfortunately Jamie was epileptic. Lorretta had to watch him continuously and he needed a lot of care and attention. I really admired the way she handled Jamie's fits. She had a totally calm approach. I would get panic-stricken, but she would effortlessly do the necessary things to make him comfortable. Because Jamie was only six years old and needed to get his sleep, most evenings we stayed in and listened to music. I enjoyed watching films on television, but Lorretta was more of a reader and it was hard to get her away from a good book. She always read newspapers and magazines from cover to cover.

'I like to stay informed,' she explained. I wasn't much of a reader at this time in my life, but we both shared a real passion for black-and-white suspense films from the thirties.

Lorretta had started to experiment with cooking, not having done much in the past, and really enjoyed baking cakes and pastries. And I loved eating them, as did Alec and Jamie. Because Alec and I were out all day working, she didn't mind cooking us an evening meal and she got quite good at it after a while.

I had not seen my parents for ages and decided to phone them to let them know that I had moved and was living with another woman. They were, in fact, coming to Newport within days to apply for passports to go away on holiday. We agreed to meet in town and when we did I invited them to come home with me. It was an awkward affair. We hadn't seen each other in a very long time. Jamie had a toy pistol, quite a realistic one. It was lying on top of one of the speakers above the stereo system. My father spotted the pistol when he sat down and, thinking it was real, he said to me:

'Jesus, you haven't got a gun now, have you?'

I explained and we both had a good laugh, which broke the ice a little bit.

Lorretta was very sensitive to the situation. She offered them a cup of tea which they didn't accept because they claimed to be in a hurry, then she went out and sat in the kitchen to leave us to talk. I was glad that my parents seemed to be getting on with their lives. Hearing that they were going on holiday (instead of being on nerve tablets) made me happy for them. We didn't have a hell of a lot to say to one another, but I wished them a really good trip, and they gave me a few quid, which I appreciated. We said 'Ta-ra' and it was to be another long stretch of time before I saw my parents again.

In love as we were, Lorretta and I were gradually running into difficulties. Part of the problem was that I was so involved in my relationship with Carl, or the lack of it, I found it impossible to form a bond with Jamie. Much as she understood it, it was quite hurtful for Lorretta to see this. She was often left on her own while I was off seeing Carl. Newport wasn't her home town and she didn't know anyone. How I wish I had been more sensitive to her needs at the time. I was too wrapped up in disentangling myself from the immediate past, and it soon became apparent I wasn't really ready for the responsibility of a new relationship.

I was out working with Colin most days, which left Lorretta on her own with Jamie. When I was home, Alec or other friends were around, which meant that we had very little privacy.

Lorretta and I didn't communicate very well verbally, but there was an innate understanding and sensitivity between us. It was that same feeling I had had about her the very first time I met her, years earlier. That feeling of already knowing her, of being able to sense her thoughts and feelings and she, mine. In the privacy of our bedroom we tended to communicate more on the physical plane, and if we had a moment alone in the house during the day we couldn't keep our hands off each other. We also laughed a lot together, about everything and nothing. We shared the same sense of humour and knew how to have fun together. As long as we had each other we felt we didn't need anyone else. Still, it would have helped if we had talked over what was happening at the time and our feelings about it, but we couldn't see any solutions, and there were too many conflicting emotions, hers and mine, to make any sense out of it. So we avoided these important issues. The responsibilities and the hassles of the real world seemed too complicated, and we didn't want to know.

Also, some of Irena's family enjoyed trying to cause trouble between us. They would hint to Lorretta that my visits with Carl weren't all that innocent. I walked in through the door once, being late coming home from Irena's house, and overheard Alec saying to Lorretta, 'He'll be in no hurry coming back from *her* house.' My feelings towards Alec changed considerably after this. I took the incident very seriously. I lost trust in the people I thought I could trust. It couldn't have been easy for Lorretta either, not knowing exactly what was going on when I went to Cleo's house. Predictably it was putting a strain on our relationship.

In fact, I hardly ever saw Irena; she was out and going wild, doing her own thing, and Carl was looked after by Cleo. It seemed Carl had not only lost me, but he wasn't seeing all that much of his mother either. He used to be very upset at the end of my visits and when I dropped him off he would stand in the driveway crying and screaming, 'I want *you* . . . I want *you*,' not wanting me to go. I hated leaving him there crying and many times I'd drive around the roundabout and go back for him.

'It's a pity that he should be left crying here with you, when his mother isn't home,' I'd say to Cleo and offer to take him out for the rest of the day. Once I had words with Irena when I caught her at home. 'You shouldn't be leaving him with your mother all the time. He needs you.' Her response was that it was none of my business. I heard that Irena had contacted Carl's natural father, and that he had met his son, but Carl's feelings for me were unaffected. More than ever, Irena was using my commitment and my affection for Carl to exert power and control over the situation, letting me see Carl only when she was in the right mood for it. I sensed she was punishing me for having brought Lorretta to live with me.

The situation was affecting Carl as much as me. As Irena was gradually withdrawing my right of access to Carl, Lorretta had to put up with my grief and my anger about it. I ranted and raved, and she got the brunt of it. She always tried to calm me down and put things into perspective. Her ability to reason things out logically would quickly make me realize that I was overreacting. My emotions often clouded my sense of judgement and Lorretta was very good for me in this way. Having said this, we still refused to talk about it in terms of its effect on our relationship. We colluded in never raising the issue and spoiling the mood between us, if we could help it.

All this was quite wearying for Lorretta. Not only did she have me to contend with, but also she had Irena and Carl thrown into the bargain, and her son as well. In her own mind she must have wondered how she fitted into my life. She tried to tell me what she saw was happening. She said, 'You either have to go back and be with Irena or you have to sever the links with Carl completely.' Being a mother herself, her appraisal of it all was very perceptive. Although I did listen, whenever I saw Carl I was thrown back into the same emotional turmoil.

'That woman is being really cruel to you,' Lorretta would say, exasperated. 'Can't you see what she is doing to you and what you are doing to yourself? *Why* do you let her go on doing it?' She would be really blunt with me: 'You're not Carl's natural father. Why are you holding on to this situation when you know it isn't good for you any more?' She was at the end of her tether, and I myself felt completely drained.

The situation was nearing an end. I felt I couldn't take much more of it. I was starting to realize that I wasn't able to cope with all the different aspects of my life. At the same time Lorretta was coming to the conclusion that she would have to let me get on and sort my life out, and that I didn't need the complications of a relationship.

'You're a man with a mission,' she said, knowing there were things about me which I had to set right before I would be any good to anyone, and she didn't know how to help me any further. Alongside all the other problems that were happening around us, Lorretta knew that I was struggling as much as ever with my dislike and alienation from my own physical form. Although I had had some surgery, for which I was very grateful, I still could not rest in myself. Even love-making with Lorretta was starting to frustrate me, which was the one thing that had always been extra special. There had never been any sexual inhibition between us, but somehow my inadequacy about not being able to father children started to affect me sexually. Every time I thought of sex, I thought of children. Every time I thought of children I thought of this ugly, fragmented body of mine, and its inability to father. Lorretta felt my anger and my frustration. I was much more aggressive and forceful when we made love, and she said a few times that she felt as if she'd been physically assaulted. It wasn't a reproach but I could hear the concern in her voice. I couldn't explain my behaviour, I just looked at her as I always did when I couldn't express myself. At this point I think she needed to really talk about what was happening to me, but I couldn't talk and kept believing that she understood.

I became much more agitated and restless with each day, and withdrew into myself. Dr Popper had been right: it was getting harder and harder to live with myself with each day. My responsibility towards Lorretta was weighing very heavily on me. If I couldn't cope with my body and the grief at gradually losing my association with Carl, how could I be stable enough to give Lorretta and Jamie the depth of commitment I wanted to give?

One day, almost a year after we moved in together, I couldn't take the pressures of my life any more. I packed all my belongings into the car and left. Our separation was badly handled. It was not as a result of any argument or disagreement; Lorretta and I never had it out with each other or said goodbye or anything – I just walked out. Lorretta stood in the kitchen window looking at me putting my stuff into the car. She looked completely blank. I couldn't believe myself that I was leaving her, but I was driven by a grim sense of fate. God, how I wished I hadn't caused all this turmoil in her life. Will she hate me for this? Will she ever be able to forgive me? I couldn't bring myself to look up at her, even though I knew she was standing there in the window. I drove away in my Beetle, which was full of bin-liners, feeling totally empty. My emotions had drained away and I felt completely flat.

I slept in the back of a friend's work van for a couple of weeks, and dossed on people's floors. I walked up and down the streets, knocking on doors, asking if I could rent a room. At the bottom of a dead-end street there was an empty house. It seemed just right for me. The woman in the house next door gave me the name and address of the owner. I found him in the garden of a massive house. He was certainly wealthy enough to let a property sit empty and rot.

'Please can I rent it, even if it is just a room?' I pleaded with him. No, he didn't want to, he was hoping for the housing association to buy it from him.

'Oh, come on, I could keep an eye on the place.' I was desperate to live in this house. There was something attractive about being on my own. 'Surely you wouldn't turn away a bit of rent?' Finally he relented and rented me a tiny room at the back of the house.

My old Beetle was falling apart, and I couldn't afford to spend the money it needed to be put right. I sold it and bought a small motorbike. This should have been a special moment for me, getting the bike that I had always wanted as a boy, but in my present frame of mind, all it represented was cheap transport.

I felt very depressed and desperate, but I kept working with Colin. I missed Lorretta and I knew I would go back for her one day. But that could not happen until everything in my life had been sorted out: all the surgery that I needed and everything else that caused me internal stress. If I ever went looking for her again, I would have to know what I was doing, and be really committed to her. Until this was possible I felt I had to stay away from her. Whether or not I had managed to explain this to her, I knew she understood me. Trying to see her would just rake up the wounds for both of us.

In the years to come I thought about her frequently and realized what I had lost: the potential depth of the physical, emotional and spiritual bond between us. She has always been on my mind and I think I was unfaithful to every woman I was with, thinking about Lorretta. I have never felt so passionately about another woman. One day I was going to be ready, and then I would go in search of her.

In the meantime, I had to resolve, once and for all, my physical condition. My frantic dislike of my body and the painful rejection of myself, plus my longing to find my real identity as a man have had peaks and troughs throughout my life, but they have never left me alone for a minute.

I confided to Colin how low I was, and how I felt I couldn't go on much longer unless there was some hope for me of getting out of this body, and fully becoming a man. Not long before this Dr Popper died. I had kept him on as my doctor when I moved to Newport. We had communicated by letters and he kept sending me my prescriptions for hormone tablets. When I heard that he had died I was very sorry. He had been supportive to me and accepting of me as a person, and he was obviously a dedicated doctor; sometimes I had walked past his surgery late in the evenings, and the light was still on in his window.

I had signed on with a doctor in Newport a few months earlier, and got my prescriptions from him for a couple of months. One day I received a letter from him, asking me to go and see him. He had not been sent my records yet.

His manner was blunt: 'Unless you tell me why you are on these hormones, I am going to stop giving them to you.'

I didn't like his approach, and was on my guard.

'I'm not prepared to tell you.'

'Why not?' he asked.

'I don't trust you.'

'For God's sake, what am I doing as your doctor if you don't trust me?'

'You have no right to stop my prescriptions. They are prescribed from Charing Cross Hospital, and if you want to know anything about me, you'll have to contact them.'

He didn't like my attitude, that was obvious. He insisted that I should tell him.

'It is too personal,' I said. 'I don't feel comfortable talking to you about it.'

I didn't feel he was someone I could learn to relax with and trust, but he continued to supply me with prescriptions for about a year.

I explained this situation to Colin, and how I desperately needed to talk to someone who would know something, anything, about my condition and what was happening around the world in terms of surgery or treatment. Colin and his wife tried to help me. They got me an appointment with a doctor they knew.

'He is very open-minded and easy to talk to,' Colin reassured me, but I was anxious about meeting the man and talking about my condition. At the same time I couldn't afford to turn away any offer of help, so I asked Colin to break the ice and explain to Dr Merritt my position before I went to see him. Even so, I was very tense when I saw Dr Merritt. He sat me down and asked me to tell him a little bit about myself. All the anxiety, the unhappiness and desperation welled up in me all at once and I burst into tears. I sat there and cried and cried and cried in front of this man, a total stranger. He let me continue for a while and then said that he could see it was difficult for me to talk about my distress. It was true; I had spoken sketchily to some people about my condition, but I had never ever sat down and told anyone exactly how it felt.

I explained in the best way I could about the constant emotional turmoil I was experiencing. I told him how restricted I felt; how my condition was preventing me from getting on with my life; how I needed an end to it all; and how alienated I felt from myself and my whole body. He was very understanding but said he didn't know anything at all about the condition that I had described and that he'd never had another patient like me.

'I'll do all I can to obtain the information you require,' he told me. 'First I'll write to the Medical Research Council. They meet every six months to share and discuss new developments and new surgical techniques in medicine, and maybe they'll be able to provide some information.' He said he would ask them to let him know if any operation such as the one I needed was being performed anywhere at all, privately or otherwise. He told me regretfully that this was as far as his help could go. At least now there was something, however meagre, for me to wait and hope for.

My link with Carl had not yet been completely severed. One night when I was babysitting Carl at Cleo's house, a friend of Irena's stayed behind to keep me company. Carl was in bed and we were alone in the house. We had a drink or two, and one thing led to another. When Irena came home she caught us asleep on the sofa, in a rather compromising position. She went berserk. Although Irena and I were no longer in any kind of a relationship she felt it was a betrayal and threw me out, saying I was no longer allowed to see Carl.

A few weeks later she softened. She phoned me up one day and told me I could see Carl if I wanted to. The further her pregnancy progressed the more help she needed with Carl, and I was still useful as a babysitter. It was evident that if I had accepted Irena's second baby as my own she would have taken me back. But I wasn't that stupid: I knew all too well the position and the rights I had as a stepfather to her child.

As it happened, I was present at the birth of Irena's second son. Our friendship was going through a slightly better phase, and I was in her house when her labour started. I and two friends of hers took her to the hospital. I wanted to see the baby's birth and, since she didn't want to go through the birth alone, she asked me to stay with her.

Cleo was furious with me for not having phoned her quickly enough. We had all tried to ring her but she was out. She gave me hell when I saw her, but by this time I had had a gutful of her attitude and told her where to go. She didn't like it and a couple of days later I had a run-in with her again. Irena had just come home from hospital, and I was helping look after Carl. Cleo let me know yet again that I was allowed in their house only for their convenience, and Irena was too cocky about what she imagined was her control over me. She never got it into her head that I was only there because of my love for Carl and my need to spend time with him. It had nothing to do with her. I had had my nose rubbed in this once too often by both of them. This time I lost my temper. I opened the back door and started throwing bottles out where they smashed on to the patio. I ranted and raved at both of them, shouting at Irena, 'The way you are carrying on, you're going to grow old and ugly like your fucking mother!' (I didn't mean it – she wasn't ugly – but in the heat of the moment anything goes.) Cleo didn't take very kindly to this and ran to the kitchen and grabbed a carving knife out of the drawer and ran at me with it. Irena jumped between us to stop her mother. Then Irena went for me as well. It was an almighty commotion. Carl was crying and Cleo was shouting, 'Get Neil, get Frank' (these were two of Irena's brothers whom she used to sort out 'trouble'). When Neil came to her assistance things had cooled down a bit and in the midst of all the shouting I just walked out of the house.

Now I had to face up to the facts; it was obvious that my relationship with Carl could no longer continue. A couple of days after the confrontation at Cleo's I was passing their house on my motorbike. Alec spotted me and waved me down to have a chat. All of a sudden I thought I heard Carl's voice. He had seen me and ran across the road to me. The two of us were able to have a few moments together on the green across the road.

When he was younger I used to ask Carl, 'Who loves you, baby?' and he would answer, 'You do and Mum does.'

'Who loves you, baby?' I asked him now, sitting there on the green. He looked at me blankly.

'I don't know,' he said, and shrugged his shoulders.

'Look, Carl,' I said, 'if I never come to see you again, it is not because I don't love you, because I really do love you. It is because your mother and I don't get on, and that is the only reason I have to stay away.'

'Everything will be all right,' he pleaded with me, 'it'll be all right as long as you don't smash any more bottles.'

I felt gutted. I wanted to explain to Carl about the possibility that he might not be seeing me in the future, but I couldn't bring myself to do it properly, and he didn't want to know. My only consolation was that he was young and would get over his loss quite quickly. For me, it would take much longer.

I never saw him again, that is until I saw him in a Newport pub thirteen years later, having a pint with one of his friends. Alec pointed him out to me. He was a tall, strapping lad, not much like the kid that I had been so crazy about.

I kept working with Colin, but while I was pinning my hopes on some kind of positive news from Dr Merritt, I stopped socializing or meeting people altogether. If there was electricity where we were working, I would often continue working till late at night. My depression was gathering momentum and, apart from working with Colin, I started spending longer and longer periods of time without leaving my room. For the first time in my life I suffered severe insomnia. I was often awake all through the night. Sometimes my predicament and my condition didn't leave my mind for days and nights on end, coupled with grief about Lorretta and Carl. Soon even this sense of loss faded. Nothing seemed to matter much.

I had been waiting and hoping to get a letter from Dr Randall with the miraculous news that they were now in a position to do the surgery, but the letter never came. I frequently contacted Dr Merritt, my only life-line, and finally he had some news for me. I was phoning him from a house I was working on with Colin, constructing some French windows.

'I'm sorry to say there is nothing that anyone can do for you at the moment, anywhere in this country,' were Dr Merritt's words. 'There is only one doctor who might possibly consider doing the surgery, but he wants £10,000 on the table before he will even discuss it, and he says that if he did perform the surgery there is a very good chance of gangrene and paralysis from the waist down.'

I barely heard him out. I put the phone down and just left everything without a word to Colin, and went to my room. My last hopes had been dashed. I could never find that sort of money, and the thought of those risks . . .

I hit the worst depression I have ever experienced. It may even have been a nervous breakdown. I stayed in my bedsit and never surfaced at all. I didn't want to go on since there seemed to be no possibility of being able to live with myself. Without hope, I could see no future. I didn't think I had anything to offer anyone, myself or the world. The more I thought about the little I had to offer, the worse I felt about myself and everything about me. Children were on my mind, and the fact that I could never father any of my own. My self-esteem had gone completely and with it my will to live. I just stayed in my bed. Why should I get up only to face the misery of my life?

In my youth I used to feel embarrassed and vulnerable if I ever cried in front of anyone and thought it was a sign of weakness, but then I found out that crying was good for you, and that the tears of sadness are chemically different to the tears of laughter and that they actually help release the pain and the build-up of stress. That changed my feelings about crying and I could cry for hours, sometimes eight hours at a stretch. My whole body and my insides used to ache; I thought my heart would collapse on me. It was all down to grieving, grieving for the boy inside me. But by this stage and with the state I was in, crying only compounded the feeling of helplessness and frustration and instead I wanted to slash my face or punch myself to bits.

Thoughts about life after death, and whether or not I believed in it, occupied my mind. I did believe in a spiritual dimension, because I felt I lived in it most of the time. I felt as if I were inside this body looking out through the holes of the eyes; this was my only contact with the world.

'Maybe it's better for me to go now,' I thought. 'Maybe my spirit has a better chance in another life.'

I didn't really want to die, all I wanted was to be able to live, but my condition was preventing me from living my life with confidence and pride. I felt completely stripped of any confidence that I had gained in my youth. When I left home at fifteen, I learned to cope by not caring, by being reckless and detaching myself from people's opinion of me. I had more ability to bounce back from difficulties, in spite of my physical and emotional limitations. As I could never have a break from myself, I gradually lost that ability, and my predicament loomed large in my mind, no matter what I was doing. I always felt gutted by it, but now all my resources had gone.

Mixed with these thoughts and regrets were more irrational feelings, even delusions. I wanted to find my place as the Red Indian that I imagined myself to be. I have always seen them as being very spiritual people with a profound understanding and appreciation of the earth. They didn't take anything from the land that they didn't need and they used everything they obtained from the land to full advantage. Their way of seeing the world has appealed to me ever since I was a young boy. I liked the simplicity of their lives; it was also what I saw in my grandfather. He liked the simple things in life, such as observing flowers and walking in the countryside.

I dreamed of the day when I could live like that, riding horses bareback and living off the land. Of course I was influenced by the old cowboy and Indian films I saw as a child, but the message that I absorbed was that the Indians were the ones who knew what life was all about. They seemed to have such a lot of freedom, whereas the white men in their uniforms were the ones conforming, blowing trumpets and all marching in order.

During battles, I was always struck by the contrast of the Indians riding wild, coming in packs, just going for it, each and every one an individual and yet in solidarity with each other. There the white men were, all in line and obeying every command: 'Aim! Fire! Step back! Next!'

My childhood and adolescent dreams of living in the wild were unrealistic, but I didn't want to live in this world as it was and in this body as it was. If I were to survive at all, I would have to live away from materialism and the constraints and pressures of society.

Even that seemed unlikely to save me now. I was in the grips of physical and spiritual torture. I felt I could no longer keep insanity at bay. I needed to be out of my body, to be free. It felt as if my 'inner body' was forcing itself to the ends of my limbs. It was growing ever larger inside of me, making me feel I was bursting at the seams and wanting out ... out ... *out!*

Because this was impossible, this process would abruptly reverse and I would start to shrink inside myself. My whole inner body shrank until I became very small inside. It was as if I became so small I had to find some safe place to hide inside myself. My tiny inner body was in unfamiliar surroundings, in a place it didn't belong and I felt utterly unsafe. I became like a little shadow inside my physical body, a shadow running around everywhere trying to find somewhere to hide. Inside I was screaming, 'Get me out of here!' At the same time my heart ached and ached and ached.

This became a cycle. The fear, and feeling of being unsafe inside my body created a state of anxiety which in turn made me want to burst out of my body. Because that wasn't possible, I would start shrinking again. It was as if, because I couldn't live in my body, I was trying to kill myself off. My spirit couldn't take any more. It was broken.

Lying on my bed I was also brooding a lot about the state of the world and our destruction of the planet, my thoughts getting darker and darker. I thought about the way in which certain tribes of Indians used to end their lives when they no longer felt useful or fit enough to partake in life properly. It was perfectly normal for them to go away and wait for death somewhere on a mountain, not eating or drinking anything in order to facilitate their bodies leaving the earthly dimension. They willed themselves to die. It was a natural and painless process, since they knew that their spirit would live on after the death of the body.

The idea appealed to me. This is what I had to do. I felt it was becoming a matter of urgency. My spirit was being smashed, and if I were ever to have another life I would have to give my spirit a fighting chance and remove it from this place before it was too late. I would be taking it to a place where it could live and be free. The process seemed natural and quite easy. I was in such a state of depression that lying on my bed without getting up for anything was no hardship at all. I decided to wait until I expired.

A few days passed; I'm not sure how many. A couple of times I heard Colin knocking on the door and calling my name, but I ignored him. The third time he came he gave the door a hard shove and it gave way. He sat by my bed talking for a long time. I vaguely remember him saying something about another guy who had been through a depression and didn't want to get out of bed, and how lucky I was that there were people who cared. Failing to get any response from me, he listed all the reasons why I should want to live. I pricked up my ears: for every reason that I should live, I had a logical objection why I shouldn't. The more he numbered, the more objections I found, and the more convinced I became that I was doing the right thing. I kept it all to myself and didn't say a word, except for a few grunts to the negative. Finally he left. His visit hadn't made me feel any different.

I was weak and listless but my determination stopped me from eating or drinking anything. Occasionally I swilled my mouth with water to get rid of the discomfort and dryness. My lips were cracking from dehydration but I didn't mind. Something was happening to my face. Every time I touched it, my hand got wet. I was pretty certain that it wasn't tears, but I couldn't be bothered to get up to look in a mirror.

A couple of days or so passed, and early one evening the door opened and in walked my mother, my uncle and my cousin Patrick.

'What the fuck do you lot want?' I asked.

'We've come to take you back home with us for a while,' my uncle said.

'Look, do you think this is the only time in my fucking life that I've felt like this?' I said sarcastically. 'I didn't need you then and I don't fucking need you now.'

In spite of my bitter words, through the layers of despair and hopelessness, there was a feeble ray of light at the end of my very dark tunnel. These people were my family, and a small part of me was thinking that maybe I could get up, and maybe I could go with them and get to know them all over again.

'You simply must come with us,' my mother insisted and, finally, I was too weak to argue. I badly needed a shower so I got out of bed and on shaky legs made my way to the little shower room down the corridor. There was a small mirror on the wall. I caught sight of my face and was shocked by what I saw. My face was pale and gaunt and covered in weeping blisters. That explained the wetness I had felt on my face. My lips were cracked. There was a big ugly red patch on my face where weeks earlier I had tried to scrub out a tattoo with a scrubbing brush and salt. I had been losing weight steadily over the last ten months, since leaving Lorretta, but now I was positively emaciated.

It was the first time that my internal stress had shown on the outside. Usually I was stressed out like hell, but I looked as if there was nothing wrong with me. People often said to me, 'You're looking good', when inside I felt like dying.

Later I found out that Colin had been in touch with Dr Merritt and then Irena, who phoned my parents.

'If you feel anything for Raymond at all, come and see him now,' was all she said to them.

It was very strange to be back in my home town and in my parents' house.

'I don't know you at all, and you don't know me. I feel like a total stranger,' I said to my parents on that first day. 'For all you know I could have murdered someone around the corner, and you wouldn't be the wiser.'

'It feels a bit strange for us as well,' my father said to me, 'but we are your mother and father, after all, and we do care about you.'

After a couple of days of being in my parents' house I started noticing that my mother was locking the doors securely, both front and back. My parents never used to keep the doors locked during the day, and relatives and friends felt free to wander in whenever they wanted to.

'Why are you locking the doors?' I said, although I knew perfectly well why.

'I don't want anyone to just walk in and see you,' she said. Perhaps she meant my ravaged face, but more likely it was my male appearance. Whatever it was, it brought back all my anger and resentment towards my mother.

'Of course, I forgot you've got a fucking monster in the house.'

One morning, within days of my coming home, my mother got my old GP to come for a house call. She wanted him to give me a mental assessment, but she didn't want me to go to the clinic to see him there. No doubt she had her reasons. I didn't know anything about it and was lying on the sofa in my jeans and a T-shirt with a blanket over me, when he walked in with my mother.

'I just brought the doctor here,' said my mother, 'to have a look at you and to see that you are all right.'

I remembered him vaguely from my childhood, so even though I was surprised to see him there, I sat up and greeted him. I tried to explain to him what was wrong with me: I had gone through a difficult time and the only thing that was going to help me was to have the surgery that, as a man, I needed. My mother kept interfering and referring to me as 'she'. Suddenly I leapt up from the sofa in a rage.

'Between locking the doors around me, and now referring to me as "that", why didn't you just leave me to die where I was?' I screamed at her.

I started to rip my clothes off. My mother was shouting at the doctor: 'Do you see what I mean? There is definitely something wrong with her.' I was half undressed.

'Look at me!' I screamed. 'Look at me, for fuck's sake! Just look at me. Do I look like what you are referring to me as?'

The bewildered doctor tried to calm my mother down.

'He is only asking you to look at him, he is only trying to make his point.' He took her aside. 'There is nothing wrong with him mentally, he is perfectly sane and intelligent and he knows exactly what is wrong with him.' I think my mother felt slightly better after the 'consultation'.

I felt very strongly that I needed to hang on to my pride and all the things I had achieved after leaving my home town so many years ago. But it wasn't easy. Between my mother's feelings about me, and all the other things that reminded me of my past, I barely felt better than I had back in my room in Newport, where at least I had a goal in mind. It was obvious that I wasn't going to be staying there for long, but for the moment it gave me a chance to recover my strength and my bearings.

My sister, Anna, whom I hadn't had any contact with since she was a child, was trying in her own way to get to know me a bit and asked me questions about myself. We had not met or spoken for at least eight years, and at first it was very strange for her to relate to me as a brother. She wanted to know what had been happening to me over the years, and I in turn wanted to explain to her why I had never come back home. We never had a proper chance to talk about it all. My mother wouldn't let us and tried to shut us up: 'We don't want to talk about things like that now.'

'She wants to know,' I retorted. 'You've kept telling me how I have ruined my sister's life, now at least let her have some understanding about who I am and what I have been going through.'

As it was, Anna hadn't been allowed to know anything or understand anything because I had been a taboo subject, not to be spoken about. If my mother had known something about my condition and understood it, she might have been able to hold her head high and say, 'Yes, my son is a transsexual, and so bloody what!' and perhaps all the gossip and speculation would never have had the power that it did. Part of the reason for the silence and secrecy that my mother created was to protect me. Also, she had nothing to retaliate with if confronted. She didn't want to hear anyone voice an opinion about me. I was her child, after all. Nevertheless, I'm sure that it was the secrecy about me and my whereabouts, which my mother insisted on maintaining, that caused most of the problems for my family.

To get out of the house, I took up my cousin Patrick's invitation and went over to his house to meet his wife and my two nephews. He came to get me, and when we walked down to his house I told him a bit about what I had been going through, and how I needed surgery but didn't have the money for a private operation. He listened to my story without making any comment. Then he said about his two boys, 'From now on, they'll know you as Uncle Ray, and nothing else, OK?' I thanked him for that. It was such a contrast from my mother's house!

I really enjoyed the afternoon with Patrick and his family, and our conversation turned out to have profound consequences. He asked me, 'Since you can't have the surgery you need just now, why don't you do something that you would really enjoy, something that could help you get on with your life?'

'The only thing that I can remember enjoying is drawing,' I said, after some thought. It was the first time that thoughts of my artistic talent had entered my head for a long, long time.

'But I can't do anything with it, can I? I have no O levels.'

'Don't be so sure,' Patrick said. He had been a fitter in the steel works, but changed direction and went back to college and became an art teacher. 'I had only three O levels. You can do it too,' he said encouragingly, and offered to look into it for me.

We talked about it for a long time, and when I went back to my parents' house that evening, it was as if a seed had been sown in my mind; Patrick had really given me something to think about. I felt inspired and uplifted by the idea, although I was sceptical that any college would ever consider me. Something so different could, perhaps, change the direction of my groundless and disorientated life.

When I went home that evening, my parents brought my paternal grandmother to see me. I hadn't seen her since I was a child and didn't know her at all. She was very warm and affectionate towards me, and said how she looked forward to getting to know me all over again.

The next day I went back to Newport, back to my room. I felt differently though. The sores on my face had dried up and were now scabs, I was skin and bones, but inside me something had shifted. I went back to work with Colin and reconnected with some of my friends.

The Wednesday after going back to Newport I had a letter from my mother, to tell me that my grandmother, whom I had just met, had died suddenly of a stroke. It shocked me and, at first, I was worried that it had something to do with seeing me. One moment she was alive and telling me how much she was looking forward to getting to know me, the next thing I knew she was dead. I did cry for her, and for the lost opportunity of getting to know her. Within a few days I went back to attend her funeral. The church where the service was held brought back memories. Walking through the graveyard I recognized the nooks and crannies where, as a child, I had looked for grass snakes. I also remembered the many Palm Sundays my father and I came to lay flowers on my grandfather's grave. Now my grandmother was there to be buried with her husband. I met some of my father's brothers and sisters, who told me that I would be welcome in their homes at any time. I didn't know them very well, but I appreciated their kind offers.

Patrick had told me that I would need to have a portfolio of drawings if I wanted to get into art college without any O levels. The more drawings I could present the better chance I would have. I started to draw furiously. When I wasn't working with Colin, I was in my room, not to ruminate on my condition, but to produce drawing after drawing and I really enjoyed it. I was constantly on the look-out for old books with topics to inspire my drawings. The first drawing I did was of Odin, the father of the gods. Odin went to see Mimir, the old giant who guarded the fountain of wisdom. Odin wanted to drink from the fountain but Mimir said to him, 'Whosoever drinks from this fountain must be willing to give much in return.' Odin gave his eye.

I had just read the story in an old encyclopaedia and it had made an impact on me. It made me think about the wisdom contained in my life and experiences. Maybe my future had to be earned in some way. The words of the priest in prison came back to me: perhaps it wasn't my time yet, and all things happen when you are ready for them. Maybe I should concentrate on the future that was within my grasp, and try to be patient about the one which wasn't. In any event, it seemed I had no choice. I also thought about my anger at God, for having deprived me of my very essence as a human being. I had forgotten that he had given me something, my talent and creativity. Becoming educated in something I was good at and enjoyed could not fail to open doors for me, give me more choices and bring more quality into my life. Even though I was still emotionally fragile and I didn't really socialize with anyone, the future didn't look so black any more. Patrick had reminded me about the talent I had shown as a child. 'You were much better at drawing than me,' he said, 'and I got through art college. There is no reason why you shouldn't.'

I also knew I could be good at other things. I used to feel such an affinity to nature and animals, surely in some capacity I could do some good for the environment? I knew that given a chance I could be totally devoted, and that it would give me great pleasure to contribute constructively. It had been a while since there had been any room in my soul for anything natural and beautiful, the things that I used to love: nature, animals, the elements, the sea. I started to notice these things around me again. It definitely meant that I was getting better and coming out of the blackness.

I became quite obsessed with my drawing, to the point where I would get up in the middle of the night to work on some detail that I couldn't get out of my head. The next thing I knew, it would be six o'clock in the morning. I didn't mind this kind of insomnia. I was creating something and it gave me a good feeling.

After a few weeks, working with Colin during the day and

drawing at night, I started to feel there was less and less reason for me to stay in Newport. Also, in spite of the difficulties I had with my mother, it seemed important that I connected with my family and got to know them better. I felt the need to explain myself to them and for them to accept me. After having been a stand-in parent to Carl, I had a bit more compassion and understanding of what it meant to have children, and to lose those children. You feel powerless and victimized and unable to do anything at all. I suppose my parents must have felt like it to some extent where I was concerned.

I started to make some trips back to my home town, just to get a feeling for it, and to see whether I could consider coming back. On the one hand, these visits reminded me of so many painful incidents and so much shame and humiliation, but on the other, I could see that there were people there who wanted to help me, who cared about me. I visited my parents occasionally and gradually we began to feel more comfortable with each other.

I found Anna hard to get to know, she seemed so self-contained, but I'm sure she thought exactly the same about me. We were quite awkward around each other at first, although I didn't sense any animosity from her, just shyness. Only once do I remember her making a cutting remark when my mother and I were in one of our heated discussions.

'You're too much like him, you are,' she said, referring to my father. 'You're too loud and aggressive.'

'My father is not aggressive,' I replied, a bit taken aback. 'We just have deep voices and sound more aggressive than we mean to.'

She used to stick around to listen to my discussions with my parents, although she didn't often join in. Only occasionally would she ask me questions, like: 'Why did you keep getting into trouble and getting arrested? How did you suppose this would help your condition?' Her questions were valid enough, and I was glad for a chance to explain myself to her.

During one of these discussions between the four of us, my mother spoke on behalf of Anna.

'The thing is, Joe,' – most people that knew me from the past still called me Joe – 'it's been very difficult for your sister. Since none of us have spoken about you since you left home, Anna's friends and boyfriend know nothing about you.' I knew what she was getting at and stopped her in her tracks to make it easy for her.

'Don't worry, I understand,' I said, turning to Anna. 'If I ever see you out with your friends I won't approach you or speak to you.'

Anna had trained as a data processor just as my mother had done years earlier. She had also worked as a personal assistant within the same company where she now worked. She had been with this company since she had left school. Anna was a very private person; in this, at least, we were similar.

For quite a few months my mother felt uncomfortable speaking about anything to do with my past, except my childhood. It was around this time that my father and I had the conversations about the giant turtle, and about our differences regarding the cowboys and Indians. Although it was fun to reminisce about these things, it was also frustrating not being able to talk about the things that really mattered. A few times my father and I broached the subject of my time in prison or my operations.

'We don't want any of that now,' my mother would insist. 'Don't talk about that now, leave it alone.' My father and I would look at each other in exasperation. He knew I needed to talk, but my mother was the most powerful of us and her word was law. Even when she was in another room, she would object to us talking. My father and I have very similar voices, very deep and intense, and we both found it difficult to tone them down.

'Enough about that now,' she would call. 'That's all over now, it's all gone.' Or else, 'The both of you sound like a pair of foghorns. Stop that now.' Alternatively she would come in and perfunctorily shut the doors to 'block out the din'.

I didn't let my mother get away with it: 'You can't shut us up. My father is asking me a question and I want to answer it.' I would get quite worked up. 'You have brought me back here, and now you don't want me to say nothing to no one. You're living in dread that I'm going to cause you embarrassment because you're still totally preoccupied with the fucking neighbours.'

I felt quite bitter and if she tried to shut me up I would retaliate by reminding her of some of the things she had said about me over the years. There were many reasons to be bitter as far as I was concerned.

'I know only too well about the stress and unhappiness I have caused you and the whole family, you've reminded me about it every time we have spoken since I left ten years ago. How distressed you are about me, how you can't hold your head up in the street, and how my name cannot be mentioned, et cetera. I know I'm your very own private nightmare.

'But think about me,' I would say to her. 'Not only have I had to live with my condition which has caused me more unhappiness and distress than you could ever imagine, but also I've had to carry the burden of your shame and disgust too. Have you ever wondered what it feels like for me?'

When I felt more composed I often tried to reason with her, and ask her not to try and stop me from talking about myself.

'Can't you see that my past and all the experiences I've ever had amount to the person I am today? This is the person you can sit and talk to (if you would allow it), which is something we were never able to do before.' We were both equally touchy and found it difficult to talk sensibly and rationally. My mother has a quick wit but I automatically took the wrong way anything at all she said to me or about me.

'Well, we all know what you think of me, don't we, Ma?' I would respond sarcastically. 'I belong in a circus, where people can sit and laugh at me.' Maybe she had forgotten some of the things she had said to me over the years, and being reminded of them must have saddened her. Sometimes my mother would slip up and refer to me as 'she' and I would go into an instant rage.

'Don't you understand what you're fucking doing to me, the distress you're causing me, saying things like that?' I would shout at her. 'You're not happy with your weight. How would you like it if I constantly reminded you of how fat you're getting. You'd be feeling the pits in no time.'

'All right, all right,' she would shout back. 'It's not easy for us either. You haven't been around for years. I'm doing my best.' Angry as I was, I also understood how hurtful and distressing some of these things were to her. I wasn't oblivious to what she had been through on my account. I really wanted and needed my parents' understanding. I wanted them to relate to me as a person, not just put up with me because I was their flesh and blood and because they felt they had to. I knew that my parents had blamed themselves and each other for having created a child in the 'wrong body', but I tried to explain to them that my condition was not their fault, that it had nothing to do with them. I tried to tell them what specialists had told me, that as parents they had done nothing wrong. These things just happen sometimes.

Gradually, we were able to speak about it more, and I think my mother was beginning to take some of it on board and understand my predicament.

During these visits to my parents, Patrick came to see me so that I could show him my drawings. 'They are excellent,' he told me enthusiastically. 'Why don't you consider applying to do an art course?'

'Yes, I was going to apply in Newport, but I am thinking of moving back here.' He was very encouraging about me coming back and promised he would look into art courses in the area.

On one of these trips I stayed for a couple of days and met up with a few friends from my teenage years. We went out for a few drinks and I felt quite comfortable in their company. I set off on my bike on the long journey to Newport that evening, having had a few beers too many. I thought I had sobered up enough. There was no traffic on the motorway and it was windy and raining heavily. I felt awake and alert. I was only five minutes away from my bedsit, when all of a sudden there was a police car after me, and they pulled me over.

I was arrested for being over the limit and taken to the police station. It was the same police station where I had suffered a lot of humiliation about five years earlier, after being arrested at the jeweller's with the stolen credit card. I felt very uneasy about this place and didn't want to give them my name in case they had it on record or remembered me. One of the police officers threw me against the wall and said, 'You better give me your fucking name, or else.' His aggression immediately put me on the defensive, and I kept my mouth shut.

'You might as well give me your name, I'll find out anyway in the morning when I check the registration of your bike.'

'Then you'll have to do that, won't you?' I said.

'What's the matter with you?' he shouted. 'For fuck's sake, sign your name on this paper.' But I wouldn't.

'Right, you are going to give me a urine sample.'

'No, I won't.'

'You have two choices, you have to give a urine sample or a blood sample, take your pick.'

Finally I relented. Giving a urine sample felt too threatening. I didn't know how and where this would take place, so I consented to giving a blood sample. A doctor was called to come and take the blood sample. I had a hell of a shock when I saw him. He was the same doctor who had forced me to strip and bend over with all the coppers present. I had a flash-back of that scene and it brought on sheer panic. I reacted out of blind fear and went berserk.

'Get me out of this fucking room, you bastards!' I shouted.

'What the fuck's the matter with you?' the copper screamed back. 'Are you off your fucking head?'

I refused to let the doctor or anyone else near me, so the copper just pushed me down some stairs into a detention room.

I calmed down after a while and took off my heavy army coat that I always wore for riding the bike. I wrapped the coat around my head to block out the light and went to sleep. The next thing I knew, someone came into the cell and ripped my boots off my feet and my coat from around my head.

'Take them, for fuck's sake,' I said. 'If you want them that badly, just take them. Where do you think I'm going anyway? I don't need them.' They just left them outside the door.

In the morning they found out my name, but they had no choice but to let me out at this point, having kept me overnight.

I was getting my possessions back from the desk, and the guy sitting behind it said, 'Wait a minute, I am just going to check that there are no outstanding charges against you, or that you are out on bail.' He got on the phone. 'I've got a Raymond Thompson here. Any warrants out for him? . . . No? . . . There isn't . . . OK.' He listened a few seconds and all of a sudden his expression changed and he looked up at me. A smile spread all over his face.

'Put your hands on the top of the table,' he ordered, smugly. There was no mistaking the scars of my tattoo removals, my most distinguishing marks.

'Well, well, well,' he said slowly. 'Haven't you got something to tell me?'

'I've got fuck all to tell you,' I said, 'and one more word comes out of your mouth about anything to do with me, I'll have my solicitor up here to deal with it.'

My belongings were already on the desk. 'Take your stuff and go,' he said with a grin on his face. I was just grateful that they had not been in possession of the facts the night before and that the doctor had not recognized me. I vowed to do my best not to act so recklessly again – I was old enough to know better. Six months later I had to go to court and I paid the price for my stupidity. I lost my licence for fifteen months.

A couple of weeks later I rode the bike back to my home town again. I stayed with the barmaid who used to put me up when I was in trouble as a kid. I told her I was thinking of moving back to the area, and she told me of a friend of hers who had a flat in the city, ten miles away. The flat was about to be vacated and the owner was looking for a new tenant. She got on the phone immediately, and the owner said that if I wanted to rent it, I had to make up my mind right away since there was someone else interested in it. I hadn't wanted to make a decision quite so hastily, but we drove to the city to have a look at the place. It was a furnished one-bedroom flat. It was fine, and I stood in the middle of the lounge, hesitating. Should I or shouldn't I? Patrick had told me that there were a couple of colleges offering art courses nearby, and the location of the flat was excellent. The landlord was arriving within an hour, and I had to make up my mind.

I thought about my resolution years ago, that I was never

coming back here to live, not ever. I had seen some of my old friends, and although it had been good to see them, what were they going to be like in the long run? Where was I going? I was divided between hope for a new beginning, and a vague foreboding about going back to the past and all that it held.

The landlord arrived while I was still in the middle of this quandary. I had to make an instant decision. The flat was nice, central, cheap.

'Right, I'll take it,' I told him apprehensively, and handed him all the money I had in the world, which amounted to one month's rent. I phoned my mother immediately to give her the news. She was pretty shocked. She didn't even know I was in town. I had some idea of the sort of thoughts that must have been going through her mind, but she must have been relieved that I had rented a flat away from my home town. Still, I was near enough, perhaps too near for comfort. I asked her how she would feel about helping me move. I had very few belongings, only my clothes and some books.

I got a lift back to Newport to collect my stuff and to say goodbye to my friends. A few days later, when I was ready, my mother came to pick me up.

'You won't be getting into any trouble, I hope,' she said to me as we were driving down the motorway.

'I haven't been in any trouble with the police for years, I have been working,' I reminded her, omitting to mention my driving offence.

'When I come back to live near you, you've got to agree to leave me alone, to just be,' I said to her. 'Why don't you try to accept who and what I am, because I'm your flesh and blood and in that sense I will never go away.

'I don't want you advising me about the right and the wrong things to do. This is my life and I want to be responsible for my own actions. I don't want anyone telling me at the end of the day, if anything goes wrong, "I told you so". I want my actions to be my actions, and my mistakes to be my mistakes.'

'My God, that was a mouthful,' my mother blurted out spontaneously, and we both laughed. 'OK, fair enough,' she said at last. 'If that's how you want it.'

In my own mind I was determined to stay out of any kind of trouble. I had already been in the press once, and that was something I could not afford to let happen again in my home town. Not just for the sake of my family, but for my own self-confidence and peace of mind.

9
Tolerating Ignorance

I moved into my flat with my few possessions. My life so far had been mostly aimless, living from day to day, carrying the sadness and hopelessness of my predicament. Now it took on a new perspective. The crimes I had committed and my time in prison had faded from my memory and I had gradually changed. This move was yet another turning point in my life. I wanted different things for myself; I wanted peace and quiet; I wanted to be creative; I wanted to have freedom of choice, to be able to travel and visit other countries; I wanted to do my bit for nature and the environment. But I needed to build up confidence in all areas of my life in order to be able to create my own environment. My mind was opened to everything I had shut out and shut off; there was a whole world of new experiences and I was ready to learn. I was drawing anything I could lay my hands on. I hardly saw a soul.

The first few weeks in my new home were a time of confronting the new as well as the old. The new opportunities and possibilities presenting themselves were very exciting, but stepping back into my past was daunting. I knew it was there, but I had put that past behind me completely. In recent years I had been accepted as the man I was, and I was not prepared for the inevitable curiosity of the people that remembered me from my childhood and adolescence. Over the next few years I was to be confronted with this inquisitiveness time and time again. People enjoy gossiping and the subject of my condition was something new for them to get their teeth into. I was going to have to learn to cope with this intrusion if I was going to be able to live with my past.

I still felt withdrawn after my breakdown and found it difficult to settle. I missed my friends in Newport and for the first few months I went there quite often on my bike to stay with them. I always had a good welcome, whomever I stayed with. There was always a hot bath and a meal for me if I wanted it. There was no need to talk or explain anything. I could just be myself and say nothing, if that was how I felt. Although I was stimulated intellectually by my new interests, I felt emotionally drained. To the outside world I smiled, laughed and joked, but I did it without knowing why, without feeling anything.

After I was rescued from my room in Newport a lot about me changed. I moved and walked differently. I slowed down and I didn't trust my instincts as I had before. My spontaneity had gone. I felt more vulnerable and alienated within my body than ever before, and here I was, contemplating a whole new future. Much as I wanted it, my confidence often faltered and I honestly didn't know how I was going to pull it off.

My mother came to see me in my flat one day. During our conversation she told me that their whole house needed decorating inside and out. With the skills I already had, I was in a position to help them. I offered to do it for her, knowing it would save them a few quid. Also, I knew it would do me good to try and involve myself in some physical work to give me back some confidence in my abilities. I painted the entire outside of their house, most of the inside and did a few repairs, such as replacing a ceiling above a bay window and the kitchen ceiling. It gave me great satisfaction to be able to help them out with this and the weather was glorious for the duration. My mother always cooked me a meal before I went back to my flat and insisted on paying me a bit for the job.

'I would have to pay someone else to do it, so I prefer to pay you to do it so that you can have some money for yourself to get out and about.'

She was always telling me to get out and about, probably worrying that I might shut myself in again. The state I had been in when she found me in Newport had shocked her greatly. I wasn't interested in getting out and about, but I met up with a guy called Alan whom I had known vaguely when I was young. I spotted him painting the outside of a house in town and we recognized each other. We got together and soon we became good mates. He needed accommodation and I found him a flat down the road from me. In return he tried to get me the odd job painting and decorating with him.

One day my mother drove to the city to see me.

'I've got a message from Patrick,' she told me. 'You are to go for an interview at the art college tomorrow at three o'clock, and ask for Paul Cook.' This was it. I got all my drawings together and tried to prepare myself mentally for the interview.

'Look, I'm really interested in art,' I told Mr Cook. 'I've got no O levels, but would you take a look at my drawings?' I took my drawings out of my cardboard folder and he looked at them for some time.

'Have you ever done anything with clay?' he asked me.

What I didn't know until that moment was that the course I was applying for was an HND diploma course in industrial ceramics.

'I am going to offer you a place on the course, on the strength of your drawing ability,' Mr Cook told me, and although I didn't know exactly what I was letting myself in for I wanted to accept his offer there and then. He took me round the college and showed me the kilns and work that other students had done. I was impressed. The idea of turning a two-dimensional drawing into a three-dimensional object, from start to finish seemed very exciting to me. Mr Cook told me that the course involved silk screen printing, hand building pottery, drawing, mould making, design and business studies. He then told me about all the options there would be once I qualified. I could work in industry, or as a studio potter, or keep entirely to design work and never touch clay. My mind took off in all directions. I could start a business of my own, work for myself in the privacy of my own home. I accepted the offer of a place on the course and felt very excited about it all.

I went straight down to the dole office where Alan was painting to tell him all about it. He grabbed hold of me and was equally excited. 'See, I knew it,' he said. 'You're an artist, not a painter and decorator.' He was really pleased for me, and that night we went out and got steaming drunk.

Next, I had to apply for my grant, but here I ran into difficulties. It seemed I wasn't meant to go to college. When I applied I had to put down what jobs I had had for the last ten years. Well, I couldn't account properly enough for the last ten years, and I didn't want to divulge my prison terms.

'All we can offer you is £480,' said the man behind the desk.

I was confused. '£480 – for what length of time?'

'Oh, for the year,' he answered.

'For the year?' I said, incredulous. 'My rent is £20 a week. How can I live on £480 a year?'

The man got quite stroppy. 'Well, that is all we can offer you.' My heart sank and I stormed out.

A couple of days later when I had cooled down, I went back and asked to see someone else. Another, more reasonable, official came and talked to me.

'Look,' he said, 'if you write a letter stating exactly how you have spent the last ten years, I'll see what I can do. With the new regulations coming into force, it is quite possible that you may get a full college grant regardless of what you've been doing.'

So this is what I did. I put down Borstal and prison and everything else in this letter and brought it back. Then I waited and waited and didn't hear anything. So I went back again. A young guy sat me down in front of a desk, while he stood up beside it.

'What's happening with my grant application?' I asked him.

He smiled. 'The thing is, you can't have a grant.' Just like that.

'What do you mean?'

'You can't have one.'

I lost my rag. This was one of those times in my life when my aggression was of no help to me at all. My grant meant so much to me, and so little to him, I just couldn't help myself and I was insulted and incensed by his arrogance. He wouldn't even sit down to give me a reasonable explanation, so I got up and sat on his table and said, 'I refuse to leave here until I see someone in authority.'

The man from my previous visit was coming around the corner. He must have recognized my voice, because he said, 'Mr Thompson, is it? Come on now,' he then said, 'get off my table.'

'I'll get off your table when you sit down on the same level as me and tell me why I can't have my college grant.'

'Yes, of course,' he said, 'I'll sit down with you, Mr Thompson. I'm afraid you can't have the grant, you don't qualify.'

A combination of rage, disbelief and disappointment flooded through me and I banged my fist on the table.

'I want my letter back!' I shouted, referring to my disclosures about my past.

'I refuse to speak to you like this. Go out and cool down a bit and then we can talk about your letter,' he said coldly.

'No, what I want to say I want to say now.' I was beyond being reasonable. 'You pay me £52 a week to sit on my fucking arse and do nothing, and you won't give me the same amount of money to go to college. I can't get a job unless I go to college, and you're telling me that I can't go to college unless I get a job.'

'We don't pay you, it's the government,' he argued.

'Come off it, the money all comes from the same place, doesn't it? What the government is telling me is that they would prefer me to sit on my arse all week rather than give me the money to better myself. Now, I want that fucking letter back. There is no reason why you should have a personal document about me on your files, since you're not giving me the grant.'

He slammed my folder shut. 'You can't have it. The letter is college property now.'

'I want the fucking letter,' I insisted.

'You can have a photocopy,' he said, and sent the young guy off to copy it.

I had calmed down a bit, and I didn't want to give up. This meant too much to me now.

'Look, I'm not satisfied. I want to see the director, or whoever is in charge. I also want the original letter back.'

'Listen here,' said the man, 'you just can't come in here demanding to see the director.'

'What have I got to do to see him, then?'

'You've got to write a letter asking for an appointment.'

'Don't tell me – more bits of fucking paper.' I snatched the photocopy from the desk and ripped it into tiny pieces.

'Here you go, here is what I think of your fucking bits of paper.' I tossed the paper into the air and walked out of there. A friend was waiting for me outside. He said it looked like I came out in a flurry of snowflakes.

My performance didn't get me anywhere, but I didn't think it would anyway. I was not going to get the grant, and that was all there was to it. I was gutted by it all. It had never occurred to me that I wasn't going to get a grant. Everybody else seemed to get one, and Mr Cook seemed to assume that I would too.

My parents also must have been disappointed because, the next thing I knew, my father offered to subsidize me. It was a very nice gesture, but I didn't want his money and I didn't like the idea of being beholden to them. It was the compensation money for his lost fingers, but I knew my mother had that money earmarked for a few things, including an extension on the house with a new kitchen.

I had not come through my life by the normal route, I had been down a different road, and I realized that getting back into education was not easy for someone like me. It was purely on account of my father having lost his fingers that the opportunity to make something out of my life became a possibility. I was deeply grateful for the chance but at the same time I doubted my ability to go through four years of college. I was fearful enough of letting myself down but, since it was my father's money, I would be letting him down as well. I explained to him that my concentration was poor and I still wasn't sleeping well.

'What if you're wasting your money? I'm not sure I can go through with it, much as I want to,' I said to him. He tried to reassure me.

'Don't fret about it. You can only do your best. It's only the interest on the money I got, so don't worry so much. It's going to be yours one day anyway so you might as well have some of it now that you really need it.'

My father insisted that I should accept his help, claiming it would make him very happy to be able to do this for me. I'm sure the college course was the best piece of news my parents had had about me, ever. I saw no other way of realizing the future in which I had put so much store and built up so much hope. It was now or never, so in the end I accepted my father's offer. I did live to regret it a few times: if my mother and I argued, she would call me ungrateful and say, 'Do you realize how much we are giving up for you?'

Gradually I had been seeing more of old friends from my past. One of them introduced me to a young woman named Katie. I got on with her although I was not in the least interested in forming any sort of relationship with a woman. I couldn't be bothered with the idea of going through with all the explaining I would have to do about my condition. Katie was living with her parents in my home town. Her main interest was a horse she owned, and she had a job in Tesco. She was very straight, in fact, apart from liking the occasional joint. We would go for a drink sometimes and she would come to my flat for a smoke. It turned out that she did know about my condition. I was more interested when I found this out, since it cut out all the tedious explanations I would have to put myself through.

One evening she came with me to my flat, and we were both quite high. She was adamant that she didn't want to go home that night, even though she was concerned about not having fed her horse. It was OK by me that she stayed the night; I didn't think anything of it. We were lying on the sofa together when suddenly, at about midnight, there was a terrific banging on my door. It was her parents.

'We know you're in there,' they shouted. Katie begged me not to open the door.

'I've got to open the door,' I said to her. 'They're worried about you. I can't just not open the door.'

Katie flung her clothes on in a hurry. She was stuffing her bra into her handbag just as I was opening the door. Her mother came charging into the flat like a bull and gave Katie a good whack on the head with her umbrella, calling her a 'little slut'. Her father walked in after and just stood there glaring at me. I was looking at the table because there, for all to see, was the dope.

'Hey, come on. Nothing's going on here,' I lied. 'She is all right.'

They dragged Katie out of the door while she shouted, 'Phone me! Phone me!'

'Don't you bother,' said her mother menacingly. 'I don't want you phoning my daughter.'

'Yes, yes, phone me!' Katie shouted as she was being dragged out by the scruff of her neck.

After Lorretta, it was difficult for me to feel very much for a woman. On the whole I was quite cool about Katie, but she was a nice girl and a fun friend and we became lovers. Soon I made peace with her parents too.

Katie and I had been out to a friend's house, having a few drinks. I was miles away from my flat so, in my drunken state, I went home with Katie and ended up sleeping in the spare room. When I woke up the next morning and found myself in her parents' house I felt very awkward and embarrassed. Dinner was cooking, and I had no choice but to come down the stairs and join the family for Sunday dinner. It was the first time that I had met them since the incident at my flat and I was worried about their reaction. I knew they didn't like it that their daughter was involved with me, but as the meal progressed I think they warmed to me.

Katie didn't want to offend her parents by moving straight in with me, so she first moved in with a couple of girlfriends from work. Sometimes I stayed with her there, and sometimes she stayed with me in the flat.

'I hope you are not telling her to leave her parents,' said my mother, probably thinking I was exerting a corrupting influence on her. Soon enough she moved into the flat with me. I hadn't ever meant it to happen, but then I don't have a very good record of controlling these things.

While I was waiting to start college, my parents were going on a fortnight's holiday, and to my surprise they offered to take me along and pay for me. They were going to Mallorca.

'You don't have to stay in the same hotel as us,' my mother offered graciously, knowing how I valued my privacy. I was very grateful for the offer, although I felt a bit guilty about my parents paying for me. There didn't seem to be any reason why they should. They saw it differently. I had had no Christmas or birthday presents for years and years, and had never cost them a penny since I had gone to Borstal at the age of fifteen. I think they also felt that a break would do me good, seeing that I was about to start a four-year college course. Katie had just moved in with me, but I had no choice but to leave her behind.

I really enjoyed the holiday. It was the first time I had been abroad and the change of environment did make me relax. It was great to be in a place where absolutely no one knew anything about me. I didn't see all that much of my parents, but we did get together a few times for meals and excursions and we met most days on the beach for a few hours. It was an opportunity to get to know them a little. At the same time, I enjoyed being on my own, although almost right away I got to know an Irish couple. I was sitting in a bar having a drink and they came up to chat to me. They soon wanted to fix me up with a girl they knew, but I wasn't into having a holiday fling. The girl came along anyway, a loud, rowdy sort of person. In the end, she insisted on coming with me to my hotel room. I was so drunk by this stage I didn't care. In my room she made herself comfortable with a bottle, while I went to have a shower to cool down from the tremendous heat.

I was standing in the bathroom with a towel wrapped around me, about to put my shorts on, when the woman burst in and roared, 'C'mon, whassa matter with you?' and sprang forward to rip the towel from around my waist.

'Out!' I shouted. 'What do you think you're doing? Out!'

She ended up staying the night, but nothing happened between us. Drunk as we both were, I could see that she found me a strange kind of guy.

I did enjoy the time I spent with my parents too. We went to a large night club that had a flamenco dancing show and acrobats. We also visited the famous caves of Drach. I was intrigued by the fact that Jules Verne got the inspiration for his book *Journey to the Centre of the Earth* from these caves. The whole experience of going down into these caves with a large underground river took me back to my childhood fascination with wanting to find places to hide. If there had been a cave like this back home, I would have disappeared into it and never been seen again.

After three days I met a couple, a black guy and a white girl sitting in a bar by the beach. They seemed likely to know where I could get hold of a bit of blow. Finding a smoke would make the holiday complete. I caught a whiff of it in the air and decided to ask them. No problem, they called the barman over who sold me a stick for 2,000 pesetas. I stayed for a few drinks, and the barman kept leaving me joints in the ashtray. I got zapped. I went to that bar every day and every day I ordered the same meal: hot dogs, salad and chips, and my face would not leave the plate. My appetite was definitely coming back. The barman would laugh at my intense enjoyment of his food and shout over the bar that I would make a great advertisement for his place.

It was incredibly liberating to be able to swim in the ocean and feel relaxed about it. It was different from going to a swimming pool at home, where I would feel conspicuous and self-conscious about my body – the whole thing was too much to contemplate. Here I didn't mind so much and nobody knew me. I hadn't had a swim in ages and it felt great.

I came home on a Friday from Mallorca, and my course was to start on the Monday. Between feeling elated and being very excited about it, there was also plenty of apprehension. Would I be able to keep it up? Was it going to be like school which I used to hate so much? Would I be able to discipline myself enough? It turned out to be quite different from what I had expected. There was freedom to get on with what you were doing, and I really started to enjoy it.

In the first year we had to do a lot of objective drawing. It meant going out into the streets or on to the beach or out into the countryside to draw. We also had quite a bit of work to do in our own homes, experimenting with drawing and painting. One day a week we had a live model to practise drawing the human form, and another two days a week we spent at another college to learn printing and hand building pottery.

I started to put some of the painful past few months behind me, and my confidence started to grow. I began to feel as if I was involved in the process of my self-development once again, not just being pulled along, dragging myself through life.

Carl was still in my heart and I thought about him often. I sent him a card for his birthday with some money for him to buy himself something. Soon after I got a sarcastic letter from Irena telling me that she now had two children (didn't I know it?) and if I was going to send birthday cards to one, I should do the same to the other. That was it. If I didn't know it before, I knew now that I had to accept the loss and see the experience for what it was. Carl was just a little boy I had helped to bring up for four and a half years, and that was the extent of it. Once I had come to terms with the loss, I was very glad that I had been able to experience seeing a child grow and develop, and glad for the emotional involvement with him. I never again felt the same level of pain and inadequacy about not being able to have children. After making a resolution not to put myself in that position ever again, I put the whole issue right out of my mind.

I didn't see much of my parents while I lived in the city. Sometimes my mother used to pick up some fish and chips and bring them to me at the flat. She never actually used to come up but would pull up and park her car and call me down. We still didn't know each other all that well and I think she didn't want to interrupt me in case I had any friends over.

'Your choice of friends leaves a lot to be desired,' she used to say to me, but then she also said, jokingly, that I left a lot to be desired. I started to take my mother's comments much less seriously. She has such a dry, wicked sense of humour, that I came to realize I wasn't the only one who got the sharp end of her tongue. I had started to get to know my parents as people and I enjoyed seeing my mother at these times. Sometimes she brought my grandmother along, to give her a day out to the seaside.

Money was tight living on the small allowance that my father had given me, but I had gone back and accepted the £480 offered to me as a grant. I soon found a few other ways of adding to my income. One was to photocopy drawings I had done. My mother knew someone who made frames cheaply and I sold the framed photocopies for a reasonable profit. A drawing of Bob Marley was particularly successful. I also had some success painting a large spliff on rush beach mats and selling them to friends and acquaintances. It was a time-consuming job, but I made quite a few of them. Later on I had a job washing dishes in a restaurant a couple of nights a week.

At college I mingled with and talked to most of the other students. There were a couple that were around my own age but most of them were younger than me. Our projects inspired lots of conversation and interaction between us and sent my imagination in all directions. I felt very excited by the design process and was fired up with enthusiasm. The whole process fascinated me, from the preliminary research through to the finished articles. We learned to make moulds to produce tableware, bakeware, tiles, sculptures, everything to do with ceramics and printing. I would go out and talk to people in the streets or in shops and ask them why they thought certain articles were not being sold in the shops, and if I were to make such and such a thing, would they be interested in buying it. I was always asking questions. I noticed myself becoming more articulate. Learning to express myself through my intellect was probably my way of compensating for the lack of identification I had with my body. I was asserting myself better and felt more at ease communicating with all kinds of different people.

For the first two years nobody knew about my past and treated me like any other man. A couple of the students became good friends, in particular one called Stewart. We had got to know each other within the first week of starting college, and we worked very well together. Since I lived near the college we would often go back to my flat at lunch time and talk about our hopes and aspirations and why we had come to college. After a few of these intense conversations Stewart and I started plans of going into business together as soon as we had finished our diploma.

Happy as I was about the work, I wasn't used to discipline as such. I had not worked for a long period of time anywhere. The only real discipline I'd had was being locked up in prison, and it's a different discipline to one where people choose to be and work together.

I didn't lack the willingness to work hard, but my ability to communicate with teachers wasn't exactly developed. I was so used to being on the defensive, and also to saying what I felt without being diplomatic. It was such a long time since I had been in school, and the idea of trying to impress or even be liked by teachers was something that had never been my thing, to put it mildly. I soon found that I was more direct and outspoken than my fellow students. Sometimes that worked for me (as when I was elected student representative in the third year) and at others it worked against me. The natural tone of my voice has always been strong and loud, and was sometimes misunderstood.

At this level of education you're expected to get on with it on your own, without much assistance, which was OK by me but, at the same time, one or two of the teachers seemed to think that learning was entirely up to us and that they had little need to teach us. One of them was particularly difficult to get along with. I found her impatience and sarcasm hard to ignore. Soon I had a showdown with her. She had been giving another student stick for not being careful with the expensive materials we were using. It had nothing to do with me, except that she was always trying to make us worry about the materials and about not wasting things. I was there to learn as much as I could and this woman seemed to begrudge us any information. Through her lack of explaining things to us, materials inevitably got wasted. We needed the practice and I was irritated by the way she loomed in the background, waiting for us to make mistakes.

'What the hell are you doing?' she snapped at my mate.

'What the hell do you expect him to do?' I snapped back on his behalf. 'I get the impression that nobody around here can be bothered to explain anything more than once. We're supposed to be here to learn. How can we experiment without using materials? We're bound to make more mistakes when you're making everyone feel nervous. You also keep using words and terminology that I have had no use for in my entire life. It's like me coming in here and throwing you a couple of floor joists and telling you, don't forget to put the tusk tenon in on the trimmer joist, and then pissing off for the rest of the day, expecting the floor to be laid by the time I get back.'

She went quite red in the face and said, 'It's you, it is. You're just disorganized, that's what you are.'

'No, it's you,' I said. 'You haven't been around here all day, and you haven't explained yourself very clearly.'

I soon discovered that even some of the other lecturers found her intimidating and would hide their own wasted materials from her, which we found very amusing. As time went by we all took her more lightly, but she didn't make learning a comfortable experience. Her lack of encouragement was compensated for by her colleague in the department. He was much more helpful and would often stay behind after hours to help us if we needed it. I found the best teachers were those who ran their own ceramics businesses and were employed as lecturers on a part-time basis. They had a lot of practical experience and enjoyed what they did for a living. They didn't mind passing on any information, technique or trick of the trade that would help us. One said, 'Your very first lesson is on how to cook your books. You have two different books, one for yourself and one for the taxman.' We had a lot of laughs with this guy. He was in touch with the real world and gave us a lot of useful information.

Outside college I got to know a few people around the neighbourhood and sometimes I used to sell the odd bit of dope to pay for my own supply. As a result, people would come and hang out at my flat, which I didn't mind at first, but I was astonished at the prejudices some of them had.

'God, where have I come to?' often went through my mind. It was like another culture altogether, compared to where I had come from; even young people were very narrow-minded. I didn't feel comfortable with the way conversations would sometimes turn. It was difficult to tolerate remarks being made about people's skin colour or sexual preferences, and the sexist and racist jokes. If they only knew what I was. I tended to be on the defensive about anything to do with discrimination.

'What's the matter with you?' I'd say. 'Why can't you let people be the way they are? Live and let live, for fuck's sake!' I was well aware of the enormous amount of stigma and prejudice attached to a condition such as mine. On one hand I felt very uneasy with this, and on the other I felt a strong urge to justify myself and put them right on a few things. But what was the point? Just as I had a few rigid ideas when I was younger, I couldn't expect these people to change their views because I wanted them to.

There were times though when, in a group of people, I felt the indignation and resentment building up in me so much that, if one more comment were made, I would stand up and say: 'Well, what do you think of me? I'm a fucking transsexual, and what about it?' But I never had the courage to give up my need for privacy. I had to hang on to my anonymity for my peace of mind. I only tolerated the situation because I needed an extra couple of quid and I didn't encourage them to stay long. I often had to remind myself that I had not come here to socialize or to put down roots. I had come here to study, to give me something to build a future with.

There were still moments when I wondered if I could keep it up for four whole years. Between my difficulty in conforming to college plus the ever-increasing workload, and living in a place where my concentration was being broken continually, I had my doubts. For that reason, Katie and I decided it would be a good idea to move away from this environment and try to buy a house – not with the intention of setting up home together, but as an investment. If our relationship came to an end, it would be something for both of us to move on with. In fact, I had no intention of staying on home ground past the end of my course. We started to keep our eyes open for a house in my home town.

I saw less and less of the friends from my time in Cardiff and Newport. I went to see Ty in Cardiff one day. It had been two years since I had last seen him. I wanted to avoid any in-depth conversation with him about the women from my past, especially Lorretta. I didn't want to hear about her being happy with someone else. Nevertheless he told me that she had found another man, and that she treated him badly. I didn't comment on it but on the journey home I couldn't avoid thinking about what he had said. Was she happy? Would she be there for me in the future if I ever came back? Was I still in her thoughts, like she was in mine? I put her out of my mind as quickly as I could. After all, I was in a relationship with Katie, and I had promised myself that I would not contact her until I had solved my problems and was at peace with myself. It was good to see Ty, however, and he invited me to go to Amsterdam with him in his caravanette. I said I would as soon as I had a break. Three years passed before I made it back to see him.

Alan became a close friend, but an unfortunate incident made a big dent in our friendship. As he knew me from childhood he was aware of my transsexual condition, but he was an easygoing, open-minded person and he didn't think anything of it. I trusted him implicitly but he took it upon himself to tell another acquaintance, Nigel, who lived in the flat above mine.

Nigel used to come to my flat quite frequently. Perhaps he had guessed that something about me was different, particularly the way I defended minority groups. I had all my paintings and drawings tacked to my walls, and there was one he was always quizzing me about, a water colour of Mother Nature. I had written a simple poem on the painting which had a meaning only for me:

> Mother Nature come to me
> and make me what I'm supposed to be
> come and take me in your care
> because life till now has been unfair
> Mother Nature, you'd be a Godsend to me
> if you could recreate me as I'm meant to be
>
> Mother Nature now I know you care
> because life now is more than fair
> Mother Nature I'm your ardent fan
> because now I'm truly a Man

'Who's it about? What does it mean?' Nigel would often ask me. I put his questions off by telling him it didn't mean anything really, it was just something I'd made up, but I could see that his curiosity wasn't satisfied. He then tried to pump Alan for information by asking why I was always on the defensive, and Alan played right into his hands.

I knew nothing about it when, one day, Nigel came to see me. He made some critical comment about Alan, which was obviously meant to make me defend him.

'Don't fucking talk about the guy,' I said, walking straight into his trap. 'He is a friend of mine.'

'I don't know why you are sticking up for him,' he replied smugly. 'He's told me all about you.'

I was really shocked. When Alan came to see me next, there were murders.

'What kind of fucking friend are you?' I rounded on him. 'What makes you think you can speak on my behalf?'

He was very upset. 'I didn't mean to hurt you. It wasn't said like that. You often said you were on the verge of disclosing it yourself.'

'You still had no right to speak on my behalf.' I was very angry and upset, but after a cool period we resumed our friendship.

However, word soon got around and I felt more strongly than ever that it was time to leave the neighbourhood. In addition to this my flat got robbed. My little stash of dope was nicked and £200. I was livid. I suspected it was Nigel but I couldn't be sure because there were a lot of people coming and going. I marched upstairs and confronted everyone who was gathered there. 'If none of you fuckers saw anything, then surely you must have heard something.' Soon after, his own flat was broken into. He in turn suspected me of having done it. The atmosphere in the house started to turn quite ugly.

One night he came to my door in a drunken state, accusing me of robbing him. He had a bit of glass in his hand, and went for me with it. It caught me on my lip. I turned around and threw him down the stairs. Running down after him, I grabbed hold of him and held him in a bear-hug from behind while he shouted at me to let him go. I should've hit him, but I didn't.

'I know you are fucking annoyed,' I said, 'but I didn't do it, I swear.' He wouldn't let up and we ended up continuing scuffling in the street. I punched him when he was down and shouted, 'For fuck's sake, I didn't break into your fucking flat.'

My opponent spotted a mate of his across the street and called for his help. They got me down and the second guy kicked me in the face. Part of my difficulty was that I was wearing no shoes and very few clothes, having got out of bed. I put my hands up to protect my face, but another kick broke two of my fingers. My arm was useless and I couldn't protect myself any longer.

A gang of boys were coming up the hill and saw what was happening, me on the ground with the two blokes kicking me. They shouted, 'Hey, what do you think you are doing, two of you against one?' and started running to help me out. At the same time I could see a taxi coming up the street and slowing down when he saw us on the road. I managed to get up and made a dash for the taxi. I quickly got in the back and asked the driver to drop me at the end of the road.

This was the push Katie and I needed to get out. A few weeks later we moved. We found a house in my home town which had just come up for sale. The former owner had died and the place was vacant. I had a good feeling about the house when I saw it. We put in an offer which was accepted. Katie sold her horse to raise some money, and I had a bit saved up.

First we moved in with Katie's parents for a few weeks while everything was finalized and I ended up getting on very well with them. I moved into our new house the day completion took place. There wasn't a thing in there. Katie's parents weren't happy about her moving in until the place was more comfortable. Her father was helping me knock two rooms into one, so there was quite a mess downstairs. I didn't care about comfort, I was just so happy to have my own place. Katie's parents also wanted to buy a lot of things for the house, including furniture. It was a kind offer but I didn't much like the idea. I wanted us to be in charge of our home.

'What's wrong with getting things bit by bit?' I told them. 'The first flat I ever had, had only three mattresses on the floor.'

'I'm not having a daughter of mine sleeping on the floor,' her mother said. Nevertheless they did help us out and we appreciated the things that they got for us.

This was my first real home, but I wasn't to know yet that the move was truly from the frying pan into the fire. About the same time as we moved in, my ban was lifted and I was able to get my motorbike back on the road. This was good timing, since I needed transport to get back and forth from college.

Katie's parents had by this time accepted me as her partner. Katie was with me, and it was better all round if we got on. We went regularly to their house for Sunday dinner, together with her brother Leonard and his wife Alison, who both later became very good friends. We did have some stimulating discussions about all sorts of things. I was totally open with them about myself, and I think our discussions made them think. I told them I sometimes smoked cannabis.

'There is nothing dangerous about it. Can you see anything wrong with me?' I asked them innocently. They laughed heartily. In fact, we had a lot of good laughs. I don't think they really understood my condition, but they wanted to listen to what I had to say and they were always fair with me.

Katie and I got on very well together. Our love life could be described as comfortable and affectionate, but not wild and crazy. We both knew that we wouldn't last a lifetime together because there was no depth in the way we communicated. I never felt close enough to her to confide in her my innermost feelings and struggles. We interacted on a superficial day-to-day level. This was my choice, not hers, as I doubted that she could really have understood me. She probably saw me as a moody and temperamental person, which I often was.

I sent my new address to Charing Cross Hospital. I had been phoning and writing to them at regular intervals; I wanted to make sure they didn't forget about me. All they ever said was that they would let me know when something new came up in the way of surgery. I kept phoning, and they said they were still experimenting. I felt the same unrelenting need for the completion of the surgery that had been started. Everything that I was doing in my life was in preparation for my rebirth as a whole man. Only then could I rest. Nothing meant anything without this hope.

Since recovering from my breakdown, life had seemed quite good. I was twenty-six years old and had started my third year in college and I was doing things that were taking me towards a better life. I had finished the first two years of my course and received my Ordinary National Diploma with merits. I still had two years to go in order to attain my Higher National Diploma.

Stewart and I got involved in voluntary teaching at an art centre. They were running pottery classes for adults in the evenings, and helping out there meant that several of us from the college could use the facilities for free. This was very helpful, because we were involved with a big project, a commemorative wheel for the Great Western Railway. It was a group project, and each of us made a segment of the wheel. Afterwards I realized how much I had learned from showing other people how to work with clay.

In addition to being excited about my art, I also began training and became very fit. An encounter with the college caretaker got me started. I used to go into college early in the morning and park my bike in the same spot in the car park. I had been parking it there for a few months.

I had had another hectic day in college and it was the end of the week, so I wanted to be out of there and on my way home. I had just put my helmet on when somebody shouted, 'Hey, you! You are not allowed to park your bike there.'

'What's different about today?' I said. 'I usually park my bike here.'

'I'm telling you,' he said. 'I'm the caretaker, and you are not to park your fucking bike there any more.'

'I've been parking here for fucking ages, what's the matter with you, why can't I park it here any more?' Because he wouldn't give me an explanation I said, 'Oh, fuck off.'

'Right,' he said, 'you want to be funny, mate. Well, I tell you what, I'll be funny. You are not coming in here on Monday.'

Come Monday I did get in, but I parked in another spot. During the day I had to go and find the caretaker in order to ask him for some timber to fix a partition that had broken. He didn't recognize me without the helmet on but when I was talking to him he looked at me sideways.

'You are that cheeky bastard with the bike, aren't you?'

'Yeah, that's right,' I said, and laughed. He was standing in the doorway of a big room in the basement that was full of weight-training equipment.

'Is that your gym?' I asked.
'Yeah.'
'Is there any chance of me and my mate using it?'
'No, only my friends can use it.'
'All right, fair enough,' I said, but later when I was getting on my bike, he heard me starting it up and opened the window.

'If you are still interested in weight training, come and see me tomorrow morning.' He lived in the building and had turned one of his spare rooms into a gym. We became good friends in the end, and Stewart and I were allowed to train in his gym five days a week. Getting fit made me feel a bit better about my body.

Since coming back to my home town from Newport and being so uplifted by the prospect of a new life, I had gradually gained courage to meet people in social situations. I was encountering new faces in college and outside college, as well as old friends and relatives. That was all very well, but it soon became evident that the breakdown I had suffered in Newport had never been dealt with properly. I carried it all deep within myself and I never talked about my inner turmoil. I came out of that room with hope for a new life, and having embarked on it I realized that nothing about myself had been resolved. It had all happened so fast: being brought back to my parents' house and immediately having the old difficulties of relating to my family brought back to life again, and then I had a rather swift move to a new scene, college and new friends. I was in my third year of college and starting to feel the pressures that went along with exposing myself to life.

My fellow students would often get together and go out for drinks, or they would play football or go swimming. Because I was getting on well with them, there seemed to be no reason for me not to join in these other activities, but I always made my excuses and I regretted intensely that I couldn't do these things. I yearned to be able to go out and run around on the football field as any other young man would. I would have loved to go down to the leisure centre with the rest of them and take my clothes off and enjoy the water. I needed to join in and do these things as a man and as a human being, but I couldn't risk anyone finding out about me. It was difficult to maintain, with changing rooms and toilets. Much as I resented this, paradoxically these restrictions were my lifeline. Even though they held me back, they were also dear to me. Without them I couldn't preserve myself, and would be too vulnerable. I had to keep making feeble excuses why I couldn't ever join in anything and I hated refusing my mates' encouragement and insistence that I should join them.

As all my limitations and the restrictions on my freedom were worming themselves back into my consciousness, with them came the feelings of desperation. My moods started to change and I was getting morose and unpredictable. I had no outlet; there was no one to blame, no one to be angry at. Much as I tried to accept that I had to live on the fringes of life, I couldn't help feeling bitter.

Some days I could cope with the idea of waiting for my complete physical transformation. I could occasionally be high on optimism and think, 'Great, I am working towards a way of earning a living in a dignified and creative way. If I can do all this now, without a body which belongs to me, what will I be able to do when I have one? By the time I finally get to have my surgery I'll come out of it with so much waiting for me: a house, a career, a business, money and freedom.' Other days I could not cope at all with the waiting. The frustration would tear me apart. I would become irritable and difficult to be with.

I finally decided to tell Stewart about my condition. I felt I owed him that much. I had spent a lot of time with him, training and working. I trusted him totally, but it was a risky business; the incident with Alan was still quite fresh in my mind.

'Look,' I said to him one day, 'I think you should know something about me, seeing that we are friends and are thinking of going into business together.'

I told him there was a reason why I appeared to be erratic and unpredictable, and why I had been getting depressed over the last few months. It was important to me that he wouldn't think it had anything to do with him. I told him that I was a transsexual and that it meant being under a lot of stress and pressure all the time.

'I don't fully understand what that means,' he said, a bit nonplussed, 'but I don't really care, anyway. I just like you as a person. Whatever you are makes no difference to me or to our plans.' And we left it at that.

There was also the old difficulty: throughout the year the college would often rent a coach to take us to see various exhibitions, museums, factories and workshops in London and other places. These trips were usually quite wild and a lot of fun. People would bring bottles of wine and beer. After having seen what we came to see, we would all go for a meal and for drinks, often getting quite loaded. I would join in and feel part of the whole thing, but I always had to think ahead about needing to use the toilet. The anxiety would gnaw away at my insides the whole time.

The college hired really old and cheap buses to take us on these trips, and they invariably didn't have a toilet. One time when we were coming home from London I became desperate. My friends could all see I was in agony. 'Here, pee in this bottle,' a couple of the girls kept saying to me, and that is exactly what I would have done if I had been born like any other man. Stewart, knowing my predicament, said, 'Oh, don't do that. I certainly wouldn't do it.' He kept talking to me in order to distract me. I was really grateful for his support, but in the end I ran up to the driver and said, 'You better stop this fucking bus, or I don't know which end it is going to come out of.'

He pulled in on the hard shoulder of the motorway, and I plus a few other of the blokes tumbled out. They had a slash standing by the bus, but I had to run a couple of hundred yards, jump over a fence and dive into a wood, with everybody still on the bus watching and wondering. Perhaps to the reader this doesn't seem to be a much of an ordeal and probably my mates didn't notice or think much of it either, but for me it was a major trauma. The stress and humiliation of it stopped me from going on most of the trips in the future. The toilet predicament also put a damper on anything else that had to do with socializing. Whereas my difficulties in college were invisible to everyone, my experience of going out in my home town was of constantly meeting people who were curious about me and brought up the subject of my condition. I could never be comfortable or allowed to forget who I was. Who and what where they on about? I couldn't relate to the person they knew me as.

I decided to write to my old probation officer, Carole. I needed to confide in someone who knew my past and understood some of the difficulties I had encountered. I explained to her how I was still suffering from paranoia, especially now, being back in my home town. I found it difficult to confide in anyone. I told her I was a weak person, and that privately I spent a lot of time crying.

She wrote me a very nice letter in response.

'You are not a weak person,' she told me. 'When you think of all that you have experienced in your life, the humiliation, the rejection and alienation, it's not surprising to me that you are still suffering from pain and paranoia. But you must keep thinking of how much you have achieved and how far you've come.' She went on to say, 'You are a sensitive, passionate man, Raymond, and therefore you feel things more deeply than most others. The majority of people have no concept of the daunting and frightening prospect of gender reassignment surgery that you have ahead of you. Remember that 99 per cent of the population take their sexual identity for granted. You must try and learn to be tolerant of other people's ignorance.'

Her letter helped me a lot, and I did try to be more tolerant of people's ignorance. Whenever I was questioned about myself, instead of always being on the defensive I tried to explain my condition to the best of my ability, so that my acquaintances might gain more understanding and be less judgemental of transsexualism. I tried to make people understand that it has nothing to do with sex, but with personal identity, that my future surgery would help me gain unity: unity between my mind and my body.

I often regretted getting into these conversations with people in the pub, which is where most of these situations arose. I had convinced myself that I was a man with a disability, not a transsexual. I felt so detached from the subject itself, as if it had nothing to do with me. I kept wondering who and what I was defending.

Life with Katie was quite uneventful. I didn't see much of her. I was totally wrapped up in my course and didn't usually come home till about eight o'clock in the evening. Often there would be a group of people entertaining themselves in my living-room. They were mainly old acquaintances from my youth. Katie had quit her job at Tesco and spent most of her time with our mutual friends. This meant that these people came back to the house more frequently. I tolerated it at first, but as I started to feel the pressure of all my limitations, coming back to a house full of people didn't help my frame of mind. In addition, I didn't want to lose sight of why I was back in town. Even though a couple of them were good friends, now I had very little in common with them. I didn't resent them being there, but our priorities and needs were different. In fact, getting drunk with them now gave me a bad feeling. It reminded me of all the time in my youth that I had spent drinking in order to numb my disorientation and hopelessness. It also diluted my concentration; I needed all my mental and emotional resources to get on with the art course. How I would have preferred to go swimming and play football with my mates from college and not to come back to my house at all in the evenings, but that was not possible.

When I was young and reckless, we used to do a mixture of drugs, usually pills of various kinds, together with booze and a bit of cannabis. I was never into injecting myself. Fortunately I had a healthy respect for heroin and other injectables, mainly because of what I had observed with Irena, so I stayed away from the hard stuff. As I grew older my choice of drug became cannabis. I found it calmed me down and I was better able to rationalize with myself. It didn't give me a hangover or the out-of-control feeling that booze did, and it provided me with some light relief from my inner turmoil. I smoke mainly for pleasure these days, less because I need it. I would love to stop smoking cigarettes, and I am always trying to cut down.

I think that if I had turned to alcohol instead of cannabis, and continued drinking the way I had done from an early age, I would have gone back to prison sooner or later. Alcohol removes your inhibitions and makes you thoughtless and reckless, as I well remember from my teens when I was constantly in trouble.

When my mother found out that I was smoking cannabis she was very critical.

'It's illegal,' she said. 'I don't want you getting into trouble.'

'Ma, there is only ever a little bit of "personal" in the house, nothing for the law to bother with,' I reassured her. When she still grumbled about it I asked her if she would prefer me to be on a legal substitute, such as Valium, which is highly addictive. She couldn't argue with this and left it at that. We never did come to agree on this subject.

She came over with my grandmother one evening when I was painting my rush mats with a cannabis leaf on them. I had four of them lined up on the floor.

'Oh, they look lovely, my handsome boy,' said my grandmother, 'nice and colourful.'

'My God, Ma,' said my mother, annoyed. 'Do you know what he is painting there? It's bloody cannabis ... he's painting cannabis leaves.'

My grandmother didn't have a clue. 'They still look lovely,' she said, and winked at me.

What really riled my mother was when, a couple of years later, I had the shape of a cannabis leaf cut into my hair at the side of my head. I did it for a laugh, knowing it would grow out soon enough.

My mother came over to my house one day and I was talking to her in the street. I turned my head and she shouted suddenly, 'My God, what is that on the side of your head?'

'It's just a leaf,' I said.

'A leaf?' she exclaimed scornfully. 'Jesus Christ.' She nearly went berserk and drove off in a huff, but about twenty minutes later her car screeched to a halt outside my house.

'I couldn't care less,' she shouted angrily out of the car window, 'if I don't see you until that leaf has grown out.' She added, 'I swear you're getting stupider as you get older,' and roared off.

Although I spent most of my time in college working on my projects I became touchy and irritable there as well as at home, and any teacher who I felt was condescending or unreasonable would get it. I was absorbed in a drawing one day when one of the teachers came up to tell me that this was not at all what I was supposed to be doing. I acknowledged my mistake, but was reluctant to stop what I had started. For no apparent reason he started to give me a lecture about 'life'.

'Oh, come on now,' he said sarcastically, 'we realize that you're not long out of school and you've just sat your O and A levels, but as you go through life, you'll soon find out you need to be open to change.'

Having a short fuse, I responded. 'Who the fuck do you think you are speaking to? Now *you* listen. I am no kid straight out of school; as it happens I have no O or A levels but I know more about change than you'll ever fucking know.'

He stormed off and reported me. I was called up to see the head, Paul Cook, and asked to account for myself.

'He voiced his opinions and I voiced mine,' I said. 'He had no more right to speak like that to me, than I had to him.' I tried to make light of it and jokingly said, 'But it's OK, you don't have to get rid of him.'

My differences with this teacher were not quite over. I was fifteen minutes late to one of his classes because it was pouring with rain and I had had trouble starting my motorbike. As I was entering the classroom, still wearing my big yellow waterproofs that went swish, swish with every step, he was in the process of giving the students a real telling off.

'You're late on purpose, and you have no commitment to the course,' I heard him say.

'Look, I'm sorry I'm late,' I said, 'but I have a genuine reason. I couldn't get my bike to start.' I couldn't leave it alone. 'Where do you get these ideas about our lack of commitment?'

'Look here,' he said, 'I think my years in the teaching profession give me the right to tell you what I think, and when I come to mark your papers I mark them not only on your ability, but on your commitment as well.'

'Listen, mate,' I said while the class held their breath, 'when you come to mark my paper, you'd better mark it on more than your assumptions about me. And why did you report me last week? Why didn't you come to me? Why didn't you think we could sort it out between us?'

'I thought we needed a middle man,' he answered, flustered.

'But you didn't even try,' I retorted. 'You said nothing to me at all, and out of the blue I was called to the head office. Didn't you think we were adult enough to sort this out between us before running off to report me?'

The man was red in the face, but there wasn't anything else to be said.

One saving grace was that my relationship with my parents had improved. Although there was the same old spiky relationship between my mother and me, we talked more and could have a good laugh together. My mother surprised me and did take a firm stand in my favour around this time. I felt it was a turning point in our relationship.

My cousin Penny was getting married; she was the daughter of my Aunt Kathleen, whom I had always got on well with when I was young. I was looking forward to this wedding, since I had been excluded from all family occasions in the past. My mother was looking forward to having me there too, which pleased me very much. She even went out and bought me a nice outfit to wear. It was an incredibly smart black leather box jacket with a matching tie.

A week or so before the wedding there was a knock on my door. It was Kathleen and Penny standing there, looking a bit awkward.

'Oh, hello,' I said. 'Come on in.' I was surprised to see them because they had never come to my home before, and I had a gut-feeling that something was up, although I didn't show it.

'Come in,' I insisted.

'When you hear what we have to say,' my aunt said, 'you might not want us in your house.'

'There is nothing you can say that is going to stop me welcoming you into my home,' I offered graciously. 'At least come in to say what you have to say.' They did.

'The thing is,' said Penny, 'you can't come to the wedding.' She started crying.

'Don't worry about it,' I said. 'But I'd like to know why.'

'Your Uncle Peter seems to think that people would laugh at you,' they said, 'and that you may cause trouble.'

I turned to Penny and said, 'Oh well, don't worry about it. I hope you have a great day and all goes well.' There was nothing else to be said. After my Uncle Peter's visit to my home in Newport to tell me that he couldn't help me because he thought too much of my parents, I might have guessed something like this would happen.

What I didn't know was that my mother would be so insulted by it, and it ended up causing a real rift in the family. Although I appreciated my mother's loyalty it also made me feel guilty. If I hadn't come back here to live she wouldn't have had all this aggravation.

My mother said to me, 'If you're not invited to the wedding, we're not going either.' My mother had by this time started to understand a little bit more about my condition. Whereas before she was determined to block it out, now she was reading articles about transsexualism, and she would occasionally come over to my house just to tell me about someone else similar to me, whom she had read about. I think she felt better, knowing that she wasn't the only mother in the world who had been through this trauma.

'For God's sake, go to the wedding,' I insisted. 'Don't worry about me not being there. If I hadn't come to live here I wouldn't have been going to the wedding anyway. I don't want to be the cause of family problems.'

'No way!' my mother said adamantly. 'Your uncle is discriminating against you, and we are not going to sit there and celebrate it.'

I respected her for taking such a stand. I should have been happy about it, but I wasn't. It just added to my feeling of being indebted and being the cause of yet more trouble. I wished my parents had ignored the incident, gone to the wedding and had a good time.

As I had started to stay away from home more, Katie and I naturally drifted apart. She had changed quite a bit from the nice quiet girl whose main interest was her horse, and I had changed too. She was still a nice girl, but there was never an undying love between us and there wasn't a strong enough foundation to hold the relationship together. I gave her nothing really, and when I found out that she was seeing someone else it didn't come as a surprise. I wasn't jealous or even particularly angry, except about the deceit involved.

'I know that there is something going on. Why don't you just say what it is?' I told Katie.

'No, no, there is nothing going on,' she insisted.

I was sick and tired of what was going on behind my back under my own roof. What pissed me off even more was that all these supposed friends of mine who kept hanging out in my house obviously knew about it too. I was particularly disappointed in Katrina (the girl I used to write to from Borstal). We went back a long way together. When we were about twelve years old we had performed a ritual joining us as blood brother and sister. We cut our wrists and joined them together, the scar is still there today. It meant a lot to me at the time. I felt she should have been more upfront with me, but seeing that she had become a good friend of Katie's, I understood that her loyalties were torn.

One day I came home from college and went up to my door loaded up with books, bags, drawing pads and motorbike gear and helmet, so I rang the doorbell. After a moment, Katrina opened the door.

'What are you doing here?' I asked, expecting to find Katie. She looked very shifty and was evasive about Katie's whereabouts. Later I found out that Katie and her boyfriend had left through the back door as I was riding up to the house. Katie was leaving me and she wasn't coming back. When I finally found out where and with whom she was living, I packed all her belongings in bin-liners and delivered them to her in three trips, balancing them on my petrol tank. I was annoyed but I tried my best not to show it. Everything that I had suspected was true, and everyone had lied to me about it.

We had lived together for over two years. After the initial anger and disappointment, we made up as friends. I was determined for there not to be any animosity. Besides, I wanted and needed the house. For this reason I didn't mind being the injured party, and Katie gave me her word that she wouldn't try to take the house from me and would give me time to raise the money to buy her out. I eventually did this by increasing the mortgage. Even though the parting was on amicable terms, it didn't help my state of mind hearing all kinds of bullshit being spread around by others. The people who were into gossip would say things such as, she was a virgin until she met her new boyfriend, and being with me was a waste of a good woman. None of this was said to my face but it got back to me nevertheless. Ironically, Katie's new boyfriend was, in fact, quite a nice guy. I met them in the pub one evening and we had a chat.

'Look,' I said to him, 'I don't bear you any malice at all for what has happened, because you didn't take from me anything that I hadn't already given away.'

He nodded and said, 'I know it,' and bought me a beer.

Once again I was living alone.

10
Tolerating Pain

The summer term was ending so I was facing three months of the college being closed for the summer holidays. College and my continued interest in art and learning had been a good prop against my encroaching depression and I had been very much involved with my work. Now there was nothing to take me away from myself. I had a few projects to work on during the summer, but I was finding it difficult to motivate myself. I felt myself beginning to go downhill.

My old friends were calling at the house less frequently, which suited me just fine. I had made it obvious to them that I wanted to be left alone. I needed to cut myself off. I had lost faith in my friends over the way they had lied to me about Katie, and I had been bottling up a lot of anger and disappointment. Finally I had one last showdown with them. They came one evening when I was already in a foul mood. Katrina and a couple of the guys tried to be conciliatory and said, 'Come on now, come on, we'll all go out for a drink. We'll treat you.'

'Why not?' I thought, although I still felt quite resentful. We went out for an hour or two and when we got back to my house, I said to them, 'Come on in. Come in and have a joint before you go.' When they all had sat down comfortably, I just stood there and looked at them all. All of a sudden, the events of the last couple of months flooded my head, and I exploded.

'Up and out,' I said coldly, 'I want you all up and out of my fucking house ... Now!' I couldn't contain the rage that had built up in me any longer. I went up to my dining-room table and grabbed two chairs. I threw one against the back window, and it went clean through with a hell of a crash and landed in my shower. The other one I threw towards the front window, but it missed. Then I ran up to my wall unit and tipped it over, and everything on it smashed to the floor. Next, I picked up a large, heavy coffee table and hurled it towards the mirror on the wall. I smashed plates and ornaments and, worse, an ashtray that my grandmother had given me. Bits of glass and china were all over the floor.

My friends were trying to grab me to stop me. 'What's the matter with you?' they shouted.

'I want you fucking out, that's what's the matter!' I shouted back at them.

Katrina screamed at me, 'What's going on? Are you going crazy, or what?'

'Just . . . fuck off, the lot of you.'

They seemed confused. Did I want them to leave, or was I having a nervous breakdown? They didn't know what to do.

When I woke up in the morning and I saw the devastation, all the broken glass and furniture, I couldn't believe that I had wrecked my home again. It wasn't the first time this had happened. How could I be so destructive time and time again? How come I never learned from my mistakes? I always tried to contain my feelings outside of my home, where I could cause trouble for myself and embarrassment for my family. My home was my only safe haven; at least there I was only hurting myself and damaging my own possessions. I never wanted to or meant to damage my own property, but it was the only place I could let rip without repercussions. Nevertheless all that day I felt confused and very angry with myself for losing control. I couldn't bring myself to clean it up. I felt like putting a rucksack on my back and taking off for good. But I knew I couldn't run away from myself.

These people from my past finally got the message and stopped coming around. I saw them occasionally in town and we said hello, but that was about it.

Katrina came by a few times and tapped on the window. When I didn't answer she'd shout to me, 'I still love you like a brother!'

I closed the doors to my house and spent hours sitting in the dark. The house became neglected, dirty and fell into disrepair. I didn't care. The walls of protection that I had carefully built around myself, I was now breaking down. It was as if I had pressed a self-destruct button. I felt I needed to let go of so many feelings that had been building up that I almost welcomed living in the pits of my despair.

The last time I started down this slippery slope I had felt ice-cold, and this sensation came back to me. Since my body is not my own I cannot feel the warmth of it, so I am cold, very cold, on the inside. I longed for that feeling of warmth, like when your feet are freezing and you slip on a pair of really thick woollen socks. You get that wonderful sensation of warming up, of regaining the feeling in your feet again. I craved this feeling all over. I could simply never be comfortable and warm in my own skin. It's also a bit like walking into a room that you know is supposed to be familiar. You know that all the things in the room should be recognizable, but they aren't, and you're looking, looking, looking for that familiar something, always trying to look beyond, but there is nothing. There is a sense of disconnectedness and unreality, of being left out in the cold. Most of the time I couldn't get my body to move from my chair, whilst panic was raging inside me.

I was seeing no one, except occasionally my parents, but I had my cats for company. As the light-bulbs started to pop, one by one, I didn't bother replacing them. The wiring was fucked and light-bulbs never survived for more than a short time.

One day I was sitting in my living-room rolling a joint. I thought I heard paper rustling. I looked around me for one of the cats, assuming it was playing with one of the paper balls I had constructed by rolling clumps of paper in masking tape. There wasn't a cat in sight.

'That's strange,' I thought. 'I'm sure I heard something.' The noise happened again, this time louder and coming from the ceiling. As I looked up, I saw a crack starting. With a sickening sound it rushed across the ceiling. A split second later the ceiling parted in two. The two halves just swung down, bringing with them a mountain of plaster, laths and black mortar dust. I was strangely calm about the whole thing, I brushed the plaster dust off my hair and lit my joint. Then I walked out of the house and didn't come back for three days. I couldn't face having to clean up that mess, let alone replaster the ceiling.

When eventually I did come back home, I simply pushed a large cupboard against the arch dividing the living-room from the dining-room so that it blocked the living-room from the rest of the house.

The days passed like this: I would go out once a week and buy fags and other supplies, and go straight back home. I cried a lot: I needed to, it was my only outlet. Mostly I sat immobile, staring into space, my mind blank.

My parents noticed that something wasn't right and they came over to check on me sometimes.

'God almighty, this is like the house of horrors,' my father said once as he stepped inside the front door. 'Why don't you have any lights in here?'

'I don't need them,' I said, trying to be funny. 'The cats' eyes glow in the dark, and they light the way for me.' My spirits had shrunk to a state where only darkness provided safety. I couldn't see light anyway, and all I wanted was to be closed in. I knew every square inch of the house so it was easy for me to find my way around.

'My God, what's that smell?' my father asked.

'It's incense. Lovely, isn't it?'

'You've got a different sense of smell to me,' he said, 'that's all I can say. It smells like you're burning bloody wood in here.'

Finally I had no light at all except the one inside my fridge and one lamp with a forty watt bulb. But I ruined the fridge on account of the light. Every time I cooked chips I would have to open the fridge and stick the chip pan into it to see if the chips were done. Between opening and closing the damn fridge door and shoving a red-hot chip pan in there once too often, the fridge was permanently damaged. Instead of being cold, it got boiling hot.

There were only two things in my kitchen: the fridge and a washing machine, no cupboards, counters or work surfaces. The kitchen was overrun with cats. I would fill their food bowls on top of the washing machine. The big cats would be scrambling around my feet, while the kittens would run up my legs and jump off the top of my shoulders on to the washing machine, trying to get at the food. The situation could be quite hard to control.

I had six cats in all, except when one had a litter, then there'd be more. Bonnie and Clyde were my first two. Then I took in Chucksy who had been abandoned by an old man down the street. He was ill in hospital and Chucksy was about to give birth to a litter; I took her in and let her have her kittens in my house. She never left after that. She was twelve years old and had never missed a litter, but the old man used to drown them at birth. I thought she deserved to keep her litter and she was brilliant with her kittens. After that lot I used my last £19 to have her doctored.

I loved all my cats, but I had a very special relationship with Pie, Bonnie's one and only kitten. She always sat with me, purring and touching her paw to my face. This may sound crazy, but when I winked at her she would wink back; it was probably a reflex. She liked trying to bite the end of my nose. She let me know when she was about to give birth to her litter, and led me upstairs to where she wanted to have them. I made her a bed in the bottom of the airing cupboard. She had no hesitation letting me pick up her kittens seconds after they were born. She trusted me completely.

My cats were a great comfort to me, particularly at this time. I spent hours watching them play and care for their kittens. Often I was down on all fours, miaowing and playing.

My mother would come sometimes on a Sunday morning and ask me home for Sunday dinner.

'No thanks,' I would say. 'I'm all right, don't worry about me, I'm just fine.'

'No,' she would say firmly. 'You come with me. You can have a good meal and I'll drive you right back home afterwards.'

Her eyes would wander around the place. 'It's all dark and gloomy and dingy in here. I can't see what you want to sit in here for anyway.'

'I have to,' I'd answer impatiently. 'I need to. I've got things on my mind. I'm struggling a bit with myself.'

'Come on, what's the matter with you? You're young and

healthy, and you're getting on with your life. Why are you acting like this?' She could never quite grasp the difficulties that my condition heaped on me every day of my life. She felt that I had achieved so much going to college and was fearful of me throwing it all away, but she didn't understand how I hated my body and that this clouded everything I did.

'I can't talk about it, just leave it alone,' was all I could say to her. 'I'll come for dinner, but I don't want to talk or say anything, or have you ask me any questions. I'll just come for something to eat.'

On one of these occasions I got in the car with her. She stopped for a moment and looked at my house.

'Come on, what is the matter with you? You want to change those net curtains, they're black. Get those nets down and wash them at least. What must the neighbours be thinking?'

'I don't give a fuck if they think I'm eating off the cat's dishes, as long as I know that I'm not,' I answered impatiently. She started driving really slowly down the street.

'Look at everybody else's windows, look how lovely everybody else's nets are looking,' she insisted, while pointing to my neighbour's windows.

'Ma,' I groaned, 'just get me out of the fucking street. I can't cope with this. I don't want to see anybody else's curtains, I don't give a fuck about anybody else's nets. Either take me home for Sunday dinner, or I'll get out of the car now.'

My mother flared up quite easily herself. 'I'd hate to live opposite you,' she said, 'you must be the worst neighbour in the street.'

It was true that my house was a real slum. Panes of glass were broken, and I had 'repaired' them with thick Sellotape; the weights of the sashes were all gone and the windows were held open by bits of wood and deodorant cans. To shut my mother up about the nets, I took them down. Instead I put a thick coat of Windolene over the window panes to block the light and prevent people from looking in. Some of the other windows I covered with newspaper.

Occasionally I would go out and get a bottle of wine. Drinking sometimes took the edge off, but at this time it got to a point where I didn't really want anything to eat, drink or smoke. I seemed indifferent to everything. One reason why booze and dope had played such a large part in my life was that I often suffered from such internal stress that my whole inside churned, continually making me feel very agitated while physically feeling almost paralysed. Numbing these sensations in my body was as urgent sometimes as numbing my mind and my emotions. A drink or a joint would calm them down. I would sometimes go days and weeks feeling all right, but most of the time these 'body feelings' would be there, an internal anxiety that could practically double me up and make me feel crippled. It was as if I needed to hold myself in, as if I were in great pain. My insides would sometimes do a sort of somersault, a sensation of a jump, starting in the pit of my stomach and shooting up into my throat. The feeling took my breath away completely; it could happen all of a sudden, even in the middle of my sleep.

I had taken to falling asleep on the sofa, sometimes fully dressed, sometimes partially dressed. Mostly I was kept warm by the cats who would settle all over me, the kittens usually arranged like a thick scarf around my neck. One morning I woke up in a daze with a hell of a hangover, shivering, dressed only in my jeans. The cats were nowhere in sight. I turned my head and spotted one of the kittens lying in front of the hearth. It was one of Pie's kittens. She had five at the time. I got up to wake it, but when I prodded it and stroked it, it remained immobile. It was dead. It brought on a state of near hysteria. I cried and ranted and raved and ran around the house looking for the rest of the kittens. I thought the culprit was Chucksy. She must have been jealous of the kittens since I had taken hers to the pet shop (they were quite grown by this time).

I ran out into the lane and there I saw Chucksy strutting along. She had a way of walking and behaving that inspired respect. All the tom-cats in the neighbourhood would scarper when they saw her. I chased her down the lane shouting, 'I'll fucking kill you!' but then reason got hold of me. I couldn't be sure she had killed the little one. My neighbours had seen me and seemed concerned: 'What's the matter, what's the matter?' I must have been a sight, crying and running in my bare feet with no shirt on.

I looked everywhere for the other kittens and was sure they were dead too. I dug a very deep grave, I dug until I couldn't reach any further. After burying the kitten I covered it up and used old broken bits of brick from the lane as a kind of crazy paving on top of the grave. I spent hours over it, arranging and rearranging the bricks, determined to get the pattern right. Looking back on it, my behaviour was bizarre, as if the depression was making me lose my grasp on reality.

I found the rest of the kittens. They were alive and well behind a roof slate that was leaning against the wall in the lounge. All four were piled up on top of each other, completely quiet and motionless. Pie, the mother, had hidden them there for safety. Later I learned that tom-cats will kill kittens in order to bring the mother back on heat. My back door had been wide open and most likely a tom had come in and perpetrated the grisly deed.

Later on that day I ran over to Alison's house. 'You've got to help me find someone to take in the cats, I can't look after them no more. They'll all end up getting killed.' I didn't trust myself any more to keep them from harm. I wasn't doing a very good job keeping myself from harm.

'Don't be so silly,' she said. 'These things happen. It's not your fault.' I used to say some crazy things to Alison. She and Leonard, her husband, were the only people I saw, having cut myself off from everyone, including Stewart and Alan. They might have knocked on the door a couple of times, but I never opened the door to anyone if I could help it. I felt I wasn't in any fit state to see anyone. I trusted Alison and knew she understood that I was going through a difficult time. One morning I made my way over to her house.

'I am the crinkled egg that nobody wants,' I said to her, 'but I am as good on the inside as all the other eggs.'

I had seen a programme on television where they injected chickens with some substance to make the egg yolks more orange, because the public doesn't want pale yolks. Some eggs came out with crinkled skin and they are not desirable either.

The programme made me very emotional, but Alison listened without saying anything. 'If they had their way, they would inject me too, to make me different, to make me fit.' I was really slipping.

My father had a word with me: 'Now look here, why don't you come and stay with us for a few days? I can see the house is getting you down.'

'No way,' I said angrily. 'What do you mean? It's my space and I am comfortable there. My cats are there. I can't leave my cats. What are you on about? I love my cats. I can't leave my house. I am completely comfortable there.' I had taken to ranting on and on when confronted with the slightest thing. And I did feel fanatically devoted to my house. I would stay there at all cost, even if the whole thing fell down around my ears.

My bathroom was literally coming down around my ears. It was a flimsy construction, with a Perspex roof, tacked on to the lean-to kitchen. The cats used to run back and forth on top of the Perspex, which was getting brittle, and one morning Pie fell through it. As she was coming through she grabbed at the shower rail to save herself, and that came down as well. So now I had a big hole right above my shower. In the state I was in, I didn't care one bit, although with my skills it would not have been at all difficult to repair it, but nothing seemed important.

The shower head went as well, so standing under the shower was like standing under a tap. As the weather got colder it was hellish standing there trying to keep warm under that tiny stream of water. When it rained it was particularly uncomfortable, trying to dodge the cold rain and keep as much of my body as possible under the shower stream.

One night after having a large amount to drink, I took a handful of Valium. I didn't mean to try and kill myself, but I desperately needed to kill these body feelings raging inside me. I phoned a friend in Newport to tell her something and she asked me if anything was wrong, saying that my speech was slurred.

'You haven't taken any pills, have you?' she asked.

'Yeah, just a few, but I'm OK.' She must have got worried and decided to phone an ambulance. The ambulance men came in through the back door and took me to the hospital. When they realized that my life was not in danger they had a social worker take me to the psychiatric hospital.

The social worker parked the car and we walked into this very grim-looking building. I looked at the people sitting in the corridors staring at the walls. There was no doubt in my mind that, miserable as I felt, this was not for me. I was shown into a room with a psychiatrist. The interview was a farce. After I had explained myself, who and what I was, and why I had taken the pills, she kept firing questions at me which were mostly, 'Who told you that you need this operation?'

When I tried to explain that it was entirely my need and my choice, she repeated the same question. It was irritating and insulting, and I had no patience for it. After each of my answers she would ask, 'What do you mean?' I knew I was a reasonably articulate person and generally people understand exactly what I mean. This 'third degree' and being treated like a moron thoroughly pissed me off. I banged my fist on her desk a few times, as if to help her understand my point. This in turn made her angry and she threatened to send for 'the doctors'. Then she tried to pressure me into signing some papers. In no way was I willing to sign any papers, but she just wouldn't let up, she wanted me locked up in there.

The social worker who had brought me there was just as much a pain in the arse. He was nodding and agreeing with every word the woman was saying, and kept urging me to sign myself in.

'If you don't, they'll commit you against your will,' he insisted.

Suddenly a man walked through the door.

'What is going on here?' he wanted to know. Whoever he was, it was a relief to see him. I jumped up and, feeling a desperate need to explain my position to someone who would listen, I appealed to him. 'Is this the kind of procedure you think is going to help me? These two want me to sign myself in. Do you think I need to be in here twenty-four hours a day staring at the walls and talking to people like her?' I said, pointing at the stony-faced psychiatrist.

'I need to be at home. I know exactly what is wrong with me, and there is nothing that you can do for me.' He didn't entirely agree with me, but didn't insist that I should be admitted. He suggested I should go to the out-patients' for some therapy with the woman who had just interviewed me. I was willing to agree to anything so long as I could get the hell out of there.

Needless to say I never did attend the appointment I was offered. I didn't trust psychiatrists, and what good would it have done to explain it all and remind myself of my misery? I felt that therapy was mainly to satisfy their own curiosity, not to make me feel better, more whole, or to make me accept myself or give me insight. Friends had suggested that counselling might help, but I felt a 'talking solution' wasn't what I needed. What I needed was surgery, the only permanent solution to my predicament.

I went home again to continue my solitary existence. Alison had dropped over to bring me a few essentials and some newspapers for when I got back. She was there when I arrived.

'The police have been here, and luckily I happened to be here or they would have kicked the door in,' she told me.

'My God, what for?'

'They alleged that you were involved in some robbery.'

I had a hard time taking it in, I was still groggy from the booze and the tablets. The cops had told her that if she didn't let them search my house while she was there, they would come back and do it after she'd left. She decided to let them go ahead, so at least she would know what they were doing. The place was full of ashtrays with roach-ends. They emptied them all into plastic bags and took them away, for analysis, I presume. Apparently I fitted the description of the robber perfectly: a guy on a motorbike with a balaclava on his head. That was me, of course.

One of the cops ran upstairs to search for evidence. Some time previous to this I had, in one of my destructive frenzies, ripped two bobble hats to bits among other bits of clothing. The policeman appeared, triumphant, on the landing, shouting, 'I've got the evidence, I've got it!'

'Oh God, no,' Alison had thought to herself. 'He hasn't got a stash of dope upstairs, has he?'

The cop came down to where Alison was standing. 'Do you know what this is?' he said, holding up a bobble hat.

'Yeah, a bobble hat,' said Alison.

The cop put his fingers through two of the many holes in the hat and said proudly, 'Yes, but . . . *now* do you know what it is?'

'Yeah, a ripped bobble hat,' said Alison.

'These are eye holes,' said the copper.

'So he's got eyes at the back of his head as well, has he?' said Alison.

Lousy as I felt I couldn't help but laugh at Alison's vivid description of the event, and her cool handling of it. That evening when I was sitting in the darkness, the cops came back. They were quite apologetic and said that they could see that I was going through a rough time. They even brought back my bag of dog-ends. I guessed that they hadn't found any traces of cannabis. They also brought back a couple of photographs of me that they'd taken from the house. They told me they had found the guys who had committed the robbery.

The weeks passed and I soon forgot about the overdose and the hospital, and about the incident of the police search. The house was falling to bits, and so was I. I turned to God to ask him why I had to continue being in this state. I had always tried to convince myself that he had a plan for me, but what good did it do me now? How long would I have to endure myself? Inside I was screaming for help and felt that I was suffocating. There seemed to be nothing I could do to help myself although I would have gladly taken a knife and done the surgery myself, but it wasn't possible. All I could do was to turn to whoever created me and ask him to help me. I clung on to the thought that ultimately he would put me right.

It didn't help much. I kept sinking. For the smallest reason I would burst into tears. It was a soundless crying, with tears rolling down my face for hours. My emotions seemed to get totally unhinged. I also started stuttering, and found it difficult to string words together into coherent sentences. Often I struggled to get my point across in conversation with my family, which was something that had never happened to me before.

Autumn was coming, but I hardly noticed it. One morning I was sitting in my lounge, staring into space, when I heard the familiar sound of a bill dropping through the letterbox on to the bare tiled floor. It landed with a thump. Just one letter. After a few moments I got my weary bones off the couch and went to pick it up. It was from a Dr Montgomery, a psychiatrist at Charing Cross Hospital, and said in a few short sentences that they had an operation which they thought might be satisfactory and that if I was interested, they suggested a date for an appointment in about two weeks' time.

I didn't take it in properly the first time, I just couldn't believe it. I read it again. A feeling of utter joy came over me, but in the next moment I had another vision: had I taken another two or three pills that evening, this house could have been empty, and the letter would have dropped on the floor and remained there. There would have been no one to pick it up and read it. All these years of waiting and striving and trying to get by would have been forsaken for the sake of three short weeks. Even the sound that the letter had made when it dropped to the floor echoed in my mind over and over; no one would have heard it. I also wondered what would have happened if I had bricked up my front door, as I had been planning.

My next thought was of God or whoever is up there; he must have realized that it was now or never. Maybe he was prodded: 'For fuck's sake, give him the letter now or he won't make it through the year.' As the words and meaning of the letter were sinking in and flooding my mind, I was filled with elation. The blackness started to lift and over the next couple of weeks I was in a very good frame of mind, celebrating this incredible and unlikely event. The way I was acting you would have thought I was going on an extended holiday to some exotic place, not into hospital to be cut up and stitched together. Alison was the first person I told. She and the few friends that knew my situation were elated for me too.

When I went up to London for my appointment, I saw Dr

Montgomery. I was told that Dr Randall had died a couple of years previously, and I felt very sad about this.

'How do you feel about extreme pain?' he asked bluntly. 'And can you cope with being laid up for long periods of time?'

'I need to be able to relate to my body, in order to get on with the rest of my life.'

'What do you mean by "relate"?' he asked me.

'I need to feel safe.' I explained to him about my life, and how I had been overwhelmingly affected by my condition.

'Whatever it takes,' I said emphatically, 'I'm prepared for it.'

'Easy to say,' he insisted. 'It does involve a lot of pain and distress.'

I was adamant; nothing would deter me from going ahead. Dr Montgomery must have been satisfied as to my suitability to have the surgery because he referred me to Mr Davies, the plastic surgeon who would be performing the operation. I had an appointment with him very shortly after at Hammersmith Hospital. Dr Montgomery took me off the hormone tablets. He told me that there had been no need for me to be on them that long. All the structural changes, such as my voice, muscle tone and facial hair, were permanent by this time. Later, thinking about it, I wondered if my hyperanxious state and my frequent bouts of fatigue had something to do with the hormones.

My interview with Mr Davies went along similar lines. He wanted to ascertain that I was aware of the dangers and risks, and that the outcome of the operation was never perfect.

'You realize we are talking major surgery. It's not life-threatening, but it's a very lengthy and difficult procedure.'

It involved two to three days in intensive care plus a further six weeks in hospital. Again, I said with absolute conviction that I was prepared for anything, whatever it took.

'Do you want a penis for sex or to be able to urinate?' he then asked me. It had never occurred to me that there would be a choice. To be perfectly honest I knew practically nothing about it at all, and had just trusted in the thought that I could be put right. I didn't need a moment to decide.

'Sex is not the main issue for me,' I told him, 'and it never has been. I need to feel comfortable in myself all day, every day.'

Mr Davies nodded. 'I had to ask, because some people prefer it the other way,' he said and explained to me the difference between putting a stiffening device into the penis and putting the urinary channel through it. It was one or the other; both were not possible. My choice was the more difficult operation of the two.

'I need to be able to relate to my body, and for it to be functional and that involves urinating in a normal way. This is for me, to enable me to live with me. I am not having this operation for anybody else, it's purely for me.' As it turned out intercourse was possible, which was a bonus I hadn't expected.

Mr Davies then got out some photos of the surgery and its aftermath. The person in the photo had extensive scars all around his abdomen and legs, but the penis itself looked good and didn't have any visible scars. I could happily live with those results.

I thought it was a miracle that gender reassignment surgery could be had on the National Health Service. In fact it was a miracle that it could be done at all. At no other time in the history of mankind has this been possible, not even twenty years ago. Maybe, after all, I was in the right place at the right time.

Mr Davies explained a bit about what the operation would entail. He told me that a few different techniques had been used so far. This kind of surgery was in its infancy and till now they had mainly constructed a penis from a free flap of skin lifted from the abdomen. The penis and the urethra were constructed all in one operation, but there had been failures. I chose not to ask any more questions at this point, I didn't want to hear about the risks and the failures. This was too important to me. I had to think positively, I couldn't afford to let doubts and anxiety weaken my resolve in any way.

The operation was set for about a month ahead. From then on I was on a high, totally recovered from my plunge into despair.

The first term of my fourth year of college started. I had a lot of catching up to do on the projects I should have finished in the summer holidays. Now that I felt so much better I started working on them, but my interest inevitably took a back seat to the excitement about the surgery. Still, I got a fair amount done in the month leading up to my hospital date.

As always, my mother was very nervous about any talk of surgery, so I didn't talk much to my parents about it, but she bought me all the things I needed for my stay in hospital: pyjamas, a toilet bag filled with shampoo, soap, toothbrush and paste and a pair of slippers. She asked me if I wanted them to visit, but I said no.

'I'll be all right and it's too far for you to come and visit. Don't worry about me – I'll ring you when it's all over.' I needed to go through this very important landmark in my life on my own.

'It's a pity he has to go through all this,' Anna said to my mother, but told me she wished it all would go well.

Stewart and another mate had kindly offered to drive me to London for the date of my operation. They also agreed to stay in my house and look after my cats, which I really appreciated.

On the journey to London I felt tense and excited: finally, after all these years, the time of release from my prison had come. It was an amazing feeling to be on the brink of realizing my true self as a man.

When we arrived at the West Middlesex Hospital it wasn't what I had expected.

'It looks like something out of Dickens,' I said to my mates. The place was old and grim and run-down looking. We found what looked like the reception, and I walked up to the desk.

'I'm Mr Raymond Thompson,' I said to the two nurses behind the desk. 'I'm booked in for this afternoon.'

They glanced at each other and giggled. 'I don't think so, Mr Thompson,' one of them said. 'This is the maternity ward.'

In spite of the grim appearance of the place it was, in fact, the friendliest hospital I have been in. I was assigned a private room and after saying goodbye and thanking my mates for the lift, I got settled in.

The first person I talked to in the hospital was an Indian woman. She explained to me that she was the anaesthetist.

'So my life is in your hands, then?' I said to her.

'That's right,' she said and smiled. 'But don't worry, I'll take very good care of it.' She was a lovely person and very reassuring.

'Look here, now,' she said. 'We've got you down for the whole operation, but sometimes the surgeon doesn't do the whole thing at once. It depends on what happens during the op.'

Hearing her say this knocked me back considerably. I had been so certain that I'd be waking up from the anaesthetic with my penis, and that all my waiting and suffering would be over. I refused to believe that this might not be the case.

'No, he'll do it for sure,' I thought, and put it out of my mind.

'If you have the whole operation in one go, I'll be seeing you later in intensive care, if not you'll be back here on the ward.'

A couple of nurses came into my room. They told me that a person who'd had the same surgery had just left the hospital.

'Was it successful?' I asked apprehensively.

'So far so good,' they told me. I asked them how many operations like these had been done. 'I think you're about the twelfth,' one of them said. 'But don't worry, the outcome is improving all the time and Mr Davies and his team are about the best plastic surgeons in the country.'

I was very excited and impatient when I was wheeled down to the operating theatre. I still had not seen Mr Davies since our consultation a month earlier. My lady anaesthetist came to put me to sleep. I said, 'Ta-ra, I'll see you later,' with emphasis on later.

It took me a long time to become conscious. When I became aware of my surroundings I saw that I was back on the ward. In my confusion I didn't remember the implications of it, and I was afraid to move my legs, not knowing where or how much I had been stitched. Mr Davies soon came in and explained that all they had done this time was to make a new channel for my urethra and directed it forward to the position where my future penis would be, in preparation for the next stage of surgery. Everything down below was stitched up: the operation I had had at the age of twenty had removed the internal organs that didn't belong to me; this op took care of the external ones.

I couldn't help being disappointed, but Mr Davies reassured

me that I would be ready for the next stage within six months. I would have to put on quite a bit of weight within this time. Because I had been weight training for the past year I was quite lean and muscular and there was not enough flesh and skin on my abdomen to construct a penis. Although I was prepared to do anything to make surgery successful, I didn't particularly like the idea of having to put on weight. It would invariably increase my discomfort with my physical form. I was twenty-seven by this time, and I felt it was important to keep reasonably slim and fit, particularly because I'd put my body through a lot and neglected my health.

Mr Davies and I had no further in-depth conversations about how the next stage, or stages, of surgery would be done and I left it in his hands. It was the knowledge that the process would resume shortly that saved me from feeling too disheartened. Later, although I was never told so directly, it appeared that between receiving that fateful letter and the date of my op, a couple of attempts on other people had proved unsuccessful and this was probably the reason for the change in the procedure.

Although the operation was only partly done it was a lot more painful than I had imagined. I had a catheter going in through a hole below my belly button to drain off urine. I had to drink three litres of liquid a day to keep my bladder clear. Another tube went into the new channel in order to keep it open, but it had to heal up before it could tolerate urine passing through it. The wound was wrapped in bandages, which were still covered in blood, but they were not to be changed as the surgeon didn't want to disturb things at this early stage.

I couldn't bring myself to look down – the pain was bad enough to handle – but the nurses kept telling me that it was better for me to look. I wasn't moving either because I was too nervous: I didn't want to jeopardize anything. Anyway, I had to have complete bedrest for a week. I felt like an old man. My hips had locked from staying so still, and I had a bag with my urine in it hanging down my side.

Once I did get out of bed I couldn't move. My hips just didn't want to unlock. The nurses tried to walk me up and down the hall. I must have looked very weird, hobbling along at a snail's pace, holding this bag full of urine.

After a few days, the tube going into my new channel was removed, which was in itself an unpleasant experience. I still had the catheter and this was supposed to stay in for another week. I had been put into a chair for the first time and, after sitting for a while, I started to get an awful pain.

'What's the matter with me, what's happening?' I thought, feeling panicky and praying to God that nothing was seriously wrong. Coincidentally, at that moment I was sent some messages from God. They came in the shape of a little old lady from the hospital chapel.

'Here you are,' she said, and gave me a little booklet with three messages from God and a bunch of violets. It did distract me for a second, and I was quite relieved that she had come in. I was still in a lot of pain, and I was sniffing the violets to try and take my mind off it.

A patient across the corridor saw me doubled up with pain and came over. The nurses had helpfully suggested that if anyone on the ward asked why I was in, I should tell him that I had trouble passing water, and that I was here to have it sorted out. This condition was common in men, so nobody would question it.

'Are you all right, son? What's the trouble, boy? Let's have a look,' he offered helpfully.

'No,' I groaned, 'it's all right. Just get me a nurse.'

I looked at the tube that was coming out of me and the panic set in again. A nurse came to see what the problem was.

'You've got to get me back into bed. I don't know what is happening down there, but I am in severe pain.' She thought I looked fine, but helped me back into bed.

'Now don't worry. Just drink plenty, drink plenty,' she said.

Like an idiot I kept drinking, not paying attention to what I knew was wrong. I started to feel bloated and my stomach was enormous and I looked down at the damned bag. Lo and behold, it was empty.

'Nurse, look. I have just drunk three of these jugs and my bag is empty and, like I said, I'm in pain.'

'I'll get the doctor,' the nurse said and went off.

Finally the doctor on duty came in, and he saw right away that although the catheter was still apparently in place, it had somehow come out of the bladder.

New panic flooded over me. 'How am I going to pee?'

'The only way you can go now is to go through the new channel that we have made for you.'

'But I'm not supposed to do that for another whole week.'

'You're going to have to now.'

All my muscles were tense with the stress and the fear, but they kept urging me to relax and try to pee through my new urethra. Eventually I did, all three jugs and more. I was raw but I wasn't too bothered about the pain, but more by the fact that my pee was going everywhere and I couldn't direct it. As I was sitting on the commode my pee went upwards and soaked my vest, then to the side and soaked my pyjama bottoms. I was embarrassed by having all the nurses standing about, looking at me. Now I was on the commode I refused to budge from it in case I needed to pee more. I felt I had no control over the muscles around my urethra and I didn't want to cause myself any more embarrassment.

After about an hour I thought, 'This is ridiculous, I've got to get off this thing.' As I stood up, the catheter shot out of my abdomen and literally flew across the room. I thought I was about to faint; everything was dancing in front of my eyes, but I could just see the bell to ring for the nurse, and I grabbed for it.

'The tube,' I gasped.

'What is the matter with it?' she enquired.

'It's over there,' I said, pointing across the room. The doctor came running too.

'Well, that's it, you don't need it any longer,' he said, laughing, and patted me on the shoulder in a mixture of congratulations and reassurance.

Twenty minutes later I was out of bed and feeling terrific. I had a look out of the window, then I put my Walkman on and even had a little dance.

Life on the ward was quite eventful and sometimes entertaining. I got friendly with this guy called Terry who had been in the hospital for about seven months with a nasty injury to his leg. He'd had a motorbike accident and they had to transplant a muscle from his back into his calf; without it he would have lost the leg. His daughter used to bring in cigarettes, and I would give her money to get me some when I ran out.

One evening Terry and another chap, who had a hernia, told me to come down to their corner of the ward for a game of Trivial Pursuit. He quite casually opened his bedside cabinet and produced a bottle of vodka and some Cokes. I had been told to drink plenty, but just to clear it with the nurses I went up to the nurses' station.

'Look, does it matter what I drink?' I asked casually.

'No, no, it doesn't matter. Just keep drinking, drink plenty.'

Well, from then on it was one big party. Every night Terry and I got together, and the daughter was called upon to deliver more stocks of vodka, Cokes and cigarettes. One evening we were having a whale of a time getting steaming drunk and asking each other inane Trivial Pursuit questions.

'What state is Memphis in?' asked Terry.

'Terrible,' I answered, and the guy with the hernia was laughing until he was doubled up and holding on to his stomach in agony, while we fell about.

'I mustn't laugh, so I have to leave you boys to play on your own,' he said, and hobbled out. It was gone midnight. Down the corridor the doctors and nurses were having some sort of party.

'Let's go to the party,' said Terry.

'But you haven't been out of bed for ages, how am I going to get you there?' Anyway, I wasn't walking that well myself.

'No problem,' he said, 'we'll borrow Sidney's wheelchair.'

Sidney, the old man in the far bed, was fast asleep. So I wheeled Terry up to the party, but we were a bit too conspicuous to blend in unnoticed. The doctors and the nurses spotted us right away and two nurses came chasing after us down the corridor. I hobbled along as fast as my legs could go, hanging on to Sidney's wheelchair for dear life. The problem was, Terry had his bad leg stuck right out in front of him. As I was swinging the wheelchair around a door which I had opened with great difficulty, I plain forgot about his leg. It was a good thing he had quick reactions because he jammed on the brakes in the nick of time, his bad leg half an inch from being crushed in the door. That didn't stop him laughing hysterically.

That night I felt so high I didn't want to go to sleep. The night nurse was not too happy with me singing at the top of my voice along with my Walkman.

'Shhh . . . go to sleep,' she would say, periodically poking her head in the door. 'Go to sleep now, you need to rest.'

I made friends with the tea lady. She was a chatty and pleasant young woman, always happy to do little favours for me, such as getting change for the phone or passing a message to Terry. There was an old guy on the other side of the ward who was always telling her what a lovely pair of twins she had.

'I can't walk past that old man's bed without having a comment from him. He's referring to my behind, you know. He's always telling me they look like a pair of twins wrestling under a blanket.' I couldn't help but laugh; she seemed to take it all in her stride. She told me about the guy who had been in my room a few weeks earlier.

'He was a nice guy, he was,' she leaned closer to me and whispered, 'but he was a sex-change.'

'Oh, is that right?' I said, pretending to be surprised, but it left me lost for words.

A few minutes later a nurse looked in on me. 'What's the matter?' she asked. 'You look as if you're deep in thought.'

'I was a bit bothered by something the tea lady said. Does she know about me?'

'Of course she doesn't. I wouldn't worry about her or anyone else knowing about you,' she said. 'That's how convincing you are,' she added with a smile.

After my first impression of the hospital, I changed my view of it entirely. Even though it was old and run-down, it had a down-to-earth feel about it. Once I could get out of bed and go and see my new friends down the ward I realized what a good atmosphere it had. The nurses were great. They used to make us cups of tea until the early hours in the morning. Nobody objected to us sending out for a pizza on the odd late evening, using the phone in the nurses' station. The delivery boy in his striped outfit would come straight up: 'Pizza for ward eight.'

I was in hospital for a total of three weeks. When I was fit enough to leave, Stewart kindly picked me up again.

The operation and recovery period meant that I missed a month of my fourth year of college. I spent only a week convalescing at home because I was now anxious to get back to my projects. Really, I should have taken that year off and caught up on my work and started the fourth year afresh. But because they told me that I would be back in hospital within six months, I thought I might as well go hell for leather and get my diploma before I went in for my final surgery. In fact, I could not afford to do another year in college. I needed to earn a living and there were major repairs needed on the house. The idea of coming out of surgery, with my course finished and a whole new life waiting for me, was so appealing I decided that I would give it my best shot; hopefully the end of the course would coincide with going into hospital.

From the start, returning to my projects, I worked as hard as I could, but I was still not fully recovered and found it very tiring. Before going into hospital I had moved my bed down into the living-room so that I wouldn't have to climb up the stairs. Stewart, his girlfriend and my other mate were still living in the house and gave me a lift to college every day, as there was no way I could ride my bike, particularly since it had a kick start. I was very grateful for all the help and support they gave me. Often, when I got home in the evening, I would sit on my bed propped up on some cushions. By the time my friends had made a cup of tea, I was already fast asleep. Just before Christmas my friends left to join their families and I spent Christmas Day alone with a bottle of whisky watching television. It was my choice to have some time to myself to rest up. I was snug in my living-room with everything I needed: music, food, chocolates and presents from my parents.

It was a cold winter and it started to snow. I got up one morning and found the shower full of snow. It still had no roof from the time Pie had fallen through it. The shampoo bottles had tall hats of snow. I got a bin-liner and my faithful roll of heavy Sellotape and tried to stick the flimsy plastic over the hole. With all my know-how this was the best I could come up with. It would last for a day or two, then fill up with snow or water and soon come down with a whoosh. My next DIY special was to wedge a broom handle up to make a sort of tent of the bin-liner. It seemed my whole house was being held together by Sellotape, but there was no money for repairs and all my energy was accounted for in college. It would have to wait.

I gave my last project my very best shot, but in the end I wasn't happy with the pieces that I had made for the final exhibition. I felt very disappointed and annoyed with myself and that, much as I had tried, I hadn't been able to catch up properly. There simply hadn't been enough time to do all the tests on the different kinds of glaze I wanted to apply. It really rankled that I had spent four years of my life working towards this event, only to find myself dissatisfied with my pieces.

While I was setting them up in the exhibition and trying to display them to their best advantage, I was ruminating about all this and felt dejected and pissed off. Suddenly one of the lecturers approached me with some trivial issue. He caught me at the wrong time and I lost my rag. It was unfair to turn my frustration on him, and when I proceeded to take all my pieces down, he tried to persuade me to leave them. I wouldn't listen to reason, I just packed up and went home.

The next day I came to my senses. I told myself I couldn't chuck four years of college away. It had been an impulsive act and I realized I should have listened to the lecturer. As I had been in college for all that time and had merits for my art work, surely all my marks wouldn't be just on my final project. Maybe they would take into consideration that I had lost a month. So I decided to go back and put up my work regardless.

'What do you think you are doing?' asked the same lecturer. 'We marked all the work yesterday.' My heart sank.

'Look, I'm sorry about yesterday,' I said to him and he gave me a quick nod.

'When is the assessor coming?'

'This afternoon,' he replied.

'Couldn't you mark me now, before he comes?'

'We'll see,' was all I got.

All the students were on a high. It was the end of four hectic years, and they all went out celebrating. I went along with them for a few drinks, and then we went back to the college to await the results. I was there in the hall with everyone else, waiting for the head to come out with the list of names of people who had passed.

When I started college I had not been bothered about any qualifications – it was the knowledge that mattered most to me. I never wanted to work for anyone else anyway. But, in the end, it did matter to me. I thought for sure my name would be on the list of passes. When I saw that it wasn't, I was gutted.

It was the time when the diploma changed from a four-year course to a two-year course. Most of the people on the list had been there only two years, and here I was after four years with nothing. I ran out of the hall and up the stairs to where this lecturer was standing and said, 'You've done this on purpose. I've been here for four years, receiving merits for my work. Even if you didn't mark my final project, surely that isn't all you mark me on. You've never liked me, you've never liked my attitude, you didn't like me voicing my opinions – that's what it is. As far as I'm concerned you had plenty of time to mark my project.'

'Are you doubting my professionalism?' he asked, offended.

'That's exactly what I am doing,' I answered.

'Listen, you don't understand,' he said to me. 'Sometimes I go home and I cry for my students.'

'Well, that's good to know,' I said, 'because you can go home tonight and have a fucking good cry for me. Thank you!' and I walked away. But when I got to the bottom of the stairs my emotions got the better of me and I was fighting to stay composed. I knew my attitude and quick temper had contributed to their decision not to mark me, and that I only had myself to blame. No matter what my circumstances were, I should at least have been able to control myself at this important time, but my tendency to cut off my nose to spite my face had let me down again. I had fucked up, and that was all there was to it.

Stewart saw me and asked what the matter was.

'Everything is finished,' I said. 'There is no business, no nothing, it's all over.'

'Don't be ridiculous, we can still do it.'

'No, there is nothing now.'

Stewart and I never did go into business together. I think he was in some ways relieved after my outburst on the final day. He knew how I had changed since he got to know me four years earlier. I had become more unpredictable, more moody and depressed while waiting and waiting to hear from the hospital. I am sure he often wondered if we could have survived together in business. Even though he knew I had all the talent and capability of doing it, there was just too much going on in my private life. Really, he understood none of it, but he liked me as a person and we got on very well. Good friends as we were, we never discussed my condition and he ignored my difficult moods.

After a couple of months had passed and I had calmed down, I went to the college and had a chat with Mr Cook. We talked about all the factors that led up to my not getting my diploma. Mr Cook agreed that I had learned the skills and done everything that was required on the course, with the only exception of displaying my final project. He said he would look into it for me.

'I'll put your case forward,' he said, 'and I don't see any reason why you shouldn't have your diploma.'

I felt reassured by Mr Cook's words and we parted on friendly terms. While I was at the college I dropped in to see Stewart who had been offered a job there as a technician. It was nice to see him and we had a cup of coffee together talking about old times. The lecturer with whom I had had the run-in was in the staff room as well. All was forgotten and we had a chat together. We talked about how stressful the final project can be and we were able to laugh at the states that we all got into, trying to get organized. We all had our own stories to tell and joke about. We were now on equal terms, no longer teacher and students and that made all the difference.

I had practically forgotten about my diploma when it arrived through the post a year later.

With college finished I settled down to wait for the next letter from Mr Davies. More than six months had passed and I felt at a loose end, expecting to go back into hospital any day. When I didn't hear anything I phoned the surgery secretary at the hospital and was told that I was on a waiting list and that I would hear from them as soon as there was a bed available. That was all she could tell me. I felt reassured and expected to have a short wait. I thought, surely it would be no longer than nine months, definitely I would be in within twelve.

My main objective at this time was to finalize my dealings with the solicitor regarding the house and get it into my name. I felt it was important to be sure that I would have a roof over my head whilst going through surgery. I needed the privacy and security of my own home. Despite the condition of the house, I was relieved now to be the sole owner.

During this time I had no idea when I would be going into hospital – I was always thinking it was imminent – so it was difficult to plan anything. Starting a business or looking for a job seemed pointless, and I lived from day to day. I was back on the dole and, with no extra money coming in, my house sank even deeper into a state of dilapidation.

I ended up waiting almost three years to have the next stage of surgery. It is difficult to describe how I coped during these three years of waiting. What kept me going was the thought that every day of waiting was a day closer to surgery. This tenuous belief kept me sane. In the meantime there were times of crisis and doubt. In the newspapers and on television I learned of the difficulties within the NHS, and with horror and a sinking heart I heard that a dozen hospitals were going to be shut down within London. These pieces of news would make me feel more anxious and I started to doubt that I would ever have my surgery completed.

11
What Took You So Long?

Well over a year had passed since my relationship with Katie had ended. I had started to enjoy life on my own again. Relationships were complicated and demanding and life was in many ways easier without them. I had complete freedom and, alone, I had a better perspective on my life. I felt relaxed, with no intrusions, and I was living comfortably with myself. While I was waiting in anticipation to hear from the hospital I kept myself to myself and only visited people I really wanted to see.

I had bought another motorbike about two years earlier; it was a good off-road bike and I would take it up into the hills. Sitting in solitude, surrounded by nature has always made me feel good, as far back as I could remember, from the time I was five and running around collecting newts, to when I was a troubled teenager. It was a joy to rediscover this feeling.

My favourite spot was a small clearing on top of a hill surrounded by forest. On one side of the clearing there was a deep drop into nothingness, and the trees leaned into this nothingness as if about to topple. I picked a spot to sit where I purposely couldn't see the bottom of the drop and it made me feel like I was facing the universe. With the expanse in front of me, my body felt small and there was a feeling of my inner body and my mind soaring and growing. The anchors that held me down and restricted me were released. The feeling gave me an inner calm and a deep sense of well-being. Down there in the valley were all my stresses and difficulties, but up here I felt at one with myself and with life.

In my house I tried to tidy up a bit before winter set in. I finally stuck a sheet of corrugated Perspex on the roof of my shower to stop the rain and the snow from coming in. The tiled floor got ice-cold in the winter, so I put a carpet down to make it a bit more comfortable. I decided to tackle my front room, which was still blocked off since the ceiling had come down. I cleared the rubble out and moved in my weight training equipment. A mate, Jack, would call in occasionally to have a work-out with me. Although I continued training I was always aware that I was supposed to gain weight on my stomach, and avoided too many stomach exercises. Jack was always asking me to come out for a pint after our work-outs, but I always declined. I told him I wanted calm and quiet and that I had everything I needed at home.

My front door stayed closed and for privacy I always came and went through the back door. Having blocked off my windows to the front for such a long time, I forgot at times that I actually lived in a street. I knew very little about what went on in the neighbourhood.

But one early summer evening, I was outside my front door cleaning up my bike, adjusting the chain and changing the spark-plug. I was having a break sitting on the front doorstep, drinking tea and having a smoke, when I noticed a girl on the opposite side of the street walking a small dog. A fleeting thought went through my head: 'She is quite attractive.' About fifteen minutes later she came back and stopped to say hello to me. She seemed a nice girl.

'Do you live here?' I asked.

'Oh, no, I'm just visiting my sister,' she said and pointed to the house opposite mine. Blind as I was to women at this time, I suddenly realized that I was attracted to this woman and the feeling was obviously mutual. After a few minutes of deliberation I thought, 'Oh, what the hell, why not invite her in?'

'I know about you,' she said bluntly as she sat down very close to me on the sofa, and as always, I was relieved that there was no need for explanations.

Louise was good company and she would come around to my house more frequently and I enjoyed her unexpected visits. She told me she had a boyfriend but that since she had met me she had broken up with him. Soon I discovered that this was not the case. She spent the evenings with him and then came to spend the night with me, leaving early in the morning to go home and get ready for work. When I confronted her with this, her excuse for still seeing her boyfriend was that he wouldn't leave her alone and she said that she would soon sort this out. I knew that breaking up can be difficult and felt it wasn't any of my business anyway. Her boyfriend kept phoning trying to find her and her parents became suspicious of her whereabouts.

Next she told me that her family had found out about our relationship and were not at all happy about it. A couple of her older sisters came banging on my door one night, demanding that Louise come home. Louise begged me not to open it.

'We know you're in there, you two,' they shouted. 'I bet you've got her drugged up in there.' I seemed to remember having been part of this ludicrous scenario once before in my life.

'This is ridiculous,' I said, pissed off at all the shouting and commotion outside my house. 'I want to open the door.'

'Please, please, don't,' she begged me nervously. 'They'll give up in a minute.'

She would often come over upset and needing to talk. She was quite shifty about her relationship with her boyfriend and complained constantly that he was hounding her and wouldn't leave her alone. Her boyfriend's parents told her that she would probably catch AIDS from me. On one occasion her father had had her by the throat, angry about her seeing me, and she told me she couldn't bear living with her parents any more.

I was taken in by all this and, feeling sorry for her, I gave her a key to my house.

'If things get really bad, and you can't get on with your parents, you can let yourself in here to have a break,' I said foolishly. She didn't hesitate. Often when I came home in the evenings, she would have left some food for me and she took to tidying up and washing my clothes and making herself at home.

One night there was a knock on my door at two o'clock in the morning. I had been out on my own, and was dozing on the sofa in my living-room. It was Louise's oldest sister. I invited her in, and she started giving me the third degree.

'How old are you anyway?' she asked.

'Twenty-seven. Why?'

'My sister is only nineteen,' she said accusingly. 'My parents will never agree to this relationship, so you can forget about it. Anyway, I want to know what's been going on between the pair of you.'

'Don't you think you'd better ask your sister?' I asked her.

'I don't think you are right for my sister, and neither does the rest of my family,' she stated in a self-righteous manner. 'You can't get married, you can't have kids – and have you had your operation yet?'

Normally I wouldn't have tolerated someone coming into my home to talk to me in this manner, bluntly voicing her prejudices. Who did she think she was? I tried to keep calm and reminded myself of Carole's words to me: I had to learn to be tolerant of other people's ignorance. This was the ideal test.

'Lots of people can't have kids. Would you speak to them in the same manner in which you're speaking to me? If I wanted to get married I could easily do so by going to a country where the laws aren't as prejudiced and ignorant as they are here. As for any operation, it's none of your business.'

If I had been injured in an accident or in a war, and lost my ability to father children, would this woman have come into my home to insult me like this and treat me with such disrespect? It amazes me how some people think they have a right to question me about the most private things and how they dig around in my intimate life, as if it should be public property. Much as I tried to be tolerant, I very much resented this. These comments made by other people were always said so carelessly and nonchalantly, as if I had a swinging brick for a heart, but they always reminded me of my sadness and grief.

Between the boyfriend, her family and all the talk about me, I felt responsible for Louise's difficulties and started to regret that I had ever met her. Here I was, trying to keep some stability to maintain my inner equilibrium, and this situation didn't help at all. What started out as a casual relationship was becoming very complicated. But I had started to grow fond of Louise and enjoyed having her around. Because of this I tried to ignore the things she was telling me. I didn't care to get to know her family anyway; they were obviously people I wouldn't have got along with. We were too different, but neither of us had the right to sit in judgement on the other.

With all that was going on, I kept asking myself why the hell I didn't finish my relationship with Louise altogether, but she had a bubbly personality and she had brightened up my life and distracted me from my seemingly everlasting wait for 'the letter' (and where the hell was it?) I knew I was killing time, but I could have picked a simpler way to do it. I should have stayed up in the hills and given the valley a miss. But I too was subject to human weaknesses.

I told Louise what her sister had said to me; with all the disapproval from her family, I asked her if our relationship was really worth continuing.

'Yes, I still want to see you,' she said with determination. 'I don't care what my family thinks, and it's over between me and Ron. What will convince him of it, is if I move in with you.'

'You might as well move in, you're practically living here anyway,' I said, feeling some trepidation. 'Let's see how it goes.'

My attraction for Louise was more physical than emotional, and I had lacked physical intimacy for quite some time. I wished I could have enjoyed this aspect of our relationship without all the hassle that went with it.

What I soon learned about Louise was that she loved all this attention and excitement. Anything that would create a drama was right up her street. I never did come to trust her completely, not on an emotional level anyway. She seemed too fickle, she was very young after all, and I remembered how I was at nineteen, when I had just got out of prison. I myself hadn't been able to give any kind of real commitment, or stay true to a relationship. Louise and I lived quite harmoniously together, but over time things kept happening that weakened my trust in her even further. I sensed she was someone who wanted to have her cake and eat it. Living with me she had complete freedom to come and go as she wished, and I suspected this was part of the reason she left her parents. She had told me she felt very restricted living with them and felt she had to be a model child, being the youngest of six. I didn't blame her for wanting freedom, I understood her need all too well, I had always needed my freedom and was still fighting for it desperately. Louise was an attractive young girl and just because I didn't want to go out and about, didn't mean that she shouldn't. She spent a lot of effort and time on her appearance and no doubt other men found her attractive too. Flattery would go a long way with her, but I wasn't very skilled at providing it. She constantly wanted reassurance and emotional attention from me, and although I tried my best, because I did have feelings for her, I just couldn't get into it.

'Sometimes I look at you and think I know you, but other times I look at you and I don't know you at all,' she used to say. 'You're like a stranger to me.' It was true that I was wrapped up in my own world. She wanted to have a good time but I had other things on my mind.

During the three years that we lived together, her family shunned our relationship completely. I wasn't welcome in their homes. 'I don't want to be involved with you not having contact with your family,' I often said. 'Go and see them, for Christ's sake.'

'If they don't accept you, I won't have anything to do with them,' she said adamantly.

'I don't care if they don't approve of me or ever want to meet me,' I said, 'but it's your family and you may live to regret having cut them off.' The drama with her family I could have done without, but I still enjoyed Louise's company enough to want to go on living together.

During this period I didn't see much of my parents and sister. The three of them were working full time and had busy lives of their own, but my mother sometimes came by to give me a cake or a tart that she had baked for me. She tried to encourage me to get a job and get some order in my life and, although I was always anticipating a hospital date, I knew she was right.

My home was by this time really in a bad state. I desperately needed to do something about it. I knew that if I was to go in for surgery I could not come back home to convalesce. The ground floor had become too damp to live in and Louise and I moved everything upstairs. I couldn't get my sofa and chairs up the stairs so I took a sledge hammer to them and a friend took the bits to the tip. The basic facilities in the house were very crude. I had applied for a grant for the house, but at the time they were only giving grants for repairs, and I would still have to pay for the kitchen and the bathroom to be built. And in order to increase the mortgage I would have to be employed.

Almost two years had gone by without a word from the hospital and I realized I had to get a job, not just for money to repair the house but for myself too. I didn't much like being on the dole and I needed something to occupy my mind to make the wait easier. Also I had accumulated a debt on my mortgage and needed to get up to date on my payments. I had to show that I could keep up regular monthly payments in order to increase the mortgage and have enough money to repair the house, which by now would cost quite a bit.

Working for myself or for friends was one thing, but actually joining the workforce was another. I already felt I had a pretty good picture of what society thought of people like me. I had experienced humiliation and prejudice within my own family, from policemen and women, from prison officers, from the press, from acquaintances and people from my childhood. Every time I thought of the need to get a job, all these obstacles and threats stood out in my mind. I felt paranoid and my self-esteem was rock-bottom. My main problem was myself and I wasn't sure how I would handle confrontations with people who knew about me, and around these parts, chances were that someone would. I just wished that my surgery was over, so I could put my life into action. I desperately wanted to move away from the area, but fate held me here and I would have to make the most out of it.

I kept going to the Job Centre, and one day I saw there was a job going as a printer's assistant, to do silk-screen and litho printing. I applied for the job and went for an interview, armed with a few of my drawings.

To my amazement I got the job, and turned out to be quite good at it. As I knew would happen, someone did know about me. We were all sitting in the coffee room within a day or two of me starting. One of the boys was messing around, drawing a penis on a Perspex cut-out of a man.

'That's a bit small, isn't it? It looks like a sex-change,' said another one. The room went silent and everybody looked embarrassed.

'Come on, we'll go back to work, shall we?' said the guy I worked with.

'Sure, mate,' I said and ignored the comment.

Although I knew I had it coming sooner or later, I was proved wrong about their attitude. No one ever mentioned anything again. I got to know them all and we got on well together and had many good laughs; on the odd lunchtime we had a beer and a game of pool in the pub opposite. In the end they could see that I was just a man doing a job.

Even though it was a big printing company, the equipment that they used was primitive compared to the stuff we'd had in college. I quickly picked up the skills and when the head printer quit his job after two months, I was given the job as head of the department. They took on another trainee, whom I had to train in turn.

The job was interesting and varied and it kept me going. Mainly I printed signs for various businesses. It involved cleaning and degreasing the silkscreens in preparation for coating them in a light-sensitive liquid, which had to be applied in a darkroom. I prepared the artwork and cut the vinyls to the required size for the stickers to be applied to the signs. The printing was done on a variety of materials: metals, vinyl, rubber and Perspex.

Fun as the job was, the fumes from the thinners we used were sometimes a bit hard to live with, especially in the summer, when the heat would make them rise to nose level. I got used to it, but when I came home in the evening Louise would comment on how strongly I smelled: the smell would go right through my work overalls, through my clothes, right down to my underpants. One day a couple of the boys at work were at the baker's next door, where we used to take it in turn to get sandwiches.

'Who is the guy with the black hair and the black moustache?' the baker asked them.

'That's Ray, the printer,' they said.

'That explains it,' he said to them. 'When he came in here

yesterday I had to leave the door open for twenty minutes, the smell was so bad.'

Louise had got a new hairdressing job where she had more responsibility, and she was good at it. To me, things seemed to be OK between us, but it was becoming obvious that life was too quiet for her liking and I wasn't enough for her. Maybe I was becoming boring. I had taken to sitting in my backyard, rain or shine. I especially liked the rain. As soon as it started to rain I would run out the back with a cushion, a cup of tea and a joint. The old man next door once saw me walking out with my cushion and a towel wrapped around my waist.

'My God, now I've seen everything,' he exclaimed. 'Where is your bar of soap?' Whenever I came in from the rain, I would sit in a chair and 'drip-dry'. I also liked to sit on the slate roof of my lean-to kitchen with the cats for company. They loved joining me up there to look at the sky. Louise told me once she wished she were one of the cats because I paid more attention to them than to her. I laughed, thinking she was joking. Maybe my peculiarities had started to annoy Louise. Also, I didn't want to go out anywhere.

'I'm leaving,' she said out of the blue one day. 'I've already moved all my stuff out.' When I asked her why, she couldn't give me a satisfactory answer. I guessed that there was someone else involved, but she wouldn't say. Her decision took me by surprise and I felt quite sad about it.

On account of the working environment and the fumes, I talked to my employers and offered to turn the basement of our building into a new printing workshop so that I could have more room and better ventilation. It was a huge basement and it would make my job a lot more pleasant. I would do any necessary building work myself with the help of whoever else was available. My employers agreed to it and ordered all the materials I needed. I set about doing the work, but I never had the time to actually finish it.

I had been with the business for about nine months when I phoned the hospital, yet again, to ask when I was likely to be called in.

'It'll be a while. You're ninety-sixth on the waiting list,' I was told by the secretary.

'Ninety-sixth!' I exclaimed. 'I was told it would be six months, but I've been waiting almost three years.'

'That *is* a long time to wait,' she said, puzzled, and she promised to look into it for me.

A week later the longed-for letter about the continuation of my surgery arrived. The wait was finally over. I was both very excited and very anxious about having what I thought, as it had been explained to me, would be the last operation ever. Now I was actually facing the experience. I know that some people believe that this kind of surgery is playing with fire, that it constitutes self-mutilation, but they obviously don't understand the self-alienation and the misery of being trapped in the wrong body. Being detached from one's body is a very isolated and lonely place to be. The very idea of mutilation was horrifying to me, I don't relish pain, but in order to live my life with some degree of happiness and harmony, I had to go through with it.

I cut down drastically on my smoking to be better able to tolerate the anaesthetic (and after it I stopped altogether for a time) and tried to look after my health as much as possible.

I had seen little of Louise over the last six months but suddenly she came to visit me. She had been living with a friend but they weren't getting on very well and she wanted to leave. She didn't want to go back to her parents and she wasn't having any luck finding somewhere else to live.

'If you're desperate,' I told her, 'I'm going into hospital for at least six weeks, so you can move in here until you get yourself sorted out and at the same time feed the cats for me.' In the month leading up to my surgery, our relationship was rekindled in a fashion. If I'd had any sense, I wouldn't have let it happen but we were obviously a convenience to each other.

By this time I had a very good rapport with my employers. They valued my work enough to say that they would keep the job open for me until I was fit enough to go back, which I told them would be three months at the most. I left reams of instructions for my assistant on how to handle the printing machines, and what to do if he ran into any trouble.

I finished work on a Friday and went in for surgery on the following Monday. As before, my mother provided me with all I needed, plus a few nice things to eat in hospital. My family were worried about me, but I wasn't. By this time I felt that my family were one hundred per cent behind me. They were trying their best to help me in any way they could. But I hated to have to worry them unnecessarily, so I kept as much of my problems to myself as possible. Sometimes I wondered if my mother had a sixth sense, because whenever I was in a crisis of some sort, she would turn up on my doorstep.

My sister had been supportive too, in her own quiet way. I feel sad that, with my life the way it was, we missed out as brother and sister and never really had an opportunity to become close. I did admire her a lot; she was an attractive and intelligent woman who was continually studying and bettering herself. She worked very hard and was a very private individual, although she had many friends. There had been a few men in her life but for reasons of her own she had remained single and continued to live in my parents' house.

As usual before surgery I was over the moon and on a high. This was definitely it, soon it would be all over for good and I could start my life in earnest. Louise accompanied me to the train station and waved goodbye to me. I had told her not to visit, but that I would appreciate her picking me up. I had a huge bag with me containing all the things I would need to occupy my mind for six weeks. My music, drawing pads, pencils, books, and everything my mother had given me: fruit, biscuits, sweets and all the toiletries that she thought I needed. I had loads of clothes and two big bath towels; all I needed now was a tent.

When I arrived at Charing Cross Hospital and had settled in my room on the ward, Mr Saxby and Mr Davies (the consultant surgeon who'd operated on me previously) came to see me to apologize for the long delay.

'We know it is a long time to be kept waiting, and we have to confess that the reason for this was that your records went astray when we were moving units from the West Middlesex to Charing Cross,' they said. 'Also, things have happened in the meantime. We have been trying to improve the operation and unfortunately it has become a political issue as well. Some politicians want to make the operation illegal on account of them deeming it unnecessary and too expensive.'

'My God,' I exclaimed, shocked at this prospect, 'if you have a solution to my condition, a solution that would change the entire quality of my life, it doesn't seem right that it should be made illegal.'

'There is no need to convince us,' they said. 'We're working with you not against you.'

Then came the bad news: they weren't going to perform the whole operation in one go, as I had been led to believe. It was going to be done in four separate operations. They explained that, because of the risks involved, it was more likely to be successful if it was done in stages.

'Oh no, not again,' I thought, 'not more delays, more waiting, months of listening for letters to drop through the mailbox.'

'How long is this all going to take?' I asked them.

'Possibly two years, perhaps more.'

What could I say? 'Well, that's my job gone,' I thought grimly. I phoned Louise that night to tell her the bad news. I was upset and despondent; yet again I had been disappointed and it felt like a huge set-back.

I had been told I could have my last cigarette at seven that evening, so I left the ward and went outside to the green in front of the hospital where there were two long ponds with Chinese goldfish in them. Sitting on the grass having my last fag, I wondered how I was going to cope with two years of surgery, knowing I would have to endure a lot over this time, physically and emotionally. It was a daunting prospect, but if this is what it took, I was quite prepared to endure it.

Before going in for the surgery, Mr Saxby and his assistant came to the ward to examine my abdomen, the site of the operation. Mr Saxby pulled out a felt-tip pen.

'We'll cut here,' he said to his assistant, drawing a ten-inch line from my groin, along the crease of my leg, to the side of my hip, 'and here,' and he made another line, parallel to the first line, but four and a half inches above.

'How are you going to do this?' I asked nervously.

'We cut along these two lines and then lift the four and a half inch wide band of flesh and skin, along with an artery, up and away from your leg. We then make a coil, or a tube, by rolling it up lengthwise and stitching the length of the coil at the back. Both ends of this tube, your penis, will still be attached at your groin and your hip respectively, but the middle will be free and separated from your body.

'You'll be left with a four and a half inch gap in the crease of your thigh. We'll pull the skin from your leg and your stomach and stitch them together underneath your penis.

'I'll lift as much skin as I can for the best possible results,' Mr Saxby continued, 'but don't worry, your penis won't be a whole ten inches long.' He smiled.

I smiled too, and joked: 'God, I wouldn't be able to keep the girls away.'

'Will there be much visible scarring?' I asked him.

'Once your penis has been freed from your hip, you'll see the scar that runs along half the diameter of the top of your leg, and there will be a scar running up the back of your penis, which won't be noticeable.'

'That's not too bad,' I said, delighted.

'Nothing will be visible if you go for a swim in a pair of regular swimming trunks,' he assured me. 'After a few months we will have you in to partially sever the tip of your penis from your hip, and after another few months we'll cut it free completely. But for now it needs to be attached to your body at both ends to allow the blood to flow through it to help it heal up. It will need all the blood supply it can get initially for the blood vessels in the base of your penis to grow strong.'

At eleven o'clock that morning a nurse came with a gown and a hat for me to put on and gave me two Temazepam tablets to calm me down before going in for surgery. I much preferred them to an injection in my backside, as I'd had in previous operations, and they worked: I felt quite high when they came to get me.

When I woke up after the operation, I was lying flat on my back. All I was aware of was pain. Vaguely, in the distance I could hear two men talking: 'If the pressure gets too great, shove a tube in here . . .' I drifted out again. The next thing I was aware of was a nurse telling me something.

'There is someone here to see you.'

It was Louise. She had decided to come because I had been upset on the phone, even though I had strongly discouraged her. It was in the evening and I was very dozy, still not totally awake.

'Give us a look, then,' she said, and without thinking I pulled the covers back. I hadn't even looked at it myself yet. If she hadn't taken me by surprise I would probably never have allowed her to see the results of my surgery, which was quite visible in spite of the bandages. No one except doctors had ever seen me without my shorts on.

'Don't worry,' she said reassuringly after examining my groin, 'I can see exactly what they are trying to achieve, and everything looks fine.' It was quite nice to see a familiar face, after all. She was also a good person to have around in a situation like this. She always wanted to be helpful and wasn't put off by a bit of blood and gore. She had a good way with people and within a day or two she had met a Yugoslav couple who offered to put her up in their home while she was coming in to keep me company and help nurse me.

I was told that same evening that I had to get out of bed to walk. It was necessary to do it right away since my right hip joint would start to stiffen up if it wasn't used, and this would cause me additional pain. I dragged myself out of that bed in agony, all hunched up. I couldn't straighten my body because the skin was so tight – it felt like it was going to burst at the seams any second. I had to drag my leg along – I couldn't lift it at all, my mind was not in control of it.

All night long, as I lay there drifting in and out of consciousness, people came in and out of the room, lifted the blankets and pressed on my penis to see if it was getting enough blood supply.

The skin of my right leg felt very taut and excruciatingly painful. I couldn't cope with anything at all touching it. Even the weight of a tissue paper would make me jump through the roof. Nerves had been damaged in the leg and apart from the pain there were also other weird sensations in it, such as shooting electric shocks, or pins and needles all over it, or creeping sensations going in all directions. The leg was huge, very swollen. After the surgery everything was left alone for a week, but after that my dressings had to be changed once a day. It was important to keep the space between my penis and the skin underneath clean and dry. Having the nurse drag a cotton pad dipped in saline solution in between two sides of raw flesh was indescribably unpleasant. Then they had to wrap my penis in gauze strips soaked in a gel, and pack the underside with cotton pads to prevent the two areas from knitting together and to allow air to circulate around it. I would grit my teeth and hold on to the sides of the bed for dear life. The sensation was like being wiped with the burning end of a cigarette. It was almost as much an ordeal to wait for these dressing changes as to suffer them.

First thing in the morning there would be a ward round, and doctors and nurses would congregate around my bed, even before I was fully awake. The doctor in charge would grab my penis and pull it out from my body and turn it inside out, to see how it looked underneath. It was very unpleasant. One night I slept poorly, waking up hourly thinking and fretting about the ward round. I was startled awake when I saw the doctor leaning towards me. I put both my hands up and beseeched him, 'Don't pull it today, please. Can't you pull it tomorrow?'

Everyone laughed and the doctor said, 'OK I won't pull it today, but I'll have to pull it tomorrow.'

The days were clocked by pain. I waited in dread of each round and each change of dressing. In the meantime I lay absolutely still, my leg propped up on a couple of pillows.

The pain was getting worse. I told the doctors and nurses, but they had looked and thought everything was fine. The area is all swollen and numb, they'd said, and you shouldn't feel very much. Gradually the swelling started to go down and then I myself discovered the reason for the pain.

I decided to have a shower, and when I stood under the stream of water, letting it run down between my penis and stomach, suddenly a very long string of suture detached itself and came out.

'My God, where has that come out from? It's supposed to hold me together,' I thought in a panic. I'd had a total of over two hundred stitches, and I didn't like the look of that long string. When the doctor came on his round, I anxiously showed it to him. He grabbed my penis like a handle, with both hands, and turned it around, first one way then the other. I was seeing stars and groaned with pain. The area from the top of my knee up to my hip-bone, across to the centre of my stomach and down to my groin was very painful and any touch at all caused a deep throb.

'Ah, I see the problem,' he said. The skin on the underside of my penis had split and it was here that the suture had come loose. There was one hell of an infection brewing there. They took a swab and sent it to the lab to find the right antibiotics for it. That night I had a dream. In this dream the skin on my hand was opened up, right along the scar where my tattoo removal had been. Underneath this opening was a ball of fat. As I looked at it, this ball disintegrated suddenly.

The next day Mr Saxby and Mr Davies came in to tell me that they had diagnosed the problem. I was suffering from a breakdown in fat tissue (fat necrosis, or death of fat tissue due to poor blood supply), which meant that my flesh had started to rot.

'I'm sorry,' said Dr Davies. 'Sometimes this happens and it means you'll have to stay in hospital a further couple of weeks.'

They prescribed me a thousand milligrams of antibiotics a day and told me the rest was up to my body – to heal itself. The auxiliary nurses would come in and wrinkle up their noses – 'Have you spilled anything in here?' – and go straight to the window to open it. But it was me, it was my flesh that stank. It was horrible and embarrassing, and I was frightened.

'Oh please, God, what are you doing to me?' The terror of what might go wrong had been with me the whole time. Now something had indeed gone very wrong. 'You've got to do this for me, God, you've got to help me heal. This is my destiny, it cannot fail.'

I knew that the antibiotics I had been prescribed needed my assistance. I had to be calm and relaxed in order to help myself heal. Being frantic with fear and stress would only aggravate the infection and hinder the healing process. I tried desperately to will myself to stay composed. I knew I had to calm down, and yet the fear of losing what I had just gained filled me with panic.

I was now to have two dressings a day. I waited with apprehension and dread for these exercises in bravery. Unpleasant as it was, with the infection, I constantly felt the need to be properly cleaned up. They hauled me into the bath-tub in a special chair to have a shower. I asked one of the nurses if I should use soap to wash all the stinking mess off.

'Yes, use plenty of soap, plenty of soap,' she said.

The next morning Mr Saxby, who was checking me over, said, 'You haven't used soap on this, have you?' The nurse was standing there and I looked at her.

'No, of course not,' I said.

'Good, make sure you don't. Soap can get clogged up underneath and cause all kinds of problems.' Little things like that took on major proportions for me. It was my penis, my lifeline. Absolutely nothing must go wrong.

After ten days it started to heal and the split skin started to come together. The swelling went down and my penis was no longer taut against the skin, it was even hanging down a little bit. I was overcome with relief and gratitude. But I still had to go through six months of cleaning pus from the open wounds, which seemed to stay raw for ever.

It got better and better, although the pain in my leg and hip was still almost intolerable. But you get used to everything and I learned to live with it. It was a very long time before the pain started to subside, but the rewards more than compensated for the discomfort.

All this time I had a long flexible tube going into my hip, just below the incision, coiling around inside my abdomen, to drain off the bad blood. There was a bottle on the end which had a suction mechanism, and the nurses would change the bottle when it got full. Any tampering with this tube triggered off deep pains in my leg. A few days before leaving the hospital to go home, the time came to take this tube out. I dreaded this and was bracing myself for it. I had asked the nurse to tell me when she was going to pull, so that I could take a big breath. She kept pulling for what seemed an eternity. My facial muscles went out of control, going through every contortion of agony, torment and disbelief and I felt myself about to faint. I was overcome by the sheer relief of finally seeing the end of it come out: I couldn't believe the length of it, it must have been about two and a half feet.

'That must be the most disturbing sensation I've ever experienced.' I sighed with relief. 'I must be the most pathetic patient you have ever had.'

'Not at all,' she assured me. 'I did leave the suction on while I was pulling it out, it helps to pull out all the waste along with it. That must be what made it so unpleasant.'

There was another nurse who also used to change my dressings for me. She was a born-again Christian. While doing the dressing she used to take the opportunity to tell me that if I had come to the church sooner, I would have been helped and I wouldn't have needed all this. Gay people could be similarly saved.

'As far as I'm concerned,' I told her, 'God knows me, and he is working through the hands of surgeons. It's all part of God's plan.' That shut her up for a while.

After about three weeks I was well enough to go home. I had had no visitors or phone calls, but this had been my choice. Louise was still around, and had come in every day to keep me company. She had seen it all and I didn't mind too much her being there when my dressings were being changed, now that my penis was where it should be.

'I could do the dressings for you, you know,' she said to me one day. I looked at her and wondered why she wanted to do this for me. I wasn't sure about the future of our relationship, and I thought that this would make me very dependent on her.

'Are you sure you know what to do?' I asked her.

'Yes, I've been watching the nurses. I know what to do.'

As I was getting ready to leave the hospital Mr Saxby came in to have a word with me. One of the nurses offered to phone and arrange for a district nurse to come and change my dressings for me once I got home. Mr Saxby looked at Louise, who was also in the room, and said, 'Well, is there any need for a district nurse?' Surprised, I too looked at Louise. It seemed to me as if the two of them had discussed the matter and had already made the decision.

Last of all I had to have most of the stitches removed. Seeing the scalpel coming towards my skin had me gasping. The whole area was numb, similar to how your face feels after a visit to the dentist, yet any touch, even one as light as a feather, would send shooting pains, shocks and throbs through my entire leg.

We got a taxi to Paddington station. Having been in a confined sterile place for several weeks, the contrast of a very busy train station was unbearable. All I could think of was how I longed to get on that train and into my own house, between four safe walls. As people were running to catch trains I was terrified someone would bump into me; while Louise was trying to find out which platform our train left from, I was hiding among some trolleys by the side of a wall where I felt safe from all the hustle and bustle. I was limping quite badly and felt paranoid about people looking at me. The longer you take to get from A to B, the more people stare at you, or so I thought. I glared back at them with a killer look. Louise was quite good about it all, she held people at bay and made a path for me to get on to the train.

I was glad to be home and to see all my cats again. They were all making a fuss over me and wanted to jump up on me. I hated having to tell them not to, but I gave them lots of attention and stroked them and talked to them. The first night in my house I was freezing cold. Having got used to the constant heat in the hospital, I spent the night shivering while Louise piled blankets, then coats, on top of me. Coming from a sterile environment to my dark and dusty house, I worried at first about catching another infection. But soon I realized that this was my natural environment and that my immune system was equipped for it.

Even though I was very tired and physically worn out, emotionally I felt very different. Even with all the anxiety of surgery, I felt peaceful. I was almost there, finally my past would be behind me. Soon fun and laughter could be a part of my life once again. I could start to enjoy life in my rightful body. I still kept myself to myself, avoiding people as much as possible, although my mother sometimes came by with some of her home-made specials.

Louise did end up doing my dressings for me; the doctors had shown her exactly what to do. I wasn't entirely happy with this arrangement, but at the same time I was grateful to her, not least for the privacy it guaranteed. With district nurses, you could be having a different one every day. At least now it was kept between me, Louise and the hospital. It was also very stressful for her: she worried about doing it right, but I thought she dealt with it in a very efficient and competent manner.

A fortnight after we had come back to my house I discovered why Louise had been so keen to help me.

'I've got something to tell you,' she said to me uneasily. 'I'm pregnant.'

I couldn't believe what I was hearing and jumped out of bed.

'If you think for one moment that I am looking after another man's baby, you're wrong.' I overreacted, but her news had really thrown me. 'What have you fucking done?' I groaned, thinking of all the implications.

Being pregnant changed things; she did have something over me now. I had got used to her gentle care and attention, helping me with my dressings twice a day. Now I saw that there were motives behind her concern and eagerness to help me.

'I don't want anything to do with it,' I said to her.

'You looked after someone else's child,' she shouted accusingly. 'You must have loved her I suppose.'

'You know fuck all about the situation I was in, and it's got nothing to do with you and me. I've sworn that no one is ever going to put me in that position again. I can't have children of my own, and that's the fucking end of it. I'm not bringing up anyone else's child.' Nothing in the world would sway me from this conviction.

'I can't keep it anyway,' Louise screamed at me. 'I don't want to keep it. I can't.'

I softened slightly. 'For God's sake, think about it. Keep the baby if you want to. I'm sorry I went over the top but I meant what I said.' I knew in my heart that Louise and I were not meant for each other anyway, and I didn't want her to get rid of her child because of me.

Within a few days she had an abortion. Even though our relationship was on shaky ground, I did go with her to the hospital for moral support. But I didn't like the way she had sprung the news on me knowing how vulnerable I felt, knowing I had come to depend on her. She continued to help me, but it was much more difficult for me to cope with. When you are at your most vulnerable and exposed, it is incredibly important to feel safe and to trust those around you. I didn't feel like that about Louise any more. It made it hard to keep my dignity.

After a couple of months I felt better, but I was terrified of being knocked or bumped in any way. I couldn't even get any trousers on, I lived for almost two years in track suits and pyjamas. The house was in the same awful state, and I simply put a chair in my dilapidated shower since I couldn't stand for very long.

I would have liked to go back to work, but I hadn't counted on how physically weak and exposed I was going to feel. Realistically I couldn't have done it anyway, knowing that I had several more operations ahead of me, and I was only out of hospital long enough to recover before the next stage of surgery. The other factor that made it impossible was the chemicals used in the printing. There wasn't a square inch of your skin, no matter how covered up, that didn't come in contact with the cleaning fluids. My employers apologized and told me that they couldn't keep the job open for me indefinitely. They needed someone experienced so they ended up contracting the printing out to another workshop.

I took to walking a lot. My leg was very sore and I still had a limp. For that reason I liked to walk on uneven ground where it was less noticeable so I stuck to footpaths that took me up into the hills or along canal paths or river banks. On one path there were some sacks of stone chippings. I would pick a couple of them up and carry them on my shoulders, to get the strength back in my legs. Having to walk really slowly across the road at a zebra crossing, while all the cars were waiting for me gave me a foretaste of what it must be like to be old. I avoided roads and public places as much as I could. Anyway, I couldn't bear people getting too physically close to me, not even Louise. I felt I needed a wide empty space around me at all times.

Perhaps what helped the healing process were my trips out into the countryside. They lightened my thoughts, and the sounds of nature had a calming effect on me. I felt like an injured animal myself, struggling for survival. I had always been sensitive about living things, but now my sensitivity came to a point of obsession and therefore I sympathized with everything in nature that was out of control.

When I was sitting in my back garden I observed everything that went on, the comings and goings of even the tiniest creatures. I did understand and respect the laws of nature, but in my frame of mind I often took it upon myself to save smaller insects being attacked by larger ones, by lifting them away on a leaf and depositing them elsewhere where they could have another chance. When I was walking on roads I kept an eye on the pavement for living things, making sure I didn't step on any. After rainfall, earth-worms get washed on to the pavement and I would stoop to pick them up and throw them back into the grass. As when I was a child, this was my way of dealing with the stresses of my life, it had always worked for me, and I didn't care how crazy this appeared to others.

I was hypersensitive to all nuances of colours, smells and shapes anyway, taking it all in as I walked along. I particularly noticed how nature had a way of finding its way back, in spite of the fact that we are trying to push it away: clumps of grass bursting through the tarmac, plantlife growing out of every crack.

My parents used to come and visit me occasionally and at this time they were getting to know Louise better, having just met her briefly in the past. She had a very outgoing, confident personality and they got on well with her, obviously thinking she was good for me.

One day my mother came to tell me that my grandmother had fallen and broken her hip. She had found her in the kitchen where she was lying helpless. Over the years I had seen quite a bit of my grandmother. I popped into her house at regular intervals and she would always say, 'Make me a cup of tea, my handsome boy, and pour yourself a large whisky.' She would always dab holy water on my forehead and tell me, 'Don't you worry about anything, everything is going to be all right, I know it will.'

'Right,' I'd say, 'now, let me put some holy water on you.' We would sit and have long chats about the past and we still talked a lot about my grandfather.

After coming out of hospital my grandmother temporarily moved in with my parents, and Louise and I frequently walked along the canal bank to their house to visit and help out. We saved all our vegetable peelings and leftover bread to feed to the goats and the ducks along the way. We'd often sit for hours by the canal bank watching the swans and the ducks. There was a variety of animals in the fields along the canal, horses, goats and chickens. I had a particularly soft spot for a tiny goat which appeared one day among the other animals. Its coat was curly, like sheep's wool, and it had floppy ears and tiny horns. He looked so helpless and vulnerable, and the big goats would butt him to the ground whenever we came to feed them. I worried about this little goat and was very tempted to take him home. Just as I had anticipated, one day he was attacked by dogs and injured. The owner put him in a barn; I went and checked on him twice the day it happened, hoping he would survive. He didn't; the following night I took some oats to feed him, it was pitch black in the barn and there was no sound. I lit a candle and found him dead in the corner.

I sat down beside him and cried bitterly. I wished to God I had taken him home.

Six months passed before I was called to London to have my penis partially severed from my hip. Freeing my penis was to be done in two stages, as I had been told, in order for the blood supply not to be cut off suddenly. It was supposed to have been three months only, but as fate would have it, there was another person coming in for an almost identical operation, with exactly the same name and similar age who had been given my appointment by mistake. It seemed a chance in a million that such a person existed and this could have happened, but it did.

The date of my operation was set. I got on the train to go to London at a quarter to four that morning. I felt a wreck. I had been awake all the previous night, unable to get the rest which I so badly needed before surgery. Money was a problem too. My financial situation was dire, and just getting the money together for a full fare to London had not been easy. I knew my parents would have lent me money, but they had been so helpful to me in the past that I didn't want to trouble them unless it was absolutely necessary.

This part of the surgery wasn't a very difficult procedure and when I woke up from the anaesthetic, Mr Saxby was standing by me with Louise, in the middle of explaining to her what he had done and how he wanted her to dress the wound. I looked around me and saw blood spattered all over his gown. There was blood all over the blanket too.

'Just have a look at it now,' he said to me when he saw that I was awake, and he opened up all the dressings. Hesitantly I looked down. I had a hell of a shock. I don't know what it was that I had expected to see, but there was the end of my penis seemingly severed and the end totally exposed. But a bit of the underside was still attached to my hip. It looked very delicate. I hadn't expected them to cut that much, and it seemed that my penis was held in such a delicate balance that any bump or scrape would severe its fragile link to my hip.

These months were frustrating, waiting for each stage of surgery in turn. I had nothing to do except try to gain my strength back and make sure I was physically well protected. The anaesthetic took the strength out of me as well as the surgery itself, and anxiety also took its toll. I tried to moderate my favourite vices, but I longed to let rip and create a ruckus and feel really alive. I was young and I wanted fun and excitement in my life too, not having to be careful all the time. Instead I lived like an elderly person, resting plenty and always being cautious. It wasn't really in my nature to be like this and it dampened my spirits.

Things would happen occasionally to reinforce the need to be ultra-careful. One day Louise and I walked up a large hill near my home town. It was a hill I often used to scramble up in my childhood. At the top there was a very steep grassy slope where, as children, we used to slide down, sitting on bits of cardboard or plywood. Having made my way slowly to the top, the memories of my childhood flooded back. I spotted an old board, and went to sit on it to enjoy the view. As soon as I sat down and put one foot on the board, it took off. I went hurtling down the steepest bit of the hill, without any way of stopping myself. I finally crashed at the bottom and rolled over three times. All I could think of was protecting my lower body and hoping to God that I hadn't injured myself. Once that had been ascertained, I laughed for hours. The absurd irony of the situation and the expression of total disbelief on Louise's face as she ran helpless down the hill beside my out-of-control board, was priceless.

Finally the day came when I was supposed to go to London to have the end of my penis completely severed from my hip. The few days leading up to my journey to London were nerve-racking. I was frightened and restless. I no longer felt like I had ten years earlier when they could have done anything to me, and I welcomed any intervention to help me along the road to complete malehood.

Had I been able to have the surgery ten years earlier, I feel my life would have been so much easier. With each year my rejection of my body had escalated and the emotional trauma increased with it. For that reason I hope that in the future they will go on to perfect these operations so that others like me can get relief earlier in life. At twenty-one you have the ability to recover physically and emotionally much quicker. At that age there is still a strong zest for life, and people in this predicament would be able to put all the confusion and unhappiness behind them sooner and get on with living.

The success of each stage of surgery came to mean even more to me as time went on, and it was increasingly important that nothing should go wrong. I had suffered a lot of pain, and was longing for it all to come to a successful conclusion. The long stretches of time, months and years, waiting for those letters from London to drop into the mailbox had been hard for me.

Hearing stories about prejudiced politicians, about the failures of different experimental surgery, and about the fragile state of the NHS, and never knowing if I was actually going to come to the end of the road and begin a new life in the body of a complete man, had affected me profoundly.

I was called to my preliminary appointment a month before going in for the surgery that would free my penis from my hip completely, and was seen by a doctor whom I'd only met briefly before. He sat me down and said, very apologetically, 'The thing is, Mr Thompson, your local health authority has refused to pay for the rest of the surgery, which means that we can't continue surgery. I'm terribly sorry,' he added.

'My God!' I exclaimed, horrified. 'What do you mean? You can't leave me like this, man, you just can't leave me in this state.' I gestured to my groin. He repeated what he had said, but I wouldn't have any of it. Seeing my distressed state he finally said, 'Hang on a minute.' He walked out, leaving me sitting in the consulting room on my own, shocked and helpless.

When he came back in he said, 'I'm awfully sorry for distressing you, I'm really sorry. It isn't you. I thought you were somebody else.'

Thank God! Selfishly I was so happy it wasn't me. This other person was obviously the same guy they had mixed me up with before. I couldn't help feeling a twinge of regret and pity for this other Raymond Thompson. I certainly knew now exactly how it felt to be in his position and be given this news. I often wonder what happened to him and hope that he managed to get things sorted out.

A few weeks later, when Louise and I arrived at the hospital, I went straight up to ward eight as I had been asked to.

Mr Saxby happened to be on the ward at the time.

'I have been meaning to have a word with you before the operation,' he said. 'Come into my office.'

'Let's have a look at it,' he said. 'How is it healing up?'

It was obvious that he had something else to tell me and I waited anxiously.

'Right, the thing is . . . now . . . I would be the best plastic surgeon in the world if I could tell you that what I am about to do this morning will be a complete success.'

My stomach started to churn.

'There is a chance,' he continued, 'that when your penis is detached from your hip, the end of it might go black and you might lose some of it.'

I was in a daze. 'What do you mean, go black?'

'The thing is, it might get "frightened". It has had a good blood supply, and all of a sudden it is not going to have that any more. It will be a shock to it. It might not be able to survive. Let's just hope that it will stay warm and pink.'

I really had no idea that this was a possibility. I had not been told of this before.

'What happens if I lose it? Is there anything else you can do for me?'

'Well –'

Before he had time to answer I interjected: 'I suppose I have my other leg.'

'I suppose that's up to you,' he said without much enthusiasm. But he added, 'Don't worry too much, it might only be the tip that goes black. We'll sort it out somehow.'

'Warm and pink,' I thought blankly, and as I walked out of that room a mammoth panic attack set in. My stomach was like jelly, my heart was racing. I felt like I couldn't breathe. Outside in the corridor I fell to my knees against the wall, feeling sick and giddy, trying to calm myself. I don't think I have ever been so frightened.

I already saw my penis as an entity with a life of its own, like a little human being. It was as if I had to breathe life into this part of my body, which should always have been there, should have been mine from birth. This was meant to be, I was a man.

'How can I not make it frightened?' I thought desperately. 'I have put my body through so much already, I must be able to cope with this.'

Even though it had felt somewhat unnatural to have my penis attached to my leg, I had grown accustomed to it, and I felt I didn't want to lose even that. Even in its abnormal position I was more 'me' than I would have been without it. As long as it was there and it was safe, I could relax. Now I was in danger of losing it. But there was no turning back.

I eventually calmed down a bit, sitting there on my bag, leaning against the wall, and someone came to get me to take me to my ward. They took my clothes and gave me a paper gown to put on. The ward was freezing cold, and I lay there under a single sheet waiting to be taken to the theatre. Hours later, I was still lying there. I was exhausted, having not slept or eaten since the previous day, but every time I dropped off, waves of panic would shoot through me, and I'd wake abruptly with a shock. I was trying desperately to get into a frame of mind which would help my penis, rather than hinder it.

'Stay pink, stay pink, stay pink.' I chanted in my mind. I tried not to think of the word black.

'Pink, pink, pink, pink.' I stroked it and talked to it. 'Please stay pink. You have to. I need you. You can't go black on me and die now, not after what we have been through.'

In spite of all my efforts to calm myself I was in a frenzy of anxiety when they came for me. They put a blanket around my shoulders and walked me to the anaesthetics room.

The injection was administered and I waited to slip into oblivion, but it didn't happen. I stared at the clock on the wall, the seconds kept ticking by and I was still wide awake. After what seemed like an eternity, I started to mellow out. Perhaps the severe stress I was suffering from and all the adrenalin were preventing the drug from working immediately as it normally does.

'I'm starting to go now,' I said, and finally I went out.

When I woke up from the anaesthetic, I was crying. Tears had been running down the sides of my face and there was a pool of them in each ear. Mr Saxby was standing over me, saying, 'Don't worry, don't worry, everything went perfectly. The blood supply is just perfect, don't worry about anything.'

He was walking beside my bed as I was being wheeled back to the ward, leaning over me and reassuring me over and over.

'Thank God. Thank you, thank you,' was all I could say, and the tears carried on streaming down my face.

I had woken up from the anaesthetic in exactly the same state as when I went under. I was still panic-stricken. Half an hour after coming on to the ward from the operating theatre, I was getting up and putting my clothes on. I couldn't wait to get out of the hospital.

'What are you doing, are you mad?' Louise said. 'There is no rush, slow down.'

'I've got to get out of this fucking hospital,' and I meant it. Getting up so quickly made me feel sick and dizzy, but I wanted out, I wanted fresh air, I couldn't stand this environment for another moment. Louise convinced me to go up to the cafeteria to have a couple of glasses of milk to settle my stomach before leaving. I was in the hospital for one day. In spite of my sixty stitches they allowed me to go home because Louise promised to get me there safe and sound.

My penis was in a sling and temporarily taped tight to my hip. I had been told not to disturb it for at least a week. I couldn't even bring myself to look at it, I was so anxious about the outcome. Within a few days of arriving home, I went to lift myself on to my bed when I felt a rip at my hip. The scar on my hip where my penis had been severed just split open. The skin was very taut there anyway. It wasn't a pleasant sensation but I was in no mood to have any more medical attention so I decided to leave it to heal by itself. The same happened to the end of my penis, due to the swelling. Remarkably, even that didn't bother me unduly. I knew I had one more operation to come, where they would be altering the tip anyway, and Louise kept it scrupulously clean in the meantime.

A week went by and I realized that I must start to relax, take the sling off and start to live normally and enjoy the outcome of all these long and painful operations. My first bath was an amazing experience. I got in and took the sling off. What a thrill it was, sitting there and feeling my penis move with the water. It was incredible. I'd had this mental picture all my life of how my genitals were supposed to look, and now finally being able to see this very sight, was a moment I will never forget. All those years of never being able to look at myself, of baths being something to get over with as quickly as possible, of washing being a difficult and shameful procedure, of clothes being put on in a hurry – all those years were finally over. For the first time in my life I could relax in the bath and look at my malehood bobbing about in the water. It was bliss.

But then, when the water started getting cold, I panicked because I didn't know how to get up. I didn't know whether I could let it fall naturally. I needed both my hands to get out of the bath since my leg was still quite useless. So I rested my penis on my outstretched leg until I had swung my legs out of the bath and I was able to let it rest in my hand again. I was terrified of it swinging about and getting damaged. The stitches underneath were still quite sore.

For about fifteen months, from the start of the surgery, I had had to sleep on my back with my leg propped up. I would have given anything to be able to turn over and curl up on my side. Soon I could start turning on to my side; it was wonderful, and I was able to stop taking the sleeping pills I had needed to knock myself out at night.

My posture was terrible. Because I had lost so much skin on my leg and abdomen, there was a terrific pull on the whole area which made me bend over slightly. To be more comfortable I had kept my leg up as much as possible but I knew that this wasn't helpful. I started straightening myself up, and the skin gradually stretched.

Soon Louise and I finished what was left of our relationship. She moved in with a guy down the road, with whom she had already started a relationship. I didn't blame her one bit for wanting to look elsewhere. She didn't get an awful lot back from me. It was a time when I didn't have much to give someone else. I had enough on my plate trying to cope with myself. She could have done it slightly differently though. Towards the end, her lies were so obvious and so blatant, I could no longer ignore what was going on. But for all that, I was very grateful for her help after my operation, and I'll never forget what she did for me. At the same time, I would much have preferred to have gone through it on my own. I wasn't going to be that vulnerable in front of anyone again, physically or emotionally.

Looking back, the two relationships that I'd had during the

last few years had been meaningful to me but my heart and soul had not been in them. I was too vulnerable and unstable to cope with the natural friction and conflicts of a relationship. What made it more difficult was being back in my home town and never being happy there; I was as desperate to leave it as I had been as an adolescent. I never felt settled and this had a bearing on how I related to others and showed in my lack of any real commitment. I've never really gone looking for relationships. I knew that some women were attracted to me, but I never took it on board. I wasn't ever sure why women were interested in me, if it was me, for myself, or just out of curiosity. I treated women mainly as friends.

I was now waiting for the last stage of surgery. I felt as unfit as I think I ever had. I had been immobilized for so long, and I'd had so much surgery, that I had lost my youthful fitness and muscle tone and gained two stone. As well as walking I decided to start swimming. It felt good to take charge of my health. After Louise left I felt I had to take my own initiative to do things, and I felt independent once again. I also cut down on the amount I smoked as I had smoked a lot in my life and I was concerned about my cardiovascular condition.

One morning a leaflet came through the letterbox, promoting transcendental meditation. It said that it was good for combating stress and lowering blood pressure. I decided to check it out; anything that might help was worth investigating. I took the course and learned to meditate, and initially I found it very beneficial.

But a few weeks before the last stage of surgery my anxiety levels started to rise and I went on a bender. I was drinking a bottle of wine a day, some of it quite strong stuff that I knew wasn't good for me. As usual, the less control I had of my life, the more out of control my behaviour became. It was a pattern that I found difficult to break, and when I hit the bottle to try and obliterate my stress, I would drink to oblivion. Every time this happened I felt gutted and disappointed in myself. It was up to me to keep myself safe from harm and, in a state of drunkenness, how could I possibly protect and look after myself?

Part of the problem was that my safe, secure home was in the midst of extensive renovations. A substantial grant had finally been approved a few months prior to me going into hospital and the work had started. Although I was over the moon that finally my house was getting the attention it needed, the timing wasn't ideal. I had no heating, no back windows, no back door, no bathroom, no water and the floor had been stripped down to the bare earth. The place looked derelict. I was still living upstairs in two of the bedrooms and spent my evenings tossing back the wine and waiting for my last hospital appointment.

The nights were bitterly cold. The window in my bedroom had been put in, but still had a six-inch gap where the wind would howl in, bringing with it clouds of dust created by the work. I had a miserable flat pillow and two blankets to keep the wind at bay. Sleeping in my tracksuit with the hood pulled up tight around my head, I curled my body up into a ball. No wonder I had one cold after another; my immune system must have been struggling.

There was a ten-month wait for the next operation and then I went back into hospital. This was to be the very last time. I was shown to my room and soon a nurse came in.

'Hi, I'm Helen, your nurse for today.'

I turned around to say hello and when I saw her face I was taken aback. She was black and had something which was extremely reminiscent of Lorretta. I wasn't sure whether it was her eyes or her expression, but instantly I felt attracted to her. We became good friends, and she even wrote to me a few times after I went home. Helen set me thinking about Lorretta. Not that I had ever forgotten about her. As I was getting nearer to the end of surgery she had frequently been on my mind. I thought a lot about the possibility of finding her again.

The doctors improved the end of my penis further by a bit of plastic surgery. They cut away a bit on the inside of my groin on one side, in order to turn my penis slightly and make it more symmetric. The tip of my penis was fashioned with smoother skin of a somewhat darker colour.

After the operation they covered it with a seaweed dressing. It's gentle on the skin and can be taken off without pulling the skin in any way. You can soak it off, since it swells naturally and separates from whatever it is adhered to. I didn't know this at the time, and went to run myself a nice hot bath, my first bath after a week in hospital. The heat of the water made me feel quite faint and giddy. I looked down and suddenly saw the water loosening the dressing and blood seemed to be pouring from the end of my penis, making the water red. I was hanging on to the sides of the bath for dear life when a nurse came in to check on me.

'What do you think you are doing, having a boiling hot bath?' she reprimanded me and ran the tap of cold water. There wasn't anything else she could do at this point but peel the rest of the seaweed off. She gave me some plastic cling film to wrap my penis in until the doctor came on his ward round. The situation wasn't as serious as I had thought and, seeing it properly for the first time, I was quite pleased with the result of the surgery.

Before leaving, Mr Davies came in to have a word with me. He was a very big and thickset fellow, at least six foot five, but very placid and soft spoken.

'This is the end of all your surgery. I've done as much as I can do for you now,' he said.

'You have improved the quality of my life one hundred per cent. I'm really pleased.' I shook his hand warmly and thanked him for what he had done for me. Two years almost to the day had passed since my penis had been constructed, exactly as he had predicted.

He asked me to come back for a last check-up in a couple of weeks.

Sadly my very last stay in hospital was tainted by an infuriating incident. I was out of my room for a moment, and during this time someone came in and pinched my wallet. It contained my money, my train ticket home, and a new social security book. Unfortunately, I lost my rag. I wanted to run after whoever the thief was, but I couldn't even walk properly, and in a fury of helplessness I threw my table over and banged my fists on the window over and over. A nurse called the doctor on duty and he came to calm me down.

'I know that you're upset,' he said soothingly. 'Your operation was a success. You don't want to be back in surgery, having your hands stitched up, do you?'

'If I could find the guy who stole your wallet,' he said with a smile, 'I would turn my head and let you get on with sorting him out.' I couldn't help but smile at his kind offer, and I realized how stupidly and irrationally I was behaving.

So my first trip outside the hospital was not home on a comfortable train, but to the Hammersmith social security office where I spent the whole day waiting to sort out a train ticket to get me home. I had already been warned in the hospital: 'You have to talk politely to whomever you see. If you raise your voice once, they won't give you a penny.' Didn't I know it; my temper had never got me anywhere.

I still had a couple of days left in hospital, and that evening I was sitting and talking to a couple of patients in the corridor opposite the lifts. Helen, the nurse I liked, was going off duty.

'You lot wouldn't be sitting with him, if you knew better,' she laughed and pointed at me. 'You should have seen him this afternoon, he was like a demon. We were seriously thinking of hanging garlic outside his door.'

Dr Montgomery, the psychiatrist, put me on a new kind of hormone treatment which would be administered by monthly injections. It was crucial that the correct balance of hormones in my body was maintained and I would have to continue the treatment for the rest of my life. Once a year I would have to have several tests on my blood, to check my liver and kidney functions, blood pressure, bone calcium and cholesterol levels.

I was happy to be home but I had hoped that the renovations would all be finished by the time I got back. This was not the case. The floors were laid and the windows and doors were put back, but the bathroom had not been plumbed in and there was still work needed on the central heating system. Alison had proved to be a very faithful friend. During my hospital stay she had kept an eye on my house and fed the cats. She and another friend had gone into my house prior to me coming back to try and organize a room where I could be comfortable. They moved a bed into one room and got my television, stereo, books and music on a unit along the wall, plus a kettle to make tea. The gap under the window had fortunately been filled in.

Since I had no bathroom, I had to wash in a bowl. The old couple next door had kindly let me use their outside loo since the work had started, but it was a hell of a performance to get over the wall between our properties first thing in the morning. I was afraid of scraping my lower parts, so I heaved myself over with great difficulty.

It was impossible to look after myself properly and to relax in the house with workmen coming and going and the place in the state it was.

'You've got to come up to my house to bath,' said Alison, and I gratefully accepted her offer. For the next six weeks I had my daily baths at Alison's house: first thing in the morning it was an arduous walk up three hills. I was clogged up with dressings and still limping and feeling very sore. I'd have my bath and change my dressings and then proceed to a café in town for beans on toast. The rest of the day I'd hang about, mostly at a pub which was always empty. It was an exhausting routine and I yearned for the privacy of my own home. My parents tried their best to get me to come and stay with them, but I couldn't cope with that either. Although I knew I would have been very comfortable and well looked after, I hadn't lived with my parents for so many years. It was important to me to be self-reliant. Also, my cats needed me, they were already disorientated by the noise of Kango hammers digging up the floors and the demolition of the kitchen and shower lean-to.

My thirty-second birthday was coming up. The night before, my mother came up to my house with a lovely present: a thick quilt with a quilt-cover and four enormous pillows. The joy of it! I thought I was in heaven and my mother was an angel. My miserable pillow and blankets were tossed out perfunctorily.

I spent most of my birthday in solitary celebration in an empty pub. I put a couple of quid in the jukebox and had a few beers. Listening to music I got lost in contemplation, my whole life spread out before me, past, present and future. My thoughts kept going back to Lorretta. Where was she? I couldn't believe the length of time that had passed since I'd seen her. She seemed so real in my mind and in my heart, and her face and that famous smile were as clear as if I had seen them yesterday.

I continued to convalesce with the support of my friends and family. One day I walked up to my parents' house for a little visit. I was wearing tracksuit pants and boxer shorts underneath. Mr Davies had told me to 'let it hang' and not to confine it in restrictive clothing. My mother took one look at me.

'My God!' she said, and laughed. 'For heaven's sake put it away. It's coming before you do. Don't tell me you've walked up through the playground looking like that.' She was mortified. 'Get some proper underpants on, for God's sake.'

'Look, I've got to let it hang. That's what the doctor said.'

Whenever I got up from a chair to go anywhere she'd cover her face and laugh hysterically. In fact it felt great having it hang and swing about the place, and I thought to myself, 'To hell with everybody. I've waited long enough for this. It's my pride and joy. I deserve it, and it deserves to hang and be free.'

I started to think about what my new life was going to be like. The last few years had been lacking in any direction except getting the surgery over with. I was ecstatic about the way I now looked and the way it made me feel, and I was profoundly grateful to the system that had allowed me this chance to become whole. Free movement, being able to go anywhere and never having to think about my limitations, was going to be the biggest release. I could forget how I was born. I was and had always been a man; that fact was unalterable.

My childhood dream of waking up, transformed painlessly and instantly with God's help into a boy, had been replaced by a long rocky road, but a road leading to the same conclusion. Not entirely through God's help, but through my own absolute conviction and the understanding and skill of the doctors. What struck me was the uncanny connection between my childhood attempts to rectify my condition and how it was eventually achieved. The position I forced myself to hold as a small child, during the night when I was asking God to transform me into the boy I knew I was, was the same position I had to maintain all through my surgery: flat on my back and in great discomfort.

Did I know something way back then. Did I have a premonition of what was in store for me?

I always thought that when this miracle took place, there would be an instant release from my humiliation and my rejection of my own body. I would be able to make friends with myself; look at every part of my body without flinching; get myself fit; get some coordination and harmony between my mind, body and spirit. But this was indeed hoping for a miracle. To make friends with my body, I needed to build myself up. My energy levels were low and I didn't yet know what my new body could do. All my life it had undermined me and humiliated me and I'd rejected it. I would have to build the physical foundations that I should have built in childhood and adolescence. All the things that I yearned to do as a young man – boxing, swimming and playing contact sports – would have given me the confidence in my physical abilities, but now I had to start from scratch. I needed to know that my body would be working for me, not against me as it had always done before. My friendship with my body would have to grow gradually alongside my confidence and trust in it.

I had wanted to go forward immediately and begin my new life somewhere else, and put into action the plans that had been brewing in my mind from the time I moved to my home town and started college, but now I understood that I would have to recover from the experience before I could move on.

Lorretta was on my mind, and so was the promise I had always made to myself to find her when all my surgery was over.

An old friend from Cardiff came to visit me out of the blue one day. Marcy's daughter Sharlene came with her. Sharlene had been a very small girl when I knew her, now she was a young woman.

'You knew my mother, didn't you?' Sharlene asked me. 'And you knew Lorretta.'

'That's right,' I said.

'Lorretta took me under her wing when I was younger,' Sharlene explained. 'She was very good to me.'

My ears pricked up. 'Do you know where Lorretta is living now?' I asked excitedly.

'Yes I do, she lives in Cardiff,' she said and gave me Lorretta's address right there and then.

Lorretta had been the love of my life, and I felt she still was. I decided that I would go looking for her. Perhaps it was only a fantasy but, looking ahead, I wanted to start my new life in my new body with her by my side. The thought that she may be with someone else, or that she wouldn't want to have anything to do with me, was at the back of my mind. At the same time I couldn't imagine that she would deny me her wonderful smile if she laid eyes on me.

One morning I woke up thinking about her. 'I've got nothing to lose,' I thought, 'and I'm going.' I got out of bed, had a bath and put nice clean clothes on. I walked into town and had a beer in a pub to fortify myself, and then I caught the train to Cardiff.

Apprehensively I walked up to Lorretta's door and knocked. There was no answer so I shouted, 'Lorretta, it's Ray.'

'Come in!' I heard Lorretta call out excitedly and I opened the door. She had just had a bath and was coming out of the bathroom. Ten years had made no impact on her. She was as beautiful as ever and she gave me the beaming smile that I knew so well.

'Come here,' she said. 'Let me look at you.'

I went over to her. She put her arms around me and held me.

'What took you so long?' she asked.

Epilogue

In telling my story to you, the reader, I have wanted to try and generate some compassion and understanding for those who, like me, are born with a disability which casts them out from society, to attempt to discourage the stigma, prejudice and assumptions about transsexualism held by so many people, through lack of real information and a wealth of misinformation. I hope I have been successful in reaching at least a few readers with this account of the difficulties of having to survive in the wrong body.

In telling my story I was also motivated by a need to make amends to my mother, father and sister, who have all been deeply affected by my condition and the life that it prompted me to lead. I'd like to say I'm sorry for all the hurt, anguish and sleepless nights I've caused them. I love them very much and want to thank them for the help, support and understanding they've given me over the last decade. But, that said, my family, like myself, no longer live in or dwell on the past.

I want to thank Kitty for the opportunity she gave me to put my life into perspective and for writing this book with me; for the long hours, commitment and hard work that she gave to make my story unfold thus helping me put my past behind me in a most positive way. Our contrasting personalities have been invaluable: Kitty's objective, level-headed perspective has helped me maintain my own objectivity in the process of writing this book.

Many thanks also to Dr Randall, Dr Montgomery, Mr Saxby and Mr Davies who recognized my torment and believed in my need to become whole. I am also very grateful to the NHS for making the treatment available to me, and I hope that this book may in some way help to make gender-confirmation surgery available to others in this desperate and genuine predicament.

And a special thanks to my editor, Jill Waters, for believing in the book and the issues it raises, and for all her help and support, and also Penguin Books for making publication possible.

Having to recall my life experiences for the purpose of writing this book has not been an easy task, but now I feel as if I've put the final seal on this chapter of my life. I no longer feel ashamed or embarrassed about myself and my experiences.

I consider myself a very lucky man. My two greatest wishes – harmony between my mind and body, and to find yet again the woman of my dreams – have both been fulfilled. Since completion of surgery just over three years ago, I have begun a new life with Lorretta. Her son, Jamie, has grown into a young man and, despite his epilepsy, he is coping well and is making a life of his own as an independent adult. Lorretta and I now have complete faith in our love and our life together, and are looking to the future with many plans and hopes. We both share a commitment to leading a more self-sufficient lifestyle, being creative while at peace with life, keeping fit and healthy in body and mind. We are currently working on acquiring a new home in a different part of the country and starting a business of our own.

Raymond Thompson
February 1995

Afterword

The average member of the public usually obtains their knowledge of transsexualism and transsexual people from some humiliating report in the tabloid press when an event in the life of the transsexual has exposed them to the publicity of a court case or to some problem with their employment. Unfortunately another source of 'information' is when male exhibitionist transvestites, some with severe gender conflict, who are attempting to live in the female role in society (and are classified by some professionals as 'secondary transsexuals') sell their stories to the tabloid press, and the lay public begin to think that this is the predominant picture of transsexualism, thus reinforcing all their prejudices.

Fortunately some sensitively written autobiographies by Jan Morris, Caroline Cossey and others have been more informative about the nature of severe gender identity disorder and how careful and sensitive assessment and management can lead to a very satisfactory psychological and social resolution of the problem. Those who have heard of her know that Caroline Cossey was one of the bevy of beauties in a James Bond film and thus demonstrated how the 'true', 'primary', or 'core' transsexual easily and appropriately adopts the opposite gender role and blends unremarkably into society in their chosen gender.

Female-to-male transsexualism is much less publicized in the media for a number of interesting reasons, some of them to do with the psychological excitement and fascination we get at the thought of a man dressing as a woman, or wanting to be a woman and denying or giving up his manhood. This obviously resonates with the castration anxiety or castration complex that Freud tells us we all have, to some extent or other. Women have been wearing trousers, jeans and other garments which could be designated as male clothing for a long time now, and although the styling can usually indicate whether a particular garment is feminine or masculine, often current fashion or the person wearing the garment doesn't make the distinction. A woman in jeans and a T-shirt can be regarded as very feminine and very attractive as a woman. There is no discordance between her clothing and her gender, and certainly there is no social interpretation of cross-dressing or of fetishism. There is today a wide acceptance of this kind of androgynous look without any inference as to a person's gender or sexual identity.

If a man uses female clothing partially or completely with the aim of either sexual or psychological excitement or arousal, he is said to be a transvestite. This is related to fetishism. Most men who indulge in such activity are heterosexual, often married with children, and their transvestism may be quite secretive. Sometimes it can become a raging compulsion, leading to great distress called 'gender dysphoria'. Depression and other severe mood disturbances may occur; alcoholism, reactive macho defences and other manoeuvres may result from such a condition. Severe marital disruption (if marriage has occurred) is almost inevitable in such extreme cases. Some such patients seek gender reassignment by hormonal and surgical means and many show great improvement in their psychological and social well-being. Many professionals would describe patients in this group as secondary transsexuals. However, a significant number of males with severe gender dysphoria choose to make a different sort of compromise and can be helped with this compromise by skilled psychiatric and psychological management.

The incidence of transsexualism has been estimated in various western European cultures as approximately one in 30,000 biological males and one in 90,000 biological females. The statistics are obviously influenced by the readiness with which people seek professional help for their experienced gender identity disturbance, and changing cultural boundaries related to gender are beginning to influence this. Interestingly, in Holland the incidence of transsexualism is counted as three times as frequent as in the UK, but this may have a lot to do with the availability of professionals. Our experience in the Gender Identity Clinic at Charing Cross Hospital is similar to the experience of other western European Gender Identity Clinics, in that three or four biological males attend our clinic to every one biological female. This sex ratio appears to have been consistent during the thirty years' existence of the Charing Cross Hospital Gender Identity Clinic. Interestingly, female-to-male transsexualism is reported to be equal to or more frequent than male-to-female transsexualism in some eastern European countries. Some speculate that the harsher economic climate increases the social advantages of being male and thus influences this ratio. Cultural and legal attitudes may also be factors contributing to this ratio.

Transsexualism is a word that has been used only since 1949, although the phenomenon of believing that one has been born into the wrong sex and the compulsive drive to live in the opposite sex role have been recorded throughout history, from ancient Egyptian and Indian records, through ancient Greek and Roman times up to the present day. In the eighteenth century the Chevalier de Eon de Beaumont, a member of the court of Louis XVI of France, lived openly in the female role as a 'courtier' and is said to have been sent to Russia as a spy in female disguise by the French court. This character has given his name to eonism, a word previously used to describe cross-dressing, and to the Beaumont Society and the Beaumont Trust, UK organizations which provide support and counselling to transvestites (the Beaumont Society) and to those with severe gender identity disorders (the Beaumont Trust).

Nevertheless, throughout all this recorded history and more recent media interest the female-to-male transsexual remains relatively silent. Perhaps this is in part due to the ability of the primary or core female-to-male transsexual to blend into society as a young 'chap' with such natural masculine body language and presentation that they are unnoticed except perhaps for a relatively highly pitched voice and rather smooth and youthful skin. It is my particular belief (requiring further research) that approximately eighty per cent of the biological females who present to the Charing Cross Hospital Gender Identity Clinic are of the primary or core transsexual classification, and only twenty per cent are of the more gender dysphoric and gender conflicted lesbian masculine-woman variety. In biological men the figures may be reversed, where approximately twenty per cent being of the core or primary transsexual type, and perhaps up to eighty per cent being in the gender dysphoric or secondary transsexual category. As four or five times as many biological men attend our clinic as biological women, it is interesting to speculate that the incidence of true or primary transsexualism may be approximately equal in both sexes. That would certainly make us wonder if there is some unknown, as yet, biological force responsible for this condition.

Indeed, many of the professionals working in the field of sexuality and gender identity disorder have begun to have stronger suspicions that a biological factor is relevant in some people with a homosexual orientation, and in some people with severe gender identity disorders. Brain studies suggest that small nuclei at the base of the brain, near the pituitary and hypothalamus, are different in size between men and women. Research has not yet confirmed clearly reports of some researchers that homosexual men and transsexual men have brain nuclei patterns similar to those of women.

It is thought by some professionals that some biological factor has androgenized or masculinized the brains (and hence the minds) of at least some of the female-to-male transsexual patients we see. Of course the issue is tremendously complex and evidence can be brought in from family studies and other cultural factors to argue the strength of training and conditioning in forming our normal stereotyped gender roles, and in those cases where gender identity appears to have gone seriously awry. The close-binding mother and the absent father have been postulated as one psychodynamic family pattern to explain male-to-female transsexualism, and there are a number of other putative psychological theories. Some have suggested that the female-to-male transsexual child develops in a family where the mother is significantly depressed for some time after the child's birth, with the husband remaining unsupportive and disconnected from her. Into this vacuum the small female child is said to step, and becomes a husband and strength to the mother.

In ten years of working with people with severe gender identity disorders I have become less and less confident that there is one psychological, sociological or biological theory for these conditions, and that each and every patient has their unique biopsychosocial pattern to their gender identity formation. With experience I have become increasingly inclined to believe in the possible presence of a biological factor in the majority of female-to-male transsexuals. Some scientists postulate that a testosterone 'surge' occurs during the early intra-uterine life of the female child transsexual-to-be, masculinizing the brain and therefore the mind. The compulsive tomboyishness and masculinity of these children is amazing, and unstoppable. Most parents and professionals eventually come to the conclusion that psychological, social, hormonal and surgical help towards the male role is not only inevitable but absolutely necessary for that particular person's psychological and social well-being.

Those who have read Raymond Thompson's autobiography must wonder in amazement how such a masculine identity or soul got into this person born with a female body. Some may comment that the masculinity seems exaggerated, and indeed Raymond Thompson has certainly used an aggressive masculinity to defend the narcissistic vulnerability he experienced from the beginning of his gender awareness. Nevertheless most readers will remain convinced of the essential masculine core to Raymond Thompson's being. It is important that society has a compassionate and helpful stance towards such people, and is prepared to offer them the experienced psychiatric and surgical help they need.

Dr D.H. Montgomery, MB ChB FRCPsych FRANZCPsych
Consultant Psychiatrist, Director of the Gender Identity Clinic
Charing Cross Hospital

Discover more about our forthcoming books through Penguin's FREE newspaper...

Penguin Quarterly

It's packed with:

- exciting features
- author interviews
- previews & reviews
- books from your favourite films & TV series
- exclusive competitions & much, much more...

Write off for your free copy today to:
Dept JC
Penguin Books Ltd
FREEPOST
West Drayton
Middlesex
UB7 0BR
NO STAMP REQUIRED

READ MORE IN PENGUIN

In every corner of the world, on every subject under the sun, Penguin represents quality and variety – the very best in publishing today.

For complete information about books available from Penguin – including Puffins, Penguin Classics and Arkana – and how to order them, write to us at the appropriate address below. Please note that for copyright reasons the selection of books varies from country to country.

In the United Kingdom: Please write to *Dept. JC, Penguin Books Ltd, FREEPOST, West Drayton, Middlesex UB7 0BR*.

If you have any difficulty in obtaining a title, please send your order with the correct money, plus ten per cent for postage and packaging, to *PO Box No. 11, West Drayton, Middlesex UB7 0BR*

In the United States: Please write to *Consumer Sales, Penguin USA, P.O. Box 999, Dept. 17109, Bergenfield, New Jersey 07621-0120*. VISA and MasterCard holders call 1-800-253-6476 to order all Penguin titles

In Canada: Please write to *Penguin Books Canada Ltd, 10 Alcorn Avenue, Suite 300, Toronto, Ontario M4V 3B2*

In Australia: Please write to *Penguin Books Australia Ltd, P.O. Box 257, Ringwood, Victoria 3134*

In New Zealand: Please write to *Penguin Books (NZ) Ltd, Private Bag 102902, North Shore Mail Centre, Auckland 10*

In India: Please write to *Penguin Books India Pvt Ltd, 706 Eros Apartments, 56 Nehru Place, New Delhi 110 019*

In the Netherlands: Please write to *Penguin Books Netherlands bv, Postbus 3507, NL-1001 AH Amsterdam*

In Germany: Please write to *Penguin Books Deutschland GmbH, Metzlerstrasse 26, 60594 Frankfurt am Main*

In Spain: Please write to *Penguin Books S. A., Bravo Murillo 19, 1° B, 28015 Madrid*

In Italy: Please write to *Penguin Italia s.r.l., Via Felice Casati 20, I–20124 Milano*

In France: Please write to *Penguin France S. A., 17 rue Lejeune, F–31000 Toulouse*

In Japan: Please write to *Penguin Books Japan, Ishikiribashi Building, 2–5–4, Suido, Bunkyo-ku, Tokyo 112*

In Greece: Please write to *Penguin Hellas Ltd, Dimocritou 3, GR–106 71 Athens*

In South Africa: Please write to *Longman Penguin Southern Africa (Pty) Ltd, Private Bag X08, Bertsham 2013*

READ MORE IN PENGUIN

A CHOICE OF NON-FICTION

The Time of My Life Denis Healey

'Denis Healey's memoirs have been rightly hailed for their intelligence, wit and charm ... *The Time of My Life* should be read, certainly for pleasure, but also for profit ... he bestrides the post war world, a Colossus of a kind' – *Independent*. 'No finer autobiography has been written by a British politician this century' – *Economist*

Far Flung Floyd Keith Floyd

Keith Floyd's latest culinary odyssey takes him to the far flung East and the exotic flavours of Malaysia, Hong Kong, Vietnam and Thailand. The irrepressible Floyd as usual spices his recipes with witty stories, wry observation and a generous pinch of gastronomic wisdom.

Genie Russ Rymer

In 1970 thirteen-year-old Genie emerged from a terrible captivity. Her entire childhood had been spent in one room, caged in a cot or strapped in a chair. Almost mute, without linguistic or social skills, Genie aroused enormous excitement among the scientists who took over her life. 'Moving and terrifying ... opens windows some might prefer kept shut on man's inhumanity' – Ruth Rendell

The Galapagos Affair John Treherne

Stories about Friedrich Ritter and Dore Strauch, settlers on the remote Galapagos island of Floreana, quickly captivated the world's press in the early thirties. Then death and disappearance took the rumours to fever pitch ... 'A tale of brilliant mystery' – Paul Theroux

1914 Lyn Macdonald

'Once again she has collected an extraordinary mass of original accounts, some by old soldiers, some in the form of diaries and journals, even by French civilians ... Lyn Macdonald's research has been vast, and in result is triumphant' – Raleigh Trevelyan in the *Tablet*. 'These poignant voices from the past conjure up a lost innocence as well as a lost generation' – *Mail on Sunday*

READ MORE IN PENGUIN

A CHOICE OF NON-FICTION

The Happy Isles of Oceania   Paul Theroux

'He voyaged from the Solomons to Fiji, Tonga, Samoa, Tahiti, the Marquesas and Easter Island, stepping-stones in an odyssey of courage and toughness ... This is Paul Theroux's finest, most personal and heartfelt travel book' – *Observer*

Spoken in Darkness   Ann E. Imbrie

A woman's attempt to understand how and why her childhood friend became, at twenty-five, the victim of a serial killer. 'Imbrie has created a highly original and heartbreaking narrative. The ground she covers is impressive: everything from feminist critiques of cheerleaders, the pain of mother–daughter relationships to the anomalies of the American judiciary ... awesome and inspiring' – *Time Out*

Fragments of Autobiography   Graham Greene

Containing the two parts of Graham Greene's autobiography, *A Sort of Life* and *Ways of Escape*, this is an engaging, vivid and often amusing account of the author's memories of his childhood, traumatic schooldays and encounters as a writer and traveller.

The New Spaniards   John Hooper

Spain has become a land of extraordinary paradoxes in which traditional attitudes and contemporary preoccupations exist side by side. The country attracts millions of visitors – yet few see beyond the hotels and resorts of its coastline. John Hooper's fascinating study brings to life the many faces of Spain in the 1990s.

The Loss of El Dorado   V. S. Naipaul

Focusing on the early nineteenth century, when British occupants inflicted a reign of terror on the island's black population, V. S. Naipaul's passionate and vivid recreation of the history of Trinidad exposes the barbaric cruelties of slavery and torture and their consequences on all strata of society. 'A masterpiece' – *Sunday Telegraph*

READ MORE IN PENGUIN

BIOGRAPHY AND AUTOBIOGRAPHY

Freedom from Fear   Aung San Suu Kyi

This collection of writings gives a voice to Aung San Suu Kyi, human rights activist and leader of Burma's National League for Democracy, who was detained in 1989 by SLORC, the ruling military junta, and today remains under house arrest. In 1991, her courage and ideals were internationally recognized when she was awarded the Nobel Peace Prize.

Memories of a Catholic Girlhood   Mary McCarthy

'Many a time in the course of doing these memoirs,' Mary McCarthy says, 'I have wished that I were writing fiction.' 'Superb ... so heartbreaking that in comparison Jane Eyre seems to have got off lightly' – *Spectator*

A Short Walk from Harrods   Dirk Bogarde

In this volume of memoirs, Dirk Bogarde pays tribute to the corner of Provence that was his home for over two decades, and to Forwood, his manager and friend of fifty years, whose long and wretched illness brought an end to a paradise. 'A brave and moving book' – *Daily Telegraph*

When Shrimps Learn to Whistle   Denis Healey

The Time of My Life was widely acclaimed as a masterpiece. Taking up the most powerful political themes that emerge from it Denis Healey now gives us this stimulating companion volume. 'Forty-three years of ruminations ... by the greatest foreign secretary we never had' – *New Statesman & Society*

Eating Children   Jill Tweedie

Jill Tweedie's second memoir, *Frightening People*, incomplete due to her tragically early death in 1993, is published here for the first time. 'Magnificent ... with wit, without a shred of self-pity, she tells the story of an unhappy middle-class suburban child with a monstrously cruel father, and a hopeless mother' – *Guardian*